SCIENCE, COLONIALISM, AND INDIGENOUS PEOPLES

At the intersection of indigenous studies, science studies, and legal studies lies a tense web of political issues of vital concern for the survival of indigenous nations. Numerous historians of science have documented the vital role of late-eighteenth- and nineteenth-century science as a part of statecraft, a means of extending empire. This book follows imperialism into the present, demonstrating how pursuit of knowledge of the natural world impacts, and is impacted by, indigenous peoples rather than nation-states.

In extractive biocolonialism, the valued genetic resources and associated agricultural and medicinal knowledge of indigenous peoples are sought, legally converted into private intellectual property, transformed into commodities, and then placed for sale in genetic marketplaces. *Science, Colonialism, and Indigenous Peoples* critically examines these developments, demonstrating how contemporary relations between indigenous and western knowledge systems continue to be shaped by the dynamics of power, the politics of property, and the apologetics of law.

Laurelyn Whitt received a Ph.D. in Philosophy, with a specialization in Philosophy of Science, from the University of Western Ontario. She teaches Native Studies and Philosophy at Brandon University and has held visiting appointments in the Department of Maori Studies, University of Auckland; the Department of Science and Technology Studies, Cornell University; the University of Notre Dame Law School; and Osgoode Hall Law School. Professor Whitt is the coauthor (with Alan W. Clarke) of *The Bitter Fruit of American Justice* and the author of *Interstices*, a collection of poetry that won the 2005 Holland Poetry Prize.

Science, Colonialism, and Indigenous Peoples

THE CULTURAL POLITICS OF LAW AND KNOWLEDGE

Laurelyn Whitt

Brandon University

CAMBRIDGE
UNIVERSITY PRESS

CAMBRIDGE UNIVERSITY PRESS
Cambridge, New York, Melbourne, Madrid, Cape Town, Singapore,
São Paulo, Delhi, Dubai, Tokyo

Cambridge University Press
32 Avenue of the Americas, New York, NY 10013-2473, USA

www.cambridge.org
Information on this title: www.cambridge.org/9780521119535

First published 2009

Printed in the United States of America

A catalog record for this publication is available from the British Library.

Library of Congress Cataloging in Publication data

Whitt, Laurelyn.
Science, colonialism, and indigenous peoples : the cultural politics of law and knowledge / Laurelyn Whitt.
p. cm.
Includes bibliographical references and index.
ISBN 978-0-521-11953-5 (hardback)
1. Indigenous peoples – Legal status, laws, etc. 2. Intellectual property. 3. Traditional ecological knowledge – Law and legislation. 4. Sociological jurisprudence. I. Title.
K3247.W488 2009
346.04′8 – dc22 2009011815

ISBN 978-0-521-11953-5 Hardback

This book is dedicated to Waerete Norman.

E te hoa o ngä wähine whänui o te ao,
takoto mai rä i tö waka o te mate.

E te karanga maha,
e te kaipupuri i te mana wahine o te Tai Tokerau,
moe mai rä i waenga i ngä koiwi o öu mätua, tüpuna.

Ka tangi tonu atu rä mö te rironga horo atu,
kähore nei i tatari kia rongo anö
i te tangi a te pïpïwharauroa o te koanga,
i te tangi a te tätarakihi o te raumati.

Kua moe rä to tinana,
kua whakangaro atu to wairua ki tua o Te Arai,
ki tua atu o Te Reinga,
ki Hawaiki wairua.

Takoto mai rä, moea te moenga roa e Waireti,
te moenga të whakaarahia.

Pai märire.

– Patu Hohepa

The dream of reason did not take power into account.
– Paul Starr[1]

1 Paul Starr, *The Social Transformation of American Medicine* (New York: Basic Books, 1982): 3.

Contents

Preface

Since this book began many years ago, many lives have passed through mine and so through it. Before this book began, many others brought me to it. All of these are still with me, though some only in memory. Gratefulness is not enough, but it is what I have; I offer it now.

To my parents, and theirs, and theirs before them.

To my spouse and friend, Alan Clarke, for the gift of his good heart and strong mind.

To my coauthors – Waerete Norman, Mere Roberts, Vicki Grieves, and Jennifer Daryl Slack – who have generously allowed me to borrow from our work together here.

To my elders, mentors, and teachers – especially Bev and Adam Lussier, Sa'ke'j Youngblood Henderson, and Iris Marion Young – for supporting and believing in me.

To my colleague and friend, Scott Abbott, who quietly, graciously, and selflessly, makes so much possible.

To those who lent strength, advice, and encouragement, in various forms, along the way, especially Wade Chambers, Don Grinde, Dale Jamieson, David Lyons, Thomas Norton-Smith, Scott Pratt, Marilyn Vogler, and Kari Winter.

To my research assistant – Asdaadooitsada (Camille Begay Benally) – who worked on references, and told me stories, while the children slept.

To Elspeth Pope, for the shelter of the northwoods, and her indexing advice.

To Patu Hohepa, for the lovely poroporoaki in honor of Waerete.

To Lawrence Paul Yuxweluptun, for the politics in his art and the art in his politics, and especially for the use of "Red Man Watching White Man Trying to Fix Hole in Sky."

And to all the four-legged companions who have found their way to me and enriched my life. Yakoke.

Finally, various institutions extended fellowships, grants, and visiting appointments that enabled me to do the research needed to bring this book to completion. These include the George A. and Eliza Howard Foundation; the University of Auckland Foundation and the Department of Maori Studies; the Humanities Research Centre of the Australian National University; the Research School of Social Sciences at the Australian National University; Michigan Technological University; Utah Valley University; Cornell University and the Department of Science and Technology Studies; the University of Notre Dame Law School; and Osgoode Hall Law School.

Acknowledgments

Parts of this book have appeared, sometimes with updated research and revisions, in the articles listed below. In addition, several of these articles list coauthors (Waerete Norman, Mere Roberts, Vicki Grieves, and Jennifer Daryl Slack), who have kindly agreed to their use in this book. Their contributions are gratefully acknowledged.

Laurelyn Whitt, "Knowledge Systems of Indigenous America," in Helaine Selin (ed.), *Encyclopaedia of the History of Science, Technology and Medicine in Non-Western Cultures* (Dordrecht, The Netherlands: Kluwer Academic Publishers, 2008): 1184–94.

Laurie Anne Whitt, "Sovereignty and Human Rights," *National Lawyers' Guild Practitioner*, 60:3 (Spring 2003): 90–4.

Laurie Anne Whitt, Mere Roberts, Waerete Norman, and Vicki Grieves, "Belonging to Land: Indigenous Knowledge Systems and the Natural World," *Oklahoma City University Law Review*, 26:2 (2001): 701–43.

Laurie Anne Whitt, Mere Roberts, Waerete Norman, and Vicki Grieves, "Indigenous Perspectives," in Dale Jamieson (ed.), *A Companion to Environmental Philosophy* (Oxford, UK: Basil Blackwell, 2000): 3–20.

Laurie Anne Whitt, "Value-Bifurcation in Bioscience: The Rhetoric of Research Justification," *Perspectives on Science: Historical, Philosophical, Social*, 7:4 (1999): 413–46.

Laurie Anne Whitt, "Metaphor and Power in Indigenous and Western Knowledge Systems," in Darrell Posey (ed.), *Cultural and Spiritual Values of Biodiversity* (A Complementary Contribution to the Global Biodiversity Assessment for the United Nations Environmental

Programme) (London, UK: Intermediate Technology Publications, 1999): 69–72.

Laurie Anne Whitt, "Indigenous Peoples, Intellectual Property Law and the New Imperial Science," *Oklahoma City University Law Review*, 23:1 & 2 (1998): 211–59.

Laurie Anne Whitt, "Resisting Value-Bifurcation: Indigenist Critiques of the Human Genome Diversity Project,"in Ann Ferguson and Bat Ami Bar-On (eds.), *Daring To Be Good: Feminist Essays in Ethico-Politics* (Oxford, UK: Routledge, Chapman and Hall, 1998): 70–86.

Laurie Anne Whitt, "Biocolonialism and the Commodification of Knowledge," *Science as Culture*, 7:1 (1998): 33–67.

Laurie Anne Whitt, "Cultural Imperialism and the Marketing of Native America," Reprinted from *The American Indian Culture and Research Journal*, Volume 19, Number 3 (1995): 1–31, by permission of the American Indian Studies Center, UCLA © Regents of the University of California.

Laurie Anne Whitt, "Indigenous Peoples and the Cultural Politics of Knowledge," in Michael Green (ed.), *Issues in American Indian Cultural Identity* (New York: Peter Lang, 1995): 223–71.

Laurie Anne Whitt and Jennifer Daryl Slack, "Communities, Environments, and Cultural Studies," *Cultural Studies*, 8:1 (January 1994): 5–31. The Web site for *Cultural Studies* is http://informaworld.com.

First Words

This book speaks to political issues that lie at the intersection of indigenous studies, science studies, and legal studies, focusing in particular on the role of power in shaping the interaction of indigenous and western knowledge systems. Pursuit of knowledge of the natural world has long been politicized. In some cases this has been subdued, a matter of inflection; in others it has been more pronounced, a dominant and dominating agenda for research. The vital role of science as a part of statecraft has been underscored by numerous historians of science,[1] who, in the latter part of the twentieth century, began to document the "issues of cultural and economic domination involved in the pursuit of natural knowledge."[2] The rule of law, they argue, was identified with the scientific method and became, for the West, a vital means of extending empire.[3] The conduct

[1] See, especially, Nathan Reingold and Marc Rothenberg (eds.), *Scientific Colonialism* (Washington, DC: Smithsonian Press, 1987); Roy MacLeod and Philip F. Rehbock (eds.), *Nature in Its Greatest Extent: Western Science in the Pacific* (Honolulu, Hawaii: University of Hawaii Press, 1988); Roy MacLeod, "Reading the Discourse of Colonial Science," in Patrick Petitjean (ed.), *Les Sciences Coloniales: Figures et Institutions* (Paris: ORSTOM, 1996): 87–96; Roy MacLeod, "On Science and Colonialism," *Science and Society in Ireland: The Social Context of Science and Technology in Ireland, 1800–1950* (Belfast: Queen's University, 1997) 1–17; Roy MacLeod, "On Visiting the 'Moving Metropolis': Reflections on the Architecture of Imperial Science," *Historical Records of Australian Science*, 5 (1982): 1–16; David Wade Chambers, "Locality and Science: Myths of Centre and Periphery," in A. Lafuents, A. Elena, and M.L. Ortega (eds.), *Mundializacíon de la cencia y cultura nacional* (Madrid: Ediciones Doce Calles, 1993): 605–17; David Wade Chambers, "Does Distance Tyrannize Science?" in R. W. Home and S. K. Kohlstedt (eds.), *International Science and National Scientific Identity* (Dordrecht, The Netherlands: Kluwer Academic Publishers, 1991): 19–38.

[2] MacLeod, "On Visiting," 14.

[3] As Roy MacLeod notes: "If imperial unity was the desired end, scientific unity was the one universally acceptable means . . . Scientific method would . . . unite empire, in unity of truth, of tradition and of leadership" (Ibid., 12).

of imperial science by nation-states during the late eighteenth and nineteenth centuries, and its effect upon other nation-states, has led historians of science to conclude that the issue is no longer science *in* imperial history but science *as* imperial history.[4]

My concern here is with the continuation of one strand of that history into the present, with how a new imperial science impacts, and is impacted by, indigenous peoples rather than nation-states. Certain areas of contemporary bioscience, currently in the service of western pharmaceutical and agricultural industries, are enabling the appropriation of indigenous knowledge and genetic resources at a prodigious and escalating rate. Opposition to such biocolonialism has not only been vigorous, but international in scope. My aim is to further and deepen such resistance by demonstrating how biocolonialism arises from the ideology, the policies, and the practices of a new imperial science, marked by the confluence of science with capitalism – a relationship mediated by a distinctively American, increasingly international, intellectual property system.

The political role of imperial science – the ways in which it supports and sustains the complex system of practices that constitutes the oppression of indigenous peoples – figures prominently in indigenist critiques of biocolonialism.[5] These critiques directly challenge the ideology which sustains and provides the justificatory rhetoric for the policies and practices of certain areas of western bioscience. Reflecting its origins, this ideology is described in Part I as neopositivist. It relies heavily upon both assertions and assumptions of value-neutrality, wields an untenable distinction between pure and applied science, and readily and unreflectively engages in value-bifurcation, demarcating and separating the ethical from the political.

The result is an apolitical ethics of science, where issues of power in ethics are either overlooked altogether or are diverted. It has also in some cases produced an amoral politics of science, as well as a focus on science "policy" rather than on the politics of science. Talk of how politics and power enter into the origins and development of science, into

[4] Ibid., 2.

[5] Indigenism critiques the diverse power relations and dynamics that facilitate and maintain the oppression of indigenous peoples. It stresses the existence, effectiveness, and potential of indigenous agency in resisting oppression and in formulating concrete proposals for securing justice.

scientific knowledge production is effectively silenced, and the rhetorical props for legitimating biocolonialism are set in place. Part II looks closely at the operation of this neopositivist ideology, offering a case study of a recent biocolonialist research program – the Human Genome Diversity Project.

Part III takes up at greater length the pivotal role played by the rule of law, and specifically of U.S. intellectual property law, in this story. The latter enables, and provides a patina of justification for, scientific policies and practices that, directly or indirectly, service the needs of powerful corporations. The microworld "factories" of the new imperial science have become crucial outposts in the establishment of an international intellectual property rights regime primed to serve the interests of biocolonialism. The hope of ending such practices rests in part upon our ability to move past current oppressive, and well-entrenched, understandings of sovereign power. Indigenous responses to biocolonialism include efforts to transform the concept and practice of sovereignty. These are, as we will see, helping to unify and transform indigenous communities politically.

Some vexing terminological and conceptual issues will remain submerged in my discussion of these matters. I will, for example, often contrast indigenous with western knowledge systems, especially in Part I. To speak of a knowledge system is to abandon the idea that a single epistemology is universally shared by, or applicable to, all humans insofar as they are human.[6] It facilitates instead a cultural parsing of the concept of epistemology, suitable to the heterogeneity of knowledge. There are specific epistemologies that belong to culturally distinctive ways of knowing.[7]

There are multiple ways of comparing and contrasting knowledge systems. My own preference for western and indigenous, or alternatively, dominant and subordinated, as terms of contrast is a political one; it is responsive to the role of power within, and the power differential among, knowledge

[6] I do not defend my adoption of this term here, but note that my use of it is itself at odds with the view of knowledge within the dominant knowledge system. Many who accept that system will insist on an extended defense. I will disappoint them here.

[7] For further discussion of characteristics of knowledge systems, see Stephen A. Marglin, "Toward the Decolonization of the Mind" and "Losing Touch," in Frédérique Apffel Marglin and Stephen Marglin (eds.), *Dominating Knowledge* (Oxford: Clarendon Press, 1990), especially 232–3.

systems. Other commonly adopted options – articulate/tacit, theoretical/practical, scientific/traditional – seem questionable if not objectionable, especially insofar as they are intended to reflect differences between forms of knowledge within indigenous and western cultures.[8]

Although speaking of a "dominant" knowledge system aptly captures the realities of power, for various reasons – including the exportation of this knowledge system beyond the geographic confines of the West – "western" is neither exact nor fully equivalent to it. By "dominant" knowledge system, I have in mind a fairly specific but enormously influential strain of the western intellectual heritage. Referred to as "positivism" in its earliest incarnation,[9] I am more concerned here with its current "neopositivist" manifestation.[10] Although purportedly dead as a movement, the spirit of positivism continues to haunt much of western science and philosophy.

Nevertheless, the diversity and non-unitary character of both "indigenous" and "western" must be acknowledged, and indeed, stressed. There are differences within, and similarities across, western and indigenous knowledge systems that confound any attempt to cast the contrast as a simple dichotomy. Indeed, after years of supposing otherwise, there is now growing acknowledgment among scholars "that there are no simple or universal criteria that can be deployed to separate indigenous

[8] For some discussion of these issues, see Thomas Heyd, "Indigenous Knowledge, Emancipation and Alienation," *Knowledge and Policy*, 8 (1995): 63–73; Arun Agrawal, "Indigenous and Scientific Knowledge: Some Critical Comments," *Indigenous Knowledge and Development Monitor*, 3 (1995): 3–6; "Editorial," *Indigenous Knowledge and Development Monitor*, 4 (1996): 1; and "Comments on Article by Arun Agrawal," *Indigenous Knowledge and Development Monitor*, 4 (1996): 12–19.

[9] A sprawling and lingering intellectual tradition, positivism has made itself felt in one guise or another for more than a century and a half. As one notable commentator of the phenomenon observes, it is, like any other tradition, "a diverse movement, with its dissidents and stalwarts, its ortho- and heterodoxies." Robert N. Proctor, *Value-Free Science? Purity and Power in Modern Knowledge* (Cambridge, Massachusetts: Harvard University Press, 1991): 162. There are positivist theories of law, of economics, of literature, of sociology, of religion, of ethics, and of science. There is the Comtean positivism of the 1830s, the neo-Kantian positivism of the last half of the nineteenth century, and the logical positivism of the early and mid-twentieth century. Although recent developments have significantly undermined its hold on the academic community, the elements of it noted here are part of its thriving legacy.

[10] References to the "legacy of positivism" abound. For two recent examples, see Dale Jamieson, "The Poverty of Postmodernism," *University of Colorado Law Review*, 62:3 (1991): 577–95 and Steve Fuller, *Philosophy, Rhetoric and the End of Knowledge* (Madison, Wisconsin: University of Wisconsin Press, 1993).

knowledge from western or scientific knowledge."[11] Such oppositions often oversimplify, blurring "the actual fluidity and permeability of knowledge and cultural boundaries."[12] Moreover, given the global presence of some 5000 distinctive indigenous cultures, reference to an "indigenous" knowledge system – even if one confined its scope to Native North America as I tend to do here – is empirically tenuous at best. It is crucial to acknowledge the specific circumstances that have shaped and differentiated the knowledge systems of indigenous peoples, and that continue to do so. As one commentator notes,

> [I]ndigenous knowledge is formed from a complex intertwining of knowledge and traditions and practices through the engagement of indigenous and nonindigenous peoples. Far from being considered a unitary, homogenous entity . . . indigenous knowledge must instead be understood as contingent, historically situated, and particular to the specifics of locality, group dynamics, place and time.[13]

It would, however, be historically and politically myopic to see only differences. Concrete diversity does not preclude commonality or community; there is much that binds indigenous peoples together. There are shared conditions, shared responsibilities, and a shared struggle: "Indianness . . . is reinforced by the common experience of almost five centuries of [Eurocentric] domination . . . The differences between these diverse peoples (or ethnic groups) have been accentuated by the colonizers as part of the strategy of domination."[14] Or, as Gail Tremblay (Iroquois/Micmac) observes, each of us

> comes from a people who has also had the experience of facing the forces of colonization by outsiders and has been subjected to

11 Arun Agrawal, "On Power and Indigenous Knowledge," in Darrell A. Posey (ed.), *Cultural and Spiritual Values of Biodiversity* (London: United Nations Environmental Programme Intermediate Technology Publication, 1999): 177.

12 Stephen B. Brush and Doreen Stabinsky (eds.), *Valuing Local Knowledge: Indigenous People and Intellectual Property Rights* (Washington, DC: Island Press, 1996): 6.

13 Michael Davis, "Bridging the Gap or Crossing a Bridge? Indigenous Knowledge and the Language of Law and Policy," paper presented to the "Bridging Scales and Epistemologies Conference," Bibliotheca Alexandrina, Alexandria, Egypt, 17–20 May 2004. Accessible online at: http://www.millenniumassessment.org/documents/bridging/papers/davis.michael.pdf.

14 Guillermo Bonfil Batalla, *Utopia y Revolucíon: El Pensamiento Politico Contemporàneo de los Indios en América Latina* (Mexico: Editorial Nueva Imagen, SA, 1981): 37–8. Translation by Roxanne Dunbar Ortiz.

attempts at physical and cultural genocide. Each knows the pressure to assimilate to other cultural patterns, and the pain of loss that has been handed down across the generations of people since contact . . . So it is that coming from such diverse cultures, we can join together to say, *we are one*.[15]

[15] Gail Tremblay, "Statement for Exhibition of Contemporary Native American Art, 'We Are Many, We Are One,'" curated by Jaune Quick-to-See Smith (1997).

PART

I

BIOCOLONIALISM AS IMPERIAL SCIENCE

Biocolonialism is in many respects more of the same – a continuation of the oppressive power relations that have historically informed the interactions of western and indigenous cultures, and part of a continuum of contemporary practices that constitute forms of cultural imperialism.[1] The first three chapters contextualize biocolonialism over time and within the broad range of these ongoing cultural practices. The phenomenon of cultural imperialism is addressed and critiqued. It is demonstrated to be consistent with (indeed, a continuation of) earlier forms of imperialism, and a preliminary sketch of biocolonialism is offered. The latter is then situated within the larger political struggles that have long inflected the relationship between dominant and indigenous knowledge systems.

The deep offensiveness and cultural destructiveness of biocolonialist practices can only be fully appreciated by seeing how profoundly they clash with many of the values and commitments that characterize and distinguish indigenous knowledge systems. The commodification of knowledge and of genetic resources that biocolonialism facilitates is sharply at odds with the web of prescriptions and proscriptions that guide the process of knowing within indigenous contexts. It also clashes directly with the role responsibilities toward the natural world that many indigenous peoples have historically assumed. The ideology that sustains biocolonialism is, in

[1] In making this claim, however, I do not mean to imply that imperialism itself, and the oppressive power relations it engenders and instantiates, have not themselves undergone significant and extensive change over the last several centuries. A range of substantive political transformations, as well as the globalized nature of contemporary economic and cultural exchanges, have unquestionably altered how imperialism manifests itself, how it impacts the lives of those it subordinates, and how it is in turn impacted by them.

turn, rooted in the neopositivist assumption of value neutrality and in a practice of value bifurcation which together enable it to deflect ethical and political critique. It both facilitates the marginalization of indigenous knowledge systems and provides thereby a legitimating rationale for biocolonialist practice.

1

Imperialism Then and Now

Introduction: Some Exhibits

An exhibit, in a court of law, is anything other than oral testimony that is placed before the fact finder to be admitted as evidence in a case. This chapter opens with four exhibits, best marked for identification as diverse instances of cultural imperialism. Cultural imperialism[1] is one of a number of oppressive relations that may hold between dominant and subordinated cultures. Whether or not conscious and intentional, it serves to extend the political power, secure the social control, and further the economic profit of the dominant culture. Ultimately, it facilitates a type of cultural acquisition via conceptual, even material, assimilation; the dominant culture seeks to establish itself in indigenous cultures by appropriating, mining, and redefining what is distinctive in, or constitutive of, them. The mechanism

[1] Various radical theorists and social critics have alluded to cultural imperialism, although few characterize it at length. My discussion differs somewhat from that of Iris Marion Young ("Five Faces of Oppression," in Thomas Wartenberg (ed.), *Rethinking Power* (Albany, New York: SUNY Press, 1992)). I agree with her that it is one of several forms of oppression, but I emphasize its impact on the cultures, rather than the individuals, subjected to it. I move freely here between references to indigenous cultures generally, and native North American cultures more specifically, because the practice of cultural imperialism under consideration is similarly imposed upon them. However, closer analyses of how specific historical, political, cultural, and socioeconomic circumstances condition and modify such practice are needed.

Within world-systems theory, Herbert Schiller describes cultural imperialism as "The sum of the processes by which a society is brought into the world system and how its dominating stratum is attracted, pressured, forced, and sometimes bribed into shaping social institutions to correspond to, or even promote, the values and structures of the dominating center of the system." *Communication and Cultural Domination* (New York: M.E. Sharpe, 1976): 9. For an excellent collection of contemporary essays on this topic, see Bernd Hamm and Russell Smandych (eds.), *Cultural Imperialism: Essays on the Political Economy of Cultural Domination* (Peterborough, Ontario: Broadview Press, 2005).

for this, as we will see, is an oft-repeated pattern of cultural subordination that turns vitally on legal and popular views of ownership and property, as formulated within the dominant culture.

Exhibit One records two recent events. In 1991, at a large gathering in California, a leading figure of the New Age movement announced to the assembled audience that he intended to patent the sweat lodge ceremony because native people were no longer performing it correctly.[2] Several years later, at a meeting of indigenous support groups in Geneva, the young Europeans in attendance were informed of the passing of a respected Muskogee Creek medicine man, widely known for his defense of the right of American Indians to retain control of their own spiritual ceremonies. On learning of his death, "they were heard to openly rejoice."[3]

Exhibit Two documents a controversy in Kansas over the skeletal remains of 146 Smoky Hill River people that were transformed into a tourist site, known as the Salina Burial Pit, visited by thousands each year. Cultural descendants of these people – including the Pawnee, Wichita, Mandan, Arikara, and Hidatsa – protested this as a racist violation of common human decency. Some scientists and historians, however, maintain that such human remains are vital for research and education. According to one of them: "It's an issue all over the United States . . . a real clash between science and religion. . . . There is a concerted effort by American Indians to shut down archaeology all over the country."[4] Walter Echo-Hawk, a lawyer with the Native American Rights Fund, sees it differently:

> There appears to be a loophole in legal protections and social policies that tends to permit disparate treatment of dead bodies and graves based on race. . . . If you desecrate an Indian grave, you get a Ph.D. But if you desecrate a white grave, you wind up sitting in prison.[5]

Exhibit Three concerns the Guajajara. Their medical knowledge has long prescribed the use of a plant, the Latin name of which is *Pilocarpus jaborandi,* to treat glaucoma. That they are no longer able to use it is the direct result of biocolonialism. *Pilocarpus* populations have been virtually

[2] This was related by Robert Antone in "Education as a Vehicle for Values and Sovereignty," an address given at the Third International Native American Studies Conference at Lake Superior State University in October 1991.

[3] José Barreiro, "The Search for Lessons," *Akwe:kon*, Vol. IX, No. 2 (1992): 22.

[4] Cited in Larry Fruhling, "Culture Collides With Archaeology Over Ancestors Graves," *The Santa Fe New Maxican* (23 April, 1989): C4.

[5] Ibid.

depleted as Brazil has exported it for some $25 million annually, and corporations holding patents derived from it have earned far more. As for the Guajajara, they have been subjected to debt peonage and slavery by the agents of the companies involved in the trade.[6]

Exhibit Four is a photograph of a Guaymi Indian woman whose name is being kept secret. If she is alive today, she is well into middle age. Diagnosed with leukemia in 1991, she sought treatment in a hospital in Panama City. While there, samples of her blood were drawn and her cell line was "immortalized" and stored in the United States, without her knowledge or consent. Two American scientists, listing themselves as "inventors" of her cell line, applied for its patent in 1993 and placed her cell line on sale at the American Type Culture Collection for $136. They did so on behalf of the Center for Disease Control because of the cell line's commercial promise and because the government encourages scientists to patent anything of interest. According to one of them,

> I think that most people wouldn't understand all the details of all the laboratory work that was being done and I don't think anyone ever really felt it was necessary . . . So in terms of specifically notifying the Guaymi that a patent application was being put forth, I don't think that was done. But again, mainly because I don't think anyone ever felt it was really necessary.[7]

Exhibits Three and Four, concrete examples of biocolonialism, share important contextual features with the first two. All four Exhibits attest to the conflict of knowledge systems within contemporary dominant and indigenous cultures, and to the existence of oppressive relations of power which promote such conflict. All four involve struggles over the politics of ownership – respectively, of spiritual knowledge, of human remains, of plant genetic resources and medicinal knowledge, and of human genetic resources. All four demonstrate the intervention of western property law in

6 Darrell Addison Posey, "Biodiversity, Genetic Resources, and Indigenous Peoples in Amazonia." Prepared for: Amazonia 2000: Development, Environment, and Geopolitics. Institute of Latin American Studies, University of London (24–26 June 1998). Available online at: http://www.ubcic.bc.ca/files/PDF/Posey_Biodiversity.pdf.

7 Jonathan Kaplan, "Who Owns Life?: Patenting Human Genes," *Living On Earth* (World Media Foundation, transcript of 13 May 1994). See also Philip Bereano, "Body and Soul: The Price of Biotech," *Seattle Times*, 20 August 1995, B5 and Philip Bereano, "The Race to Own DNA: Guaymi Tribe Was Surprised They Were Invented: Part II," *Seattle Times*, 27 August 1995, B5. The U.S. Commerce Department abandoned its application in 1993, following extensive protests by indigenous peoples, among others.

a manner that privileges the already powerful and violates the sovereignty of indigenous peoples.

Because an important strain of the indigenist response to biocolonialism turns on spiritual beliefs about the nature of life and about human responsibilities within the natural world, it is appropriate to begin with an analysis of Exhibit One. The commodification of indigenous spirituality is a paradigmatic instance of cultural imperialism. As such, it plays a politically vital, diversionary role, serving to colonize and assimilate the knowledge and belief systems of indigenous cultures.

Marketing Native America

Whether peddled by white shamans, plastic medicine men and women, opportunistic academics, entrepreneurs, or enterprising New Agers, Indian spirituality – like Indian lands before it – is rapidly being reduced to the status of a commodity, seized, and sold. Sacred ceremonies and ceremonial objects can be purchased at weekend medicine conferences or via mail-order catalogs. How-to books with veritable recipes for conducting traditional rituals are written and dispensed by trade publishers. A succession of born-again medicine people have – with greater or lesser subtlety – set themselves and their services up for hire, ready to sell their spiritual knowledge and power to anyone willing and able to meet their price. And a literary cult of Indian identity appropriation known as white shamanism continues to be practiced. Instead of contributing to the many Native-run organizations devoted to enhancing the lives and prospects of Indian people, New Agers are regularly enticed into contributing to the continued expropriation and exploitation of Native culture by purchasing an array of items marketed as means for enhancing their knowledge of Indian spirituality.[8]

Recently, the National Congress of American Indians (an organization not exactly known for radicalism), issued a "declaration of war" against "non-Indian wannabes, hucksters, cultists, commercial profiteers and self-styled New Age shamans" who have been exploiting sacred knowledge and rituals.[9] Throughout Indian Country, eloquent, forceful critiques of

[8] For a discussion of the New Age (especially as it bears on the marketing of indigenous spirituality), and for a survey of many of its products and practitioners (and prices!), see Lisa Aldred, "Plastic Shamans and Astroturf Sun Dance," *American Indian Quarterly* 24:3 (2000).

[9] David Johnston, "Spiritual Seekers Borrow Indian Ways," *New York Times*, 27 December 1993, A15.

these cultural developments have been mounted by writers, intellectuals, activists, and spiritual leaders. The phenomena being protested are diverse and include literary, artistic, scholarly, and commercial products intended for consumption in the markets of popular culture as well as in those of the cultural elite.[10]

When the spiritual knowledge, rituals, and objects of historically subordinated cultures are transformed into commodities, economic and political powers merge to produce cultural imperialism. A form of oppression exerted by a dominant society upon other cultures, and typically a source of economic profit, cultural imperialism secures and deepens the subordinated status of those cultures. In the case of indigenous cultures, it undermines their integrity and distinctiveness, assimilating them into the dominant culture by seizing and processing vital cultural resources, then remaking them in the image and marketplaces of the dominant culture. Such "taking of the essentials of cultural lifeways," Geary Hobson observes, "is as imperialistic as those simpler forms of theft, such as the theft of homeland by treaty."[11]

It is a phenomenon that spans North America, sparking the fierce resistance of indigenous people in Canada, as well as the United States. Lenore Keeshig-Tobias, a Toronto-based Anishinabe poet and storyteller, is a founding member of the Committee to Re-Establish the Trickster, an organization devoted to reclaiming the native voice in literature. The Canadian cultural industry, she protests,

> is stealing – unconsciously, perhaps, but with the same devastating results – native stories as surely as the missionaries stole our religion and the politicians stole our land and the residential schools stole our language . . . (it) amount(s) to cultural theft, theft of voice.[12]

10 Christopher Lind misses the nature of this protest and of the "claim being made by aboriginal artists and writers of colour . . . that whites are 'stealing' their stories." See "The Idea of Capitalism or the Capitalism of Ideas? A Moral Critique of the Copyright Act," *Intellectual Property Journal*, 7 (December 1991): 69. He insists that "(w)hat is being stolen is not the story itself but the market for the story . . . or the possibility of being able to exploit the commercial potential" (ibid.) of the story. Indigenous critiques are directed against the very fact of commercialization, against the extension of the market mechanism to these cultural materials by the dominant society. The claim being made is that this continues and extends a long history of oppression, that it constitutes theft of culture, of voice, of power.

11 Geary Hobson (ed.), *The Remembered Earth: An Anthology of Contemporary Native American Literature* (Albuquerque, New Mexico: University of New Mexico Press, 1979): 101.

12 Lenore Keeshig-Tobias, "Stop stealing native stories," *Toronto Globe and Mail*, 26 January 1990, A7.

Wendy Rose makes it plain that the issue here is not that "only Indians can make valid observations on themselves" and their cultures, rather, it is "one of integrity and intent":

> We accept as given that whites have as much prerogative to write and speak about us and our cultures as we have to write and speak about them and theirs. The question is how this is done and . . . why it is done.[13]

Some forms of cultural imperialism are the products of academic privilege and opportunism. The "name of Truth or Scholarship"[14] may be invoked, the cause of scholarly progress, of advancing knowledge.[15] Anishinabe author Gerald Vizenor reproaches the "culture cultists (who) have hatched and possessed distorted images of tribal

[13] Wendy Rose, "The Great Pretenders," in M. Annette Jaimes (ed.), *The State of Native America* (Boston, Massachusetts: South End Press, 1992): 415–16.

[14] Hobson, *The Remembered Earth*, 101.

[15] Cultural imperialism is often at its apex in the academy. As a result of the stubborn influence of positivism, knowledge claims within the dominant (academic) culture continue to be regarded as value free, as we consider at length in Chapter 3. An instructive example of this is Wilcomb Washburn's "Distinguishing History from Moral Philosophy and Public Advocacy," in Calvin Martin (ed.), *The American Indian and the Problem of History* (New York: Oxford University Press, 1987). A past president of the American Society for Ethnohistory, Washburn is particularly upset about "the process of using history to promote non-historical causes." He reacts with consternation to the call for historians to "form alliances with non-scholarly groups organized for action to solve specified societal problems," which he associates with "leftist academics" and "Indian activists."(p. 95)

Washburn offers himself as an example of an historian committed to what one is tempted to call a Great White Truth, a Truth properly cleansed of all values:

> all my efforts are guided by, and subject to, the limitations of historical truth . . . There is no place in the scholarly profession of history for such distorting lenses. History to me means a commitment to truth . . . however contradictory it may be to our . . . acquired convictions about how the world should be. (p. 97)

He assumes that his work, like his conception of truth, is unburdened by such distorting lenses, and remains both value free and politically neutral. Yet note that this work includes his "recent experiences in writing Indian history, which involve combat with radical theorists on the ideological front," his letters to the *Dartmouth Review* in support of the use of the Indian as a symbol, his efforts abroad to "justify United States policy . . . to spike assertions of genocide . . . to disprove the assertion that . . . multinational corporations control the United States Government and seek to exploit the resources of all native peoples against their will." (p. 94) All this, we are to suppose, is 'value free.' He goes on to claim that some will recognize his "lifelong and quixotic pursuit of the reality of the Indian as 'noble.'" (p. 97)

cultures."[16] Their obsession with the tribal past, he contends, "is not an innocent collection of arrowheads, not a crude map of public camp sites in sacred places, but rather a statement of academic power and control over tribal images."[17] Sometimes the "cause" is one of ethical progress, of moral duty: "Given the state of the world today, we all have not only the right but the obligation to pursue all forms of spiritual insight . . . it seems to me that I have as much right to pursue and articulate the belief system of Native Americans as they do."[18] On this reading, the colonization of indigenous knowledge and belief systems (and the attendant economic profit that their repackaging brings in the marketplaces of the dominant culture) is not only morally permissible, it is morally mandated.

Whatever its form, cultural imperialism often plays a diversionary role that is politically advantageous because it serves to extend – while effectively diverting attention from – the continued oppression of indigenous peoples. Acoma Pueblo writer Simon Ortiz underscores this aspect of the phenomenon. Condemning white shamanism as a "process of colonialism" and a "usurping (of) the indigenous power of the people," he charges that:

> symbols are taken and are popularized, diverting attention from real issues about land and resources and Indian peoples' working hours. The real struggle is really what should be prominent, but no, it's much easier to talk about drums and feathers and ceremonies and those sorts of things. "Real Indians," but "real Indians" only in quotes, stereotypes, and "interesting exotica" . . . So it's a rip-off.[19]

Keeshig-Tobias refers to it as "escapist" and a "form of exorcism," enabling Canadians "to look to an ideal native living in never-never land" rather than confront "the horrible reality of native-Canadian relations."[20] The extent to which cultural imperialism turns on conceptual colonization, and what is ultimately at stake in this, has been succinctly captured by Oneida scholar

16 Gerald Vizenor, "Socioacupuncture: Mythic Reversals and the Striptease in Four Scenes," in Calvin Martin (ed.), *The American Indian and the Problem of History* (New York: Oxford University Press, 1987): 183.

17 Ibid.

18 Gary Snyder, as cited in Ward Churchill, *Fantasies of the Master Race* (Monroe, Maine: Common Courage Press, 1992): 192.

19 Simon Ortiz in an interview in Laura Coltelli, *Winged Words: American Indian Writers Speak* (Lincoln, Nebraska. University of Nebraska Press, 1990): 111–12.

20 Keeshig-Tobias, "Stop stealing," 7.

Pam Colorado. She contends that the commodification of indigenous spirituality enables the dominant culture to supplant Indian people even in the area of their own spirituality. This process moves beyond ensuring their physical subordination to securing absolute ideological/conceptual subordination. If it continues, she observes:

> Non-Indians will have complete power to define what is and is not Indian, even for Indians . . . When this happens, the last vestiges of real, Indian society and Indian rights will disappear. Non-Indians will then "own" our heritage and ideas as thoroughly as they now claim to own our land and resources.[21]

The Cultural Politics of Ownership

When confronted by their critics, those engaged in the marketing of Native America frequently do attempt to justify their behavior. From their reasoning and rhetoric, we can elicit some distinctive features of this variant of cultural imperialism. What we will find is a rationale that has reverberated throughout the history of dominant–indigenous relations, one that starkly reveals how the cultural politics of ownership are played out in the context of oppression.

Consider Gary Snyder's response to indigenous protests: "Spirituality is not something that can be 'owned' like a car or a house," he asserts. It "belongs to all humanity equally."[22] Or consider Alberto Manguel's response to Keeshig-Tobias: "No one," he contends, "can 'steal' a story because stories don't belong to anyone. Stories belong to everyone . . . No one . . . has the right to instruct a writer as to what stories to tell."[23] Yet those who write and copyright "native" stories, those white shamans who sell poetry that "romanticize(s) their 'power' as writers to inhabit (Indian) souls and consciousness,"[24] and those culture capitalists who traffic in "Indian" rituals and sacred objects are all clearly making individual profit on what "no one" (allegedly) owns. Such responses are both diversionary and delusionary. They attempt to dictate the terms of the debate by focusing

21 Pam Colorado, as cited in Ward Churchill, *Fantasies*, 101.

22 Snyder, as cited in Ward Churchill, *Fantasies*, 192.

23 Alberto Manguel, "Equal rights to stories," *Toronto Globe and Mail*, 3 February 1990, D7.

24 Leslie Silko, as cited in Michael Castro, *Interpreting the Indian* (Albuquerque, New Mexico: University of New Mexico Press, 1983): 161.

attention on issues of freedom of speech and thought,[25] and deflecting it from the active commercial exploitation, and the historical realities of power, that condition current dominant–indigenous relations. In the words of Margo Thunderbird:

> They came for our land, for what grew or could be grown on it, for the resources in it, and for our clean air and pure water. They stole these things from us . . . and now . . . they've come for the very last of our possessions; now they want our pride, our history, our spiritual traditions. They want to rewrite and remake these things, to claim them for themselves.[26]

The colonists, indeed, displayed varying motivations regarding their presence and conduct in America, and they are similar to those presently vending Native Americana. The prospect of profits from speculation lured some to seize native lands; others, wanting to escape poverty and enhance their lives, regarded themselves as merely "sharing" underused lands; most found it convenient to believe that the indigenous inhabitants of this continent "could have no legitimate claims to land."[27]

Analogous reasoning and rhetoric accompany numerous parallel tales of acquisition in contemporary western–indigenous relations. By examining some of these, we can better elicit the specious "justificatory" appeals on which cultural imperialism relies to extend and legitimize such practice. Their cumulative weight suggests that cultural imperialism, in its late capitalist mode, requires a legitimating rationale, one that enables the dominant culture to mask the fundamentally oppressive nature of its treatment of subordinated cultures. This rationale is fashioned by invoking legal and popular views of ownership and property prevalent in western culture and conceptually imposing these upon indigenous cultures. It may take one, and usually both, of two forms: an appeal to common property and an appeal to private property.

In the first, the dominant culture enhances its political power, social control, and economic profit by declaring the (material, cultural, genetic)

25 Appeals to the First Amendment are the most common response of New Agers to their indigenist critics, according to the ethnographic fieldwork of Lisa Aldred, "Plastic Shamans," op. cit.

26 Margo Thunderbird, cited in Wendy Rose, "The Great Pretenders," 403.

27 David Lyons, "The Balance of Injustice and the War for Independence," *Monthly Review*, 45 (1994), 20.

resources of indigenous cultures to be common property, freely available to everyone. Thus, whatever the dominant culture finds desirable in indigenous cultures is declared to be part of the "public domain." The second appeal accomplishes the same ends through opposing means – facilitating privatization and the transformation of valued indigenous resources into commodity form. These appeals, examples of which will be considered below, lie at the heart of cultural imperialism and commonly function in tandem, with the former preparing and paving the way for the latter. Through the development of the notion of intellectual property and the articulation of intellectual property laws, the established legal system extends and enforces the practice of cultural imperialism. The patenting of indigenous genetic resources is a case in point. Before turning to this, however, a few remarks about the historical antecedents of cultural imperialism will be of value in illustrating the continuum of expropriative strategies that are in play.

In an earlier day, imperial powers could appeal to three competing legal theories of territorial acquisition to justify their claims to sovereignty over new lands: occupation, conquest, and cession. The first of these, unlike the other two, required that the land be *terra nullius*, devoid of people. According to Blackstone, "if an uninhabited country be discovered and planted by English subjects, all the English laws then in being . . . are immediately there in force."[28] Declaring that the land belonged to no one set the stage for its conversion into private or individual property – a legally protected possession.

However, other legitimating rationales for the privatizing of property were needed, particularly to accommodate types of property other than land. By declaring the intellectual and cultural properties of indigenous peoples to be in the public domain (i.e., to belong to everyone), the stage is equally well set for their conversion into private property. These two rationales (*terra nullius* and public domain) clearly resemble each other. The notion of property belonging to no one is the functional equivalent of that of property belonging to everyone; they both serve as the terms of a conversion process that results in the privatization of property. However, whereas the concept of *terra nullius* enabled the privatizing only of lands, the notion that property in the public domain could come to be owned by

[28] William Blackstone, 1 *Commentaries on the Laws of England* (1st edition, Oxford, 1765): 107–8.

individuals applies to other types of property as well, such as intellectual and cultural property. The latter conversion process may be regarded as a legal theory of cultural acquisition, whereby western intellectual property rights are invoked in the interests of cultural imperialism in order to appropriate valued intangible indigenous resources.

The politics of property is the central historical dynamic mediating western and indigenous relations. Certainly one of the more obvious examples of this is the General Allotment Act of 1887 that privatized communally owned tribal lands. A more recent case is that of the struggle to protect Newe Segobia (Western Shoshone homelands) from further encroachment by the U.S. government. The politics of property, however, has never been confined to land, as the struggle in Exhibit Two over the ownership of human remains demonstrates. Because the United States claims title to all "cultural property" found on federal public lands, material items of indigenous cultures discovered on these lands belong to the U.S. government, provided that they are at least 100 years old.[29] This includes human skeletal materials, which find themselves – together with these other items – thereby transformed into the "archaeological resources" of the dominant culture.[30] Ultimate authority to regulate the disposition of such "resources" rests with the Secretary of the Interior, according to the Archaeological Resources Protection Act of 1979.[31] Moreover, because the

[29] Speaking of the Antiquities Act of 1906, Walter Echo-Hawk notes that

> the underlying assumption . . . is that all "cultural resources" located on federal land "belong" to the United States, and can be excavated only for the benefit of public museums. There are no provisions for Native ownership or disposition. (Walter Echo-Hawk, "Museum Rights Vs. Indian Rights: Guidelines for Assessing Competing Legal Interests in Native Cultural Resources," *Review of Law and Social Change* XIV (1986), 449. This article also offers a useful discussion of the American Indian Religious Freedom Act, and its implications for ownership of native resources.)

The Antiquities Act has never been formally repealed, though it has been superseded by the Archaeological Resources Protection Act of 1979.

[30] The term "cultural property" is generally considered to include "objects of artistic, archaeological, ethnological, or historical interest" (John Merryman, "Two Ways of Thinking About Cultural Property," *The American Journal of International Law*, 80:4 (1986): 831). An "archaeological resource" refers to any material remains of past human life and activities that have been determined to be of "archaeological interest." 16 *United States Code*, Section 470bb(1).

James Riding In offers an excellent study of professional grave desecration, particularly in the academic context. See his "Without Ethics and Morality: A Historical Overview of Imperial Archaeology and American Indians," *Arizona State Law Journal*, 24:1 (1992).

[31] 16 *United States Code*, Section 470(dd). However this Act, unlike the earlier Antiquities Act, does require that Indian tribes be notified of any excavation permit that might cause harm to the cultural sites. See 16 *United States Code*, Section 470cc(c).

majority of states do not strictly regulate the excavation of native graves and sacred sites on state or private lands, private landowners have historically been at liberty to sell, destroy, or otherwise dispose of any material remains of indigenous cultures as they saw fit or profitable.[32]

Thus, whether it is legally permissible to dig up a grave, to display or sell the contents of it, will depend in part on whether that grave is in an Indian or non-Indian cemetery. This discriminatory treatment of skeletal remains has been contested by various critics. C. Dean Higginbotham has observed that "only the burial and religious sites of Native Americans are regularly subjected to archaeological excavation and study in the United States."[33] Walter Echo-Hawk concurs:

> If human remains and burial offerings of Native people are so easily desecrated and removed, wherever located, while the sanctity of the final resting place of other races is strictly protected, it is obvious that Native burial practices and associated beliefs were never considered during the development of American property law.[34]

Cultural imperialism, then, embraces a spectrum of expropriative strategies. At one end of this spectrum we find legal theories of acquisition that facilitate the dominant culture's ownership of indigenous land and of the material remains of indigenous peoples within the land. At the other end, we find theories of acquisition that rely on laws of intellectual property to legitimate the privatization of less tangible indigenous resources. We turn next to the type of case represented by Exhibit Three, in which the legitimating rationale of public domain is invoked to provide moral and legal cover for the theft of indigenous knowledge and genetic resources.

32 Indeed, according to an article on a Colorado development known as "Indian Camp Ranch," prospective homeowners:

> can now purchase land where more than 200 Anasazi sites have been identified . . . Those who buy property . . . will also be allowed to excavate sites on their land . . . Artifacts recovered will become the property of a museum to be built in the area. Homeowners will be allowed to display recovered artifacts in their residences, provided they are turned over to the museum upon their death. (*Archaeology*, March/April 1995: 14)

According to the state archaeologist of Colorado, such land-use plans are legal.

33 C. Dean Higginbotham, "Native Americans Versus Archaeologists: The Legal Issues," *American Indian Law Review*, 10 (1982), 99–100.

34 Echo-Hawk, "Museum Rights," 448.

Genetic Imperialism and the "Common Heritage"

In what has been described as "the last great resource rush,"[35] commercial seed and drug industries are extracting, transforming, and commodifying the valuable genetic resources of indigenous peoples. This time around, it is not land or natural resources that imperialism has targeted, but indigenous genetic wealth and pharmaceutical knowledge. Indigenous peoples inhabit the most genetically diverse areas of the world, and once again

> their areas, and their knowledge, are . . . being mined – for information. Unless indigenous rights to this material and knowledge are respected, this gene rush will leave indigenous people in the same hole as the other resource rushes.[36]

Corporate and academic scientists engaged in "gene-hunting" and "chemical prospecting" first mine indigenous medicinal and agricultural knowledge. They then identify and extract selected plant materials, process these in laboratories and finally through the legal system – ultimately transforming them into commodities and legally protected private property, for whose use indigenous people must pay. The key first step is to declare that these indigenous genetic resources belong to everyone. As the "common heritage of humankind . . . to be traded as a 'free good' among the community of nations,"[37] they are "not owned by any one people and are quite literally a part of our human heritage from the past."[38] Thus, they are "looked upon as a public good for which no payment is necessary or appropriate."[39] One may then convert these free "public" goods into private property and a source of enormous economic profit.

A recent example is the use by the Uru-eu-wau-wau Indians of Brazil of the bark of the Tike-Uba tree in a preparation that acts as

[35] Jason Clay, "Editorial: Genes, Genius, and Genocide," *Cultural Survival Quarterly* 14:4 (1990), 1. See also Al Gedicks's discussion of resource colonialism in his *The New Resource Wars: Native and Environmental Struggles Against Multinational Corporations* (Boston, Massachusetts: South End Press, 1993): 13.

[36] Ibid.

[37] Norman Myers, *A Wealth of Wild Species* (Boulder, Colorado: Westview Press, 1983): 24.

[38] Garrison Wilkes, "Current Status of Crop Germplasm," *Critical Reviews in Plant Sciences*, 1:2 (1983), 156.

[39] Jack Kloppenburg and Daniel Kleinman, "Seed Wars: Common Heritage, Private Property, and Political Strategy," *Socialist Review*, No. 95 (September/October 1987), 8.

an anticoagulant.[40] Reportedly, a large U.S.-based chemical company attempted to patent these properties of the plant,[41] following a study by corporate scientists of sap and bark specimens provided to them by members of the Goiana Institute for Prehistory and Anthropology.[42] The Uru-eu-wau-wau, protesting this commercialization of their knowledge, challenged that company's right to patent their traditional medicines.[43] However, as Janet McGowan notes:

> [M]uch like Columbus' voyage, when it comes to U.S. patent law, it isn't always a question of getting there first, but having the resources to control and protect your discovery . . . U.S. patent law really protect(s) (and financially reward(s)) the discovery of the known.[44]

Despite the fact that approximately 80% of the world's population relies on traditional health care based on medicinal plants, and that 74% of contemporary drugs have the same or related uses in western medicine as they do in traditional medical systems, the pharmaceutical knowledge and medicinal skills of indigenous peoples are neither acknowledged nor rewarded. As one commentator observes:

> Traditional remedies . . . are products of human knowledge. To transform a plant into medicine, one has to know the correct species, its location, the proper time of collection . . . , the part to be used, how to prepare it . . . the solvent to be used . . . , the way to prepare it . . . and, finally, posology . . . curers have to diagnose and select the right medicine for the right patients.[45]

Yet although indigenous pharmaceutical knowledge, like industrial knowledge, has been accumulated by trial and error, "it has been made public with no patent rights attached . . . What are the ethics behind recording customary knowledge and making it publicly available without

[40] Jack Kloppenburg, "No Hunting!," *Z Magazine* (September 1990), 106.
[41] Clay, "Editorial," 1.
[42] John Jacobs et al., "Characterization of the Anticoagulant Activities from a Brazilian Arrow Poison," *Journal of Thrombosis and Haemostasis*, 63:1 (1991), 34.
[43] Andrew Gray, "The Impact of Biodiversity Conservation on Indigenous Peoples," in Vandana Shiva (ed.), *Biodiversity: Social and Ecological Perspectives* (Atlantic Highlands, New Jersey: Zed Books, 1991): 67.
[44] Janet McGowan, "Who is the Inventor?," *Cultural Survival Quarterly*, 15:1 (Summer 1991), 20.
[45] Elaine Elisabetsky, "Folklore, Tradition, or Know-How?," *Cultural Survival Quarterly*, 15:1 (Summer 1991), 10.

adequate compensation?"[46] Such questions are all the more pressing given that this knowledge is often obtained from specialists in the indigenous community only after the scientist "has established credibility within that society and a position of trust with the specialist."[47] Research in ethnopharmacology[48] cannot ignore the omnipresence of pharmaceutical corporations eager "to analyze, develop, and market plant products" to secure "exclusive rights to pertinent information" collected.[49]

Whereas some ethnopharmacologists have worked to develop products managed by indigenous communities, others have been accused of "stealing valuable plant materials and appropriating esoteric plant knowledge for financial profit and professional advancement."[50] Wittingly or not, this collusion of western science, business, and legal systems is a potent extractive device:

> [C]ontemporary patent systems tend to disregard the creative intelligence of peoples and communities around the world. Thus the Western scientific and industrial establishment freely benefits from a steady flow of people nurtured genetic material and associated knowledge, and, at times, after only a superficial tinkering, reaps enormous economic profits through patents, without even token recognition, and much less economic reward to the rightful owners of such resources.[51]

Rural sociologist Jack Kloppenburg describes this phenomenon as "the commodification of the seed."[52] He notes that scientists from the advanced industrial nations have, for more than two centuries, appropriated plant genetic resources, yet

> Despite their tremendous utility, such materials have been obtained free of charge as the "common heritage," and therefore common good, of humanity. On the other hand, the elite cultivars developed

46 A.B. Cunningham, "Indigenous Knowledge and Biodiversity," *Cultural Survival Quarterly*, 15:1 (Summer 1991), 4.

47 Brian Boom, "Ethics in Ethnopharmacology," in Darrell A. Posey et al. (eds.), *Ethnobiology: Implications and Applications* (Belem, Brazil: Proceedings of the First International Congress of Ethnobiology, 1990): 150–51.

48 Defined from the perspective of the dominant science, ethnopharmacology is the "scientific study of the medicinal uses of plants and animals by human groups other than the dominant Western society."(ibid., 148)

49 Ibid., 149.

50 Ibid.

51 GRAIN (Genetic Resources Action International), "GATT, the Convention and IPRs," Econet, in the conference 'Biodiversity' (28 June 1994).

52 Jack Kloppenburg, *First The Seed: The Political Economy of Plant Biotechnology, 1492–2000* (Cambridge: Cambridge University Press, 1988): 11.

> by the commercial seed industries . . . are accorded the status of private property. They are commodities obtainable by purchase.[53]

The process wholly discounts the tremendous investment of generations of indigenous labor that is involved in the cultivation of specific plant varieties for their medicinal and nutrient value.[54] It credits solely the "chop shop" laboratory labor of corporate and academic scientists who "modify" what they have taken. Victoria Tauli-Corpuz, representing indigenous peoples at a meeting of the United Nations Commission on Sustainable Development, underscores the exploitation and skewed reasoning that is at work:

> Without our knowing these seeds and medicinal plants were altered in laboratories and now we have to buy these because companies had them patented . . . We are told that the companies have intellectual property rights over these genetic plant materials because they improved on them. This logic is beyond us. Why is it that we, indigenous peoples who have developed and preserved these plants over thousands of years, do not have the rights to them anymore because the laboratories altered them?[55]

Biocolonialism: Science and Empire

The significance of science, especially of the biological sciences, in both empire building and in maintaining imperial domination, has finally

[53] Kloppenburg and Kleinman, "Seed Wars," 24. See also Stephen Brush's discussion of the common heritage regime in his "The Demise of 'Common Heritage' and Protection for Traditional Agricultural Knowledge" in Charles McManis (ed.), *Biodiversity & the Law: Intellectual Property, Biotechnology & Traditional Knowledge* (Sterling, Virginia: Earthscan, 2007).

[54] This was acknowledged by Illinois Congressman John Porter who in 1990 introduced a resolution to discontinue the ongoing GATT negotiations regarding the extension of intellectual property rights to genetic and biological resources. The difficulty with the U.S. proposal on trade-related aspects of intellectual property rights, Porter charged, is that

> it fails to consider the value of biological and genetic material and processes in developing nations, as well as the invaluable and historic contributions of local people in the use of that material.
>
> Since these people typically do not have access to representation to ensure that their interests are protected in the General Agreement on Tariffs and Trade (GATT) process, we have an obligation to recognize their rights.

(John Porter, "A Resolution Affecting the GATT Negotiations on Intellectual Property Rights for Genetic and Biological Resources," *Congressional Record*, 101st Congress, 2nd Session, Vol. 136, No. 94 (20 July 1990), E 2425.)

[55] Victoria Tauli-Corpuz, "We are part of biodiversity, respect our rights," *Third World Resurgence*, 36 (1993), 25.

begun to receive sustained attention. Even so, as Londa Schiebinger observes in her recent study of botany and the geopolitics of plants, "historians, post-colonialists, even historians of science rarely recognize the importance of plants to the processes that form and reform human societies and politics on a global scale."[56] Yet according to Linnaeus, the very *raison d'être* of the science of natural history was to serve the state. Moreover, in the eighteenth century, political economists "taught that exact knowledge of nature was key to amassing national wealth and hence power."[57] Indeed, seeing that science served "the interests of imperial efficiency and colonial development" was an important aspect of late nineteenth-century European imperialism.[58]

Resource colonialism – the identification, appropriation, extraction, and processing, by dominant societies, of select natural resources belonging to other, subordinated peoples – quickly moved, in the Americas, from the gold and silver, which drew early conquistadors, to encompass plants and animals of numerous and varied sorts. Not only did European naturalists collect "the stuff of nature," Schiebinger notes, but they also "lay their own peculiar grid of reason over nature so that nomenclatures and taxonomies often served as 'tools of empire.'" Botanists, for their part, were

> "agents of empire"; their inventories, classifications, and transplantations were the vanguard and in some cases the "instruments" of European order.[59]

At the same time, formal scientific institutions (such as Britain's Kew Gardens) played a crucial role in the expansion of empire by generating and disseminating scientific knowledge "which facilitated transfers of energy, manpower, and capital on a worldwide basis and on an unprecedented scale."[60]

[56] Londa Schiebinger, *Plants and Empire: Colonial Bioprospecting in the Atlantic World* (Cambridge, Massachusetts: Harvard University Press, 2004): 3.
[57] Schiebinger, 5.
[58] Roy MacLeod, "Reading the Discourse of Colonial Science," in Patrick Petitjean (ed.), *Les Sciences Coloniales: Figures et Institutions* (Paris: ORSTOM, 1996): 87.
[59] Schiebinger, 11. See also David MacKay, "Agents of Empire: The Banksian Collectors and Evaluation of New Land," in David Philip Miller and Peter Reill (eds.), *Visions of Empire: Voyages, Botany and Representations of Nature* (Cambridge: Cambridge University Press, 1996): 38–57.
[60] Lucile H. Brockway, *Science and Colonial Expansion: The Role of the British Royal Botanical Gardens* (New Haven, Connecticut: Yale University Press, 2002): 6.

The term "biocolonialism," as used here, may best be regarded as one variant of neocolonialism, a relationship of dominance and oppression between nations or peoples in which a nation, or nations, maintains power over another nation through a variety of means other than direct governmental control.[61] Given the nature of contemporary globalization and of transnational corporations, the dominant group is increasingly likely to involve more than one nation-state. The subordinated society "is robbed of its historical line of development, externally manipulated and transformed according to the needs and interests"[62] of the dominant group(s). Although, as some have noted, direct colonial rule in the late twentieth century "has all but vanished . . . the persistence of neocolonial domination . . . is undeniable."[63] It relies on, and actively draws upon, complex webs of power, the intersecting strands of which buttress and strengthen one another, allowing "certain communities to assert their influence and sovereignty over other groups."[64] These webs may include the legal systems of dominant nation-states that are imposed upon or otherwise impact the subordinated peoples, trade activities (especially as conducted by transnational corporations),[65] the scientific and technological knowledge industries, and the threat (or reality) of indirect political interventions – all of which may

[61] See Kara H. Ching, "Indigenous Self-Determination in an Age of Genetic Patenting: Recognizing an Emerging Human Rights Norm," *Fordham Law Review*, 66 (1997): 687–730.

[62] Jürgen Osterhammel, *Colonialism: A Theoretical Overview* (Princeton, New Jersey: Markus Wiener, 1997): 16–17.

[63] Nicholas Thomas, *Colonialism's Culture* (Princeton, New Jersey: Princeton University Press: 1994): 1.

[64] Tony Ballantyne and Antoinette Burton, *Bodies in Contact: Rethinking Colonial Encounters in World History* (Durham, North Carolina: Duke University Press, 2005): 3.

[65] David C. Korten, in his classic study of contemporary corporate power, contends that global domination of weak by strong states did not end with World War II:

> It simply cloaked colonialism in a less obvious, more beguiling form. The new corporate colonialism is no more than a consequence of immutable historical forces than was the old state colonialism. It is a consequence of conscious choices based on the pursuit of elite interest. This elite interest has been closely aligned with the corporate interest in advancing deregulation and economic globalization. As a consequence, the largest transnational corporations and the global financial system have assumed increasing power over the conduct of human affairs in the pursuit of interests increasingly at odds with the human interest. (David C. Korten, *When Corporations Rule the World*, 2nd edition. (Bloomfield, Connecticut: Kumarian Press, 2001): 173).

serve as, or enable, "mechanisms of social control, commodity transaction, exploitation, and appropriation."[66]

Although some theorists of neocolonialism focus their accounts on the subordination of nation-states,[67] the practice may well be most egregious and destructive when visited upon peoples not recognized as forming separate states. This last brings the interests and ambitions of the surrounding state – often itself subject to domination by the more powerful – into play, especially as these states may be authorized in international fora to protect the threatened resources and well-being of the nations within their borders. Precisely what is ignored or overridden, in the conduct of biocolonialism, are indigenous sovereignty and rights to self-determination: "the sampling and patenting of indigenous genetic materials amounts to neocolonialism . . . indigenous peoples' control over their own genetic heritage is an essential part of their fight for self-determination."[68] Although the role of nation-states as imperial powers is now more complex, and involves a richer cast of interconnected actors than was previously the case, it remains a vital feature of neocolonial domination. As Keith Aoki comments:

> Despite many rumors of its impending demise in the era of globalization, news of the demise of the nation-state may be premature. Ironically, the increasingly transnational proprietors of vast (and private) intellectual property holdings must turn to the national legal regimes in order to underwrite the value of their holdings.[69]

66 David Wade Chambers and Richard Gillespie, "Locality in the History of Science: Colonial Science, Technoscience and Indigenous Knowledge," *Osiris*, 15 (2000), 232.

67 See Kwame Nkrumah, *Neo-Colonialism: The Last Stage of Imperialism* (Atlantic Highlands, New Jersey: Humanities Press International, 1965). According to Nkrumah "The essence of neocolonialism is that the State which is subject to it is, in theory, independent and has all the outward trappings of international sovereignty." (In Robert J.C. Young, *Postcolonialism: An Historical Introduction* (Malden, Massachusetts: Wiley-Blackwell, 2001): 46.)

68 Federico Lenzerini, "Biogenetic Resources and Indigenous Peoples' Rights," in Francesco Francioni (ed.), *Biotechnologies and International Human Rights* (Portland, Oregon: Hart Publishing, 2007): 197.

69 Keith Aoki, "Neocolonialism, Anticommons Property, and Biopiracy in the (Not-So-Brave) New World Order of International Intellectual Property Protection" *Indiana Journal of Global Legal Studies* 6 (1998): 50. While I agree that the concept of sovereignty is undergoing significant transformation (see Chapter 8), I am not convinced either that this has progressed as far as (or that the effective role of nation-states is as diminished as) contemporary theorists Michael Hardt and Antonio Negri suggest in their *Empire* (Cambridge, Massachusetts: Harvard University Press, 2000).

It is important that biocolonialism not be held to turn on intent.[70] A host of different agents – no doubt with a host of different intentions – contributed to the biocolonialist venture captured in Exhibit Three: the anthropologists and botanists who mined Guajajara medical knowledge to identify and locate *Pilocarpus*; the laboratory scientists who isolated the active ingredient, transforming it into a novel invention that could be converted into private patented property; and the politicians, chief executive officers, lawyers, and entrepreneurs in Brazil and those employed by the pharmaceutical corporations who processed and marketed the result as a glaucoma treatment.[71]

Whether a specific project or practice is biocolonialist depends on the consequences of agency, not the agent's intent – whether the agents in question are scientists, corporations, or states. Although intent may be

70 As Lawrence Hinman (*Ethics: A Pluralistic Approach to Moral Theory* (Belmont, California: Thomson Wadsworth, 3rd edition, 2003)) notes, when our concern is to assess the moral correctness of legislation, we focus on its effects on people, not on the intentions of those who passed the legislation (which may vary and be venal). In doing this, he suggests, we are not

> necessarily denying that individual intentions are important on some level but are rather confining our attention to a level on which those intentions become largely irrelevant. This is particularly appropriate in the case of policy decision by governments, corporations, or groups. In such cases, there may be a diversity of different intentions that one may want to treat as essentially private matters when assessing the moral worth of the proposed law, policy, or action. (p. 155)

Such a parsing of the role of intention versus consequences is also embedded in proposals for a functional definition of genocide advanced by Ward Churchill in *Since Predator Came* (Littleton, Colorado: Aegis Publications, 1995), whose discussion of it is drawn upon here.

71 Some suppose that "northern bioprospectors" cannot be held responsible for their part in such destructive practices because other agents are involved in biocolonialism: "Accusations that commercial development is inflicting environmental damage, though justifiable to some degree, should not be laid at the feet of northern bioprospectors....If jaborandi bushes are being overharvested for their pharmacologically active leaves, the depletion should not be blamed on Merck & Company. Responsibility for this plant's decline does not rest with the multinational pharmaceutical company... Rather, the government of Brazil is accountable for its failure to control access to jaborandi..." Jim Chen, "There's No Such Thing As Biopiracy... and It's a Good Thing Too," *McGeorge Law Review*, 37 (2006): 13. One problem with this reasoning is that it supposes that responsibility for foreseen harms cannot be shared. Furthermore, the likelihood of such harmful consequences cannot morally be legitimately screened off; it constitutes a reason for refraining from such practices. Whether these consequences are intended or merely foreseen is irrelevant to whether those involved are responsible for them. For a detailed discussion of these issues, see Alison McIntyre, "Doing Away with Double Effect," *Ethics* 111:2 (2001). For a simpler discussion, albeit in a different context, see Alan W. Clarke and Laurelyn Whitt, *The Bitter Fruit of American Justice* (University Press of New England: Lebanon, New Hampshire, 2007): 149–50.

relevant to an assessment of culpability, it is not relevant to the identification of some activity or project as biocolonialist. This case demonstrates the futility and inadequacy of tying an occurrence of biocolonialism to the presence, absence, or predominance of any particular intent. Rather, the impact – material, political, socioeconomic, cultural, and environmental – of such activity upon a people is central in its characterization as biocolonialist.[72] What sorts of impacts are relevant to a determination of biocolonialism? Having a workable definition of extractive biocolonialism in hand would be of practical and strategic value in resisting it. To be effectively combated, the phenomenon itself must be recognized and acknowledged for what it is.

I propose the following as an account of biocolonialism. As it pertains to indigenous peoples, extractive biocolonialism may be understood as any activity that (a) through the use of force or coercion (economic or otherwise), involves or facilitates the removal, processing, conversion into private property, and commodification of indigenous genetic resources by agents of the dominant culture(s), and (b) typically results in some or all of the following:

1. substantial damage to the environment, such that a peoples' way of life is destroyed, undermined, or threatened;
2. erosion of indigenous health and well-being, whether physical or spiritual;
3. destabilization of indigenous social, economic, and legal structures;
4. creation of new, or the exacerbation of existing, internal or external political struggles;
5. disruption or discrediting of indigenous knowledge and value systems;
6. imposition of concepts, practices, and values that further the economic and political interests of the dominant culture;

[72] There is also this essential question to address: Who calculates the consequences? Hinman observes that it makes a difference when one group in society does the calculating for another group; it is all too easy for those calculations to become miscalculations.

> This is, at least in part, an epistemological point. Many would argue that those most directly affected by consequences are in the best position to estimate the importance of those consequences for themselves. There is also a moral and a psychological point here. The moral one is that those who will bear the consequences should have a voice in determining those consequences. The psychological one is that people are more likely to bear onerous consequences when they themselves have had a voice in choosing them. (*Ethics*, 160)

7. loss of political and economic autonomy and increased dependency on the dominant culture(s); and
8. assimilation and loss of biological and cultural diversity.

This account may be of value in demonstrating how the Guajajara case in Exhibit Three, the Guaymi case in Exhibit Four, and the Human Genome Diversity Project considered in Chapter 4 may, for all their differences, appropriately be judged biocolonialist. Moreover, it is flexible enough to produce a continuum along which biocolonialist projects can be arranged by severity of impact. It is, however, a working proposal that needs and invites further development. What is clear, however, is that the term "biopiracy" (which frequently appears in the literature on this topic[73] and is often used interchangeably with "biocolonialism") fails to capture the full scope of the phenomenon sketched here. Biocolonialism is not exclusively a matter of theft or of economic deprivation undertaken by a band of scofflaws that can be ameliorated, if not exonerated, by the provision of funds.[74] It is not, as Edward Said has noted of both imperialism and colonialism, "a simple act of accumulation and acquisition."[75] The term biocolonialism, unlike biopiracy, brings the matter of indigenous sovereignty and self-determination – and its violation – directly to the fore. The protection of indigenous knowledge and genetic resources

> is not just a theoretical question of confronting misappropriation and abuse; it is a question of political status and recognition. Inherent in the protection of traditional knowledge and cultural heritage is the

[73] Ikechi Mgbeoji's *Global Biopiracy: Patents, Plants and Indigenous Knowledge* (Ithaca, New York: Cornell University Press, 2006) is one of many examples. It offers an excellent analysis of these concerns as they are posed for nation-states (i.e., primarily for the industrialized North vs. the 'westernizing' South), especially as regards intellectual property issues.

Biopiracy has been defined as "the unauthorized extraction of biological resources and/or associated traditional knowledge from developing countries, or to the patenting of spurious 'inventions' based on such knowledge or resources without compensation." Graham Dutfield, *Intellectual Property, Biogenetic Resources and Traditional Knowledge* (Sterling, Virginia: Earthscan, 2004): 52.

[74] More inadequate yet is "bioprospecting," maintaining as it does an aura of a harmless hunting about that wholly divorces itself from context, history, and consequence. In both biopiracy and bioprospecting, the presence or absence of monetary compensation may well be a determinative factor. This is not the case in biocolonialism.

[75] Edward Said, *Culture and Imperialism* (New York: Random House, 1993): 9.

> protection of the land on which indigenous knowledge is practiced and perpetuated.[76]

This is an issue that we will explore in Chapter 8.

The introduction of monocultures and the attendant undermining of plant genetic diversity (via "development" debacles such as the Green Revolution)[77] is one form of biocolonialism. Another is extractive biocolonialism – where valued genetic resources and information are sought, "discovered," and removed to the microworlds of biotechnoscience. There, they are legally christened the private intellectual property of individuals, corporations, and universities; transformed into commodities; and placed for sale in genetic marketplaces, such as the American Type Culture Collection. In this manner, the commercial seed industry and the pharmaceutical industry have commodified the plant genetic resources and traditional medicines of indigenous peoples, along with their agricultural and medicinal knowledge. The controversy over the Human Genome Diversity Project and the commodification of the cell lines of indigenous peoples, examined in Part II, is only one phase of this struggle. They are, indeed, more of the same, as law professor Keith Aoki notes:

> While patenting a cell line from an indigenous person may be a particularly egregious form of biocolonialism, it may be entirely consistent with Western practices rooted in the not too distant past. For example, a high percentage of the genetic resources that the United States uses in its own agricultural production originated from uncompensated sources in the Third World. No compensation was paid for these resources because such genetic resources were seen as a product of nature. At virtually the same moment it became technologically possible to alter these "products" genetically, the Supreme Court held them to be patentable.[78]

76 Danielle Conway-Jones, "Safeguarding Traditional Knowledge and Cultural Heritage: Supporting the Right to Self-Determination and Preventing the Commodification of Culture," *Howard Law Journal*, 48 (2005): 754.

77 See generally, Vandana Shiva, *The Violence of the Green Revolution* (Atlantic Highlands, New Jersey: Zed Books Ltd, 1991).

78 Keith Aoki, "The Stakes of Intellectual Property Law," in David Kairys (ed.), *The Politics of Law* (New York, New York: Basic Books, 1982, 1998): 273.

Legitimation

The rule of law, as we will see more fully in Part III, is an even more effective means of extending empire than is military force and occupation because it brings its own validation, its own legitimating rationale, with it. When British colonists arrived in North America, their empire's laws and legal practices arrived with them. These drew heavily on John Locke's theory of property to justify the occupation and expropriation of the lands and resources of Native America. According to Locke, the Christian God commanded "Man . . . to subdue the Earth, i.e. to improve it . . . As much land as a Man Tills, Plants, Improves, cultivates, and can use the Product of, so much is his Property. He by his Labour does, as it were, inclose it from the Common."[79] The value of land was almost entirely due to such "improvement," that is, to the labor that was mixed with land. Thus, it is labor that establishes property rights over land, and "land that is left wholly to Nature, that hath no improvement of Pasturage, Tillage or Planting, is called, as indeed it is, waste . . ."[80]

The cultural bias embedded in this account of "improvement" discounted the labor and skills of indigenous North America in pursuing an ecologically sustainable way of life; it also, conveniently, declared most of the continent a wasteland or wilderness, a *vacuum domicilium* awaiting occupation. In the words of Pilgrim apologist Robert Cushman, because Indians "do but run over the grass, as do also the foxes and wild beast . . . [and are] not industrious, neither have art, science, skill or faculty to use either the land or the commodities of it," their land was "spacious and void," free for English taking.[81]

So it was that, in classical imperialism, legal and philosophical concepts of property provided the ideological justification for colonization. The frontiers have expanded in contemporary imperialism to include intangible property – the cultural, intellectual, and genetic resources of indigenous peoples. Intellectual property laws are mediating the confluence of science and the economy, easing the merger of scientific and industrial

79 John Locke, *Second Treatise of Government*, third edition (New York: Liberal Arts Press, 1690, 1952): 20.

80 Ibid., 347.

81 Cited in William Cronon, *Changes in the Land: Indians, Colonists, and the Ecology of New England* (New York, New York: Farrar, Straus & Giroux, 1983): 56.

policy. They are doing so in a manner which sustains and advances the interests of the dominant institutions of society, especially American society – both of the federal government and of large corporations. As these interests extend to the nation-states of the Third World and the indigenous nations of the Fourth World, they shape and constrain the initiatives undertaken in the name of contemporary technoscience structuring the pursuit of knowledge. Biocolonialism is one result of this new imperialism diversifying the range of processes and policies available for establishing and maintaining an empire.

A legitimating rationale analogous to that relied on earlier is at work within the intellectual property regime. The intellectual and manual labor, and the innovative skills, of indigenous peoples are discounted, and their genetic resources treated as raw and undeveloped – ripe for the taking. Whatever value they come to have is understood in Lockean terms as the result of the labor of, and improvements or innovations introduced by, corporate and academic scientists. The process of legally sanctioned theft, alienation, and commodification of indigenous land has, with the rise of biopatents, been extended to include the legally sanctioned theft, alienation, and commodification of indigenous knowledge and genetic resources. The "colonies," as Vandana Shiva puts it, now encompass "the interior spaces, the 'genetic codes' of life forms from microbes and plants to animals, including humans."[82] This process is seen as justifiable and as justified because indigenous peoples are regarded as *sine scientia*, without science, and, therefore, without genuine knowledge of the natural world. Guajajara healers, the rationale goes, may have used *Pilocarpus jaborandi* to treat glaucoma for centuries, but they have not isolated the active ingredient responsible for its beneficial effects in the laboratory. So it is perfectly legitimate to go ahead and apply for a patent. In a similar way, early European explorers in Australia alleged that the indigenous inhabitants either lacked the language or the intelligence to classify and name the landscape, and such a purported "spatial deficiency" became a "legal deficiency":[83]

> Seeing that [the Aborigine] did not classify it, did not distinguish it from other places, seeing that he did not seem to know "it" as a

[82] Vandana Shiva, *Biopiracy: The Plunder of Nature and Knowledge* (Boston, Massachusetts: South End Press, 1999): 3.

[83] Nicholas K. Blomley, *Law, Space, and the Geographies of Power* (New York, New York: The Guilford Press, 1994): 54.

> "place," could he be said to understand the notion of possession at all? And, if his grasp of it were so tenuous, then it was hardly a crime to take possession of it. The Whites did not, in this sense, possess the aborigine's country... They possessed a country of which the Aborigine was unaware... Logically then, possession could go ahead without consultation.[84]

The imperial dynamic that governs dominant–indigenous relations continues to rely on the politics of property and the apologetics of law. Law is the means by which dominant nation-states, and dominant elites and classes within nation-states, strive to maintain, justify, and extend their power. Yet, as we will see in subsequent chapters, both law and science invoke a rhetoric of neutrality that facilitates their operation by obscuring their political face. Indigenist resistance to biocolonialism involves a sustained critique of the value-laden and value-bifurcated operation of the new imperial science; simultaneously, it demonstrates how the law's own rhetoric of neutrality acts as an ideological cloaking device. The analysis of the Human Genome Diversity Project and comparable extractive biocolonial projects developed in Part II will illustrate how the new imperial science arises from the confluence of science with capitalism, mediated by an intellectual property system that is distinctively western, essentially American, and increasingly international.

[84] Ibid., 164.

2

Indigenous Knowledge, Power, and Responsibility

An excellent antidote to the power of our Western hierarchical oppositions and the theory of knowledge upon which they ride is an acquaintance with other theories of knowledge and ontologies. – Joanna Overing[1]

Introduction

Keeping in mind the caveats voiced above about the need to acknowledge differences within, and similarities across, indigenous and western knowledge systems, the burden of this chapter is to acknowledge some of the differences between them. One of the most consequential of these is the fact that knowledge tends to be tied to the natural world in very different ways within indigenous and western knowledge systems. Among indigenous peoples, for example, the belief that knowledge and land are intimately bound to one another is widely shared, as is the accompanying belief that the natural world is alive, spiritually replete. Not only are these beliefs generally not shared by the dominant knowledge system, but they are at odds with varying aspects of it. Without some appreciation of such differences, we cannot fully grasp the force of indigenist critiques of biocolonialism, nor can we understand well how contemporary relations of power sustain cultural imperialism. The policies which legitimate biocolonialism, and the practices which constitute it, arise within a cultural milieu notable for its marginalization and dismissal of indigenous knowledge systems.

[1] Joanna Overing, "Introduction," in Joanna Overing (ed.), *Reason and Morality* (London: Tavistock Publications, 1985): 17.

This chapter and the next situate the struggle over biocolonialism within the context of indigenous and western knowledge systems, and the dynamics of power which structure their interaction. It opens once again with two exhibits, concrete examples of the type of issue this chapter will attempt to illuminate. The words that follow were spoken in the context of specific political struggles. Ammoneta Sequoyah's, in the first exhibit, appear in his lawsuit against the Tennessee Valley Authority, and Alice Benally's, in the second, are part of her affidavit in the case of *Manybeads v. United States*. Words spoken in such contexts are not offered primarily as philosophical commentary or as insight into the environmental ethics of their speakers' cultures – nor should they be heard that way. They are part of a political struggle.

Exhibit Five. Some years ago, the Cherokee mounted fierce resistance to the construction of the Tellico Dam and the subsequent flooding of the Little Tennessee Valley.[2] Many of their objections were based on the threat that it posed to their cultural heritage. Ammoneta Sequoyah, a medicine man who gathered healing plants in the Valley several times a year, explained that "[his people] believe that all a person knows is placed in the ground with that person [at the time of burial]."[3] "Flooding the Valley or digging up the [Indian graves] there will destroy 'the knowledge and beliefs of (the) people who are in the ground' and destroy what they have taught."[4] Consequently, it was Mr. Sequoyah's belief that, if the Valley were flooded, he would lose his knowledge of medicine.

Exhibit Six. In an effort to prevent their forced relocation from their traditional homelands, a number of Diné people have been involved in a lawsuit against the United States. Alice Benally, facing the prospect of removal from Big Mountain, expressed the incomprehensibility of that notion by commenting, in her affidavit to *Manybeads v. United States*, that in the proposed relocation site the plants and animals would not know her – nor would she know them. She said:

> If we are to make our offerings at a new place, the spiritual beings would not know us. We would not know the mountains or the significance of them. We would not know the land and the land would

[2] See *Sequoyah v. Tennessee Valley Authority*, 620 F.2d 1159, 1160 (6th Cir. 1980).
[3] Ibid., 1162.
[4] Ibid.

> not know us.... We would not know the sacred places... If we were to go on top of an unfamiliar mountain we would not know the life forms that dwell there.[5]

In some native languages such relocations are literally unthinkable. There is no term for them, and no concept by which they are known. As Pauline Whitesinger once stated, "In our traditional tongue there is no word for relocation. To move away is to disappear."[6]

Pluralism and Anti-Pluralism

Before attempting a working characterization of dominant and indigenous knowledge systems, it will help to clarify what is meant by "knowledge system." Drawing on Stephen Marglin's useful discussion,[7] a knowledge system can be defined in terms of four characteristics: epistemology, a theory of knowledge giving an account of what counts as knowledge and how we know what we know; transmission, dealing with how knowledge is conveyed or acquired, with how it is learned and taught; power, both external (how knowledge communities relate to other knowledge communities) and internal (how members of a given knowledge community relate to one another); and innovation, how what counts as knowledge may be changed or modified. The systemic nature of knowledge is due to the reciprocal influence of these four characteristics upon one another: how we know, how we learn and teach, how we innovate, and how power figures in this are linked. Together they provide valuable conceptual parameters for describing and contrasting dominant and indigenous knowledge systems.

Oppressive relations of power have shaped the histories of diverse knowledge systems and continue to inflect the present in ways that obscure or override their diversity. The existence and value of indigenous knowledge systems have, for example, been systematically denied. In the origin stories of the dominant culture, indigenous peoples have superstitions, myths, or belief systems based on ignorance. They do not have knowledge systems.

5 See *Affidavit of Alice Benally* ¶ 56, *at* 248, *Manybeads v. United States*, 730 F. Supp. 1515 (D. Ariz. 1989) (No. 88–410).

6 Cited in Michael Riley, "Bury My Heart at Big Mountain," *Time*, 7 July 1986. Available online at: http://www.time.com/time/magazine/article/0,9171,961656,00.html.

7 The following account is drawn from Stephen A. Marglin, "Toward the Decolonization of the Mind" and "Losing Touch," in Stephen A. Marglin and Frédérique Apffel Marglin (eds.), *Dominating Knowledge* (Oxford: Clarendon Press, 1990), especially 232–3.

Contributors to a recent volume devoted to the encounter between the dominant knowledge system of the West and the traditional knowledge systems of India found themselves stymied by a recurrent problem, by "the imperialist pretension to universality made on behalf of the western [knowledge system] . . . and the total inability of its adherents to regard competing systems with anything but contempt, the inability indeed even to contemplate the existence of competing systems."[8]

The dominant knowledge system tends to embrace an anti-pluralism, a lack of receptiveness to alternative epistemologies, to other ways of knowing the world. Other knowledge systems are usually reduced to "superstition, the very antithesis of knowledge."[9] This is especially so for knowledge systems employing forms of knowledge transmission that are regarded as suspect – such as the stories and ceremonies upon which indigenous communities heavily rely. They defy a ready reduction to factual propositions and are seen as "tainted" with a normative and spiritual component. As Stephen Marglin notes, when "the supreme confidence of Westerners or Westernized elites in their knowledge is coupled to the superior means of political and economic force at their disposal" the result is "often fatal for indigenous systems."[10]

Part of what facilitates this closure to alternative epistemologies within the dominant knowledge system is a tendency toward a reductivist scientism – the conviction that science is the best, if not the only, way of knowing, "that we can no longer understand science as one form of possible knowledge but rather must identify knowledge with science."[11] This tendency is apparent in the early Comtean version of positivism, where the movement of intellectual thought leads from superstition to the triumph of science, the "culminating stage of human knowledge" where "one devotes oneself to the search for relationships through observation or experimentation . . . the stage toward which all human history has been advancing."[12] It emerges at the beginning of the twentieth century in Max Weber's 1930 introduction to *The Protestant Ethic and the Spirit of Capitalism,* in which

8 Ibid., 25.
9 Ibid.
10 Ibid.
11 Jurgen Habermas, *Knowledge and Human Interests,* translated by J.J. Shapiro, 2nd edition (London: Heinemann, 1974): 4.
12 Robert N. Proctor, *Value-Free Science?: Purity and Power in Modern Knowledge* (Cambridge, Massachusetts: Harvard University Press, 1991): 160.

he comments that "Only in the West does science exist at a stage of development which we recognize to-day as valid."[13] It also surfaces mid-century in a logical positivism committed "to epistemology as the central task of philosophy, to science as the single best way of knowing, and to the unity of science as a goal and methodological principle."[14]

Such scientism aids and abets the kind of cultural practices displayed in Exhibit Two (see Chapter 1). Appeals to the interests of science, to the advancement of archaeological and biological knowledge, are seen by many to trump the moral objections of indigenous peoples to the desecration of ancestral graves. A key move in the development of scientism is a change in the concept of science. No longer a field of study or a realm of inquiry, it emerges primarily as a method.[15] The assumption that only the West "has" or "does" science is thereby eased. If an indigenous culture is not employing "the scientific method," it cannot be doing science. Nor can its contributions to scientific knowledge be recognized. Those scholars involved with efforts to integrate indigenous and dominant knowledge systems have observed that

> (a)ll too often it is the Indigenous researcher who is taught the scientific method and forced to adapt his or her cultural reality to that model. Western scientists need the same exposure to TEK (traditional environmental knowledge).[16]

The marked tendency of the dominant knowledge system to embrace anti-pluralism, together with its narrow reconceptualization of science

13 Max Weber, *The Protestant Ethic and the Spirit of Capitalism* (New York: Charles Scribner's Sons, 1930, 1958): 13.

14 Proctor, *Value-Free Science?*, 167.

15 Science thus becomes largely a matter of procedure rather than content, a function not of what is studied, but of how it is studied. In addition to securing as "science" proper a singular way of doing science, this move extends the power of the dominant knowledge system in another manner as well. Because the doing of science becomes a matter of adopting a certain methodology, everything can in principle be done "scientifically." Hence the proliferation of "wannabee" sciences. The book titles in any sizeable library reveal the extent and diversity of this aspiration. Cornell's holdings, for example, list more than 400 titles that begin with the invocation "The Science of." There are, it would seem, sciences of ethics, of religion, of art, of education, of money, of judicial proof, of mystic lights, of peace, of rights, of revolution, of buffoonery, of fairy tales, of housekeeping, of love, of fly-fishing, even of scientific method itself.

16 Martha Johnson, "Documenting Dene Traditional Environmental Knowledge," *Akwe:kon*, Vol. IX, No. 2 (1992): 77.

as restricted to a specific method, facilitates a variety of cultural practices, including biocolonialism. Within the dominant knowledge system, it is doubtful that the Guajajara (Exhibit Three) can be said to have any "scientific knowledge" regarding *Pilocarpus jaborandi*, or that Ammoneta Sequoyah (Exhibit Five) or Alice Benally (Exhibit Six) have any of healing. This cognitive power to determine what constitutes scientific knowledge, conjoined to the economic, political, and legal power of global corporations, is a potent combination, enabling violation of the intellectual property rights, and theft of the genetic resources, of indigenous peoples.

By contrast, indigenous knowledge systems typically place considerable significance and value on alternative ways of knowing the world, particularly on gaining access to the perspective of the other-than-human. The indigenous account of what can be known and how one comes to know tends to be immensely generous. This commitment to a non-anthropocentric epistemological pluralism, to coming to know the world through perspectives that are diverse and not restricted to that of humans, runs directly counter to the commitment to anti-pluralism typical of the dominant knowledge system.

The richness of the indigenous commitment to epistemological pluralism lies in the recognition that there are diverse "versions of existence,"[17] diverse ways of being in the natural world, and so diverse experiences to appreciate and respect. Some of these may be shared, although they are not to be appropriated. Access to other ways of knowing is something that must be given, not taken. One cannot lay claim to it or demand it as a right. It can only be received because it is shared by other beings – human and nonhuman. This is reflected in the special status of dreams and visions as vehicles of knowledge. It is in and through such means that humans are typically brought into their most direct, and often transformative, contact with nonhuman beings. Vine Deloria Jr. underscores the diverse sources of indigenous knowledge: "[t]he Indian understands dreams, visions, and intra-species communications . . . as a natural part of human experience."[18] Yet western science "discards anything that has a

[17] Yvonne Dion-Buffalo and John C. Mohawk, "Thoughts from an Autochthonous Center: Postmodernism and Cultural Studies," *Akwe:kon* Vol. IX, No. 4 (1992): 19.

[18] Vine Deloria, Jr. "Ethnoscience and Indian Realities," *Winds of Change* (Summer 1992): 16.

remote relationship with the subjective experiences of human beings and other forms of life."[19]

Intraspecies communication occurs often in dreams and visions, where human beings communicate with and learn from nonhuman beings. In "The Woman Who Brought Back the Buffalo," a traditional story of the Blackfoot Nation, a woman and her people learn to communicate with the buffalo through the mediation of the Iniskim, or Buffalo Stone. In a dream, the stone informs the woman: "I have chosen you to bring me to the camp because you are humble and I know your thoughts are good . . . I will teach you some songs and a ceremony which you must show them. If you do this then I will have my power bring back the buffalo."[20] It instructs her to tell her people that, if they wish to learn to communicate with the buffalo they "should look for one of (their) relatives and bring them home and treat them with respect."[21] Part of what the stone teaches is that humans must not kill the first, solitary buffalo they see, but wait until a whole herd has arrived.

Story: Experience and Imagination in Indigenous Knowledge Systems

There is a story connected with every place, every object in the landscape.
– Leslie Marmon Silko[22]

Within indigenous knowledge systems, knowledge is typically tied so intimately to experience and imagination as to be inconceivable without them. Stories are acts of the imagination that enable us to enact and re-enact experience. One source of their richness as pedagogical vehicles is that they permit us some access to the perspectives of other beings, often those very different from ourselves. We come to know them by relating ourselves to them, by imagining what it is like to be them and to experience the world – including ourselves – through them. Stories have

19 Ibid., 15.
20 Beverly Hungry Wolf, *The Ways of My Grandmothers* (New York: William Morrow & Co., 1982): 164.
21 Ibid., 164.
22 Leslie Marmon Silko, *Yellow Woman and a Beauty of the Spirit: Essays on Native American Life Today* (New York: Simon & Schuster, 1996): 58.

long figured as indispensable aspects of indigenous legal and political knowledge practice. As Robert Williams observes,

> Indian diplomats recognized that making connections with others was a most difficult process. Successful treaty-making required the use of great acts of the imagination so that the two sides could come to see themselves as related in their needs and sufferings as fellow human beings . . . this is why a treaty was told as a special kind of story, a way of imagining a world of human solidarity where we regard others as relatives.[23]

The integrative power of stories, the way they help us initiate and maintain relationships with others who may appear different from us, is especially needed to guide human interaction with the other-than-human world. Stories are related to convey the behavioral constraints that should guide us if we are to act responsibly, if we are to understand and respect the role of other entities and their unique contribution to the natural world we share. Many different peoples have many different stories about what happens when someone, human or otherwise, violates these constraints.

The significance of stories within indigenous knowledge systems lies as much in the telling as in what is told. The intergenerational transmission of knowledge from elders is both a responsibility and a gift. Stories are told only in the context of particular relationships and are a means of maintaining and nurturing those relationships. Part of the responsibility of telling stories lies in determining when and to whom they should be told.

> Elders often decline to have their words printed or to be videotaped because they insist that what they have to say must be communicated in person. Aboriginal people know that knowledge is power and that power can be used for good or evil. In passing on knowledge the teacher has an obligation to consider whether the learner is ready to use knowledge responsibly. . . . Teachers who allow these things relinquish the possibility of adjusting their teaching to the maturity of the learner and thereby influencing the ethical use of knowledge.[24]

[23] Robert Williams, *Linking Arms Together: American Indian Treaty Visions of Law & Peace 1600–1800* (New York: Oxford University Press, 1997): 113.

[24] Marlene Brant Catellano, "Updating Aboriginal Traditions of Knowledge," in George J. Sefa Dei, Budd L. Hall, and Dorothy Goldin Rosenberg (eds.), *Indigenous Knowledges in Global Contexts* (Toronto, Ontario: University of Toronto Press, 2000): 26.

As vehicles of experience, stories relate empirical knowledge about the relationships that connect us to the world and to one another, and about how those relationships can be well or adversely affected. Such knowledge is the product of careful observations, spanning generations, of how entities in particular places are interrelated and of the complex dynamics of their relationships. It is both temporally "deep" or historically replete, as well as spatially located, or endemic, knowledge – intimately bound to the land, to specific places and the entities located there.

> The need to walk on the land in order to know it is a different approach to knowledge than the one-dimensional, literate approach to knowing. Persons schooled in a literate culture are accustomed to having all the context they need to understand a communication embedded in the text before them . . . Persons taught to use all their senses – to absorb every clue to interpreting a complex dynamic reality – may well smile at the illusion that words alone, stripped of complementary sound and colour and texture, can convey meaning adequately.[25]

And so, to return to the Exhibits at the outset of this chapter, Ammoneta Sequoyah realizes that if the valley is flooded his knowledge of medicine – and not just the medicinal plants themselves – will be lost. This knowledge is the cultural heritage and responsibility of his people. "Cultural," here, far from sitting on one side of a nature/culture divide, extends to – and indeed from – the natural world. Mr. Sequoyah also realizes that when he is buried this knowledge will be returned with him to the land in which it is embedded, and will continue to be present within the land for others to experience. This may seem strange to someone deeply schooled in, or committed to, certain convictions that prevail in the dominant knowledge system and the science which it sustains – for example, that knowledge of nature is ultimately distinct, and separable from, nature and that what is known are true propositions about reality. One way of capturing the contrast between such convictions and those of Mr. Sequoyah would be to say that western science, western knowledge of the natural world, is representational. Indigenous science, indigenous knowledge of the natural world, is – if Ammoneta Sequoyah's and Alice Benally's comments are typical – presentational. Its continuation, its transmission, and its possibility

[25] Ibid., 29.

turn vitally upon the presence of the natural world, and on the kind of experiences that world offers. It is in this sense too that knowledge, in Luther Standing Bear's words, is "inherent in all things"[26]; it is almost literally caught up in experience, and cannot be extracted from its context.

Relatedness

In each place they lived, they learned the subtle, but all important, language of relationship.
– Gregory Cajete[27]

If knowledge *inheres* in all things, it can only properly be educed or drawn forth. So coming to know another entity or process is best approached as an eductive process that turns on establishing certain relations with it. Coming to know it well involves strengthening and sustaining those relations. Knowledge within indigenous knowledge systems is always knowledge of relations; it is not individual entities or processes which are primary or basic, but the relations that hold between them, among them. Indigenous knowledge, Marie Battiste and Sa'ke'j Youngblood Henderson note, is "the expression of the vibrant relationships between the people, their ecosystems, and the other living beings and spirits that share their lands."[28]

Construing knowledge as relatedness, as a matter of appreciating how we are bound to other entities and processes, makes integration with them possible, desirable, and necessary for survival. Our fates and futures are understood to be conjoined with theirs. Knowing them commits us to cohering and cohabiting with them. Indigenous knowledge systems enable such coherence, such holding and living together. To acknowledge affiliational ties with other entities in the natural and social worlds is to acknowledge that, and how, our lives are linked with theirs.

Such relatedness, or affiliation, is best understood in its primary – genealogical – context. One of its clearest and simplest expressions is in the Lakota invocation *mitakuye oyasin* ("I am related to all that is"). It

[26] Luther Standing Bear, *Land of the Spotted Eagle* (Lincoln, Nebraska: University of Nebraska Press, 1978 (1933)): 104.

[27] Gregory Cajete, *Native Science: Natural Laws of Interdependence* (Santa Fe, New Mexico: Clear Light Publishers, 2000): 178.

[28] Marie Battiste and Sa'ke'j Youngblood Henderson, *Protecting Indigenous Knowledge and Heritage* (Saskatoon, Saskatchewan: Purich Publishing, 2000): 42.

is reflected as well in the Andean concept of an *ayllu* – a group of related persons, human and nonhuman, who live in a particular place:

> *Ayllu* refers not only to relationships between human beings but to the relationship between all members of the *Pacha*... they are all relatives and are at once children, parents, and siblings.[29]

Genealogies provide stories of origins. They tell a person, or a people, where and from whom they are descended. In this sense, they bind through time, showing how ancestors and descendents course together through a continuous, unfolding history. Properly told, they set out the changing contours and constitution of families, including how they have branched into and out of one another over time.

A genealogy draws a family or a people together, distinguishing them from others. It also acknowledges that members of a family or clan already are drawn together, and sets out how they are related to others. To recite a genealogy, to recall affiliational ties, is to affirm a reciprocal bonding. It has the powerful function of reminding members of a family or clan of who they are – individually and collectively – and with this of their moral responsibilities to one another. A peace-making process used among the Comanche relies on this:

> Bonding was strengthened by calling on each person to track their kinship ties to the rest of the group. Cross-links between individuals and their inherent relational obligations immediately began drawing the group together and helped make tribal values and tribal identity the focus of the group's attention.[30]

The nature of a genealogy is such that an individual cannot appear in it without thereby assuming relational ties to all others within the genealogy. It is not possible to exist within a genealogy and stand outside such affiliational ties, although one may fail to acknowledge their presence. Nor is it possible to exist in such a genealogy and be "outside" of nature:

> Nature is not something apart from [the Native American]. [It is] an element in which he exists. He has existence within that element,

[29] Julio Valladolid Rivera, "Andean Peasant Agriculture: Nurturing a Diversity of Life in the *Chacra*" in Frédérique Apffel-Marglin and Julio Valladolid Rivera (eds.), *Regeneration in the Andes* (St. Urbain, Montréal, Québec: Intercultural Institute of Montréal, 1995): 25.

[30] LaDonna Harris *et al.*, "Returning to Harmony: A Comanche Effort to Reactivate the Wisdom of the People," *Native Americas* (Fall/Winter 1996): 51.

much in the same way that we think of having existence within the element of air.[31]

In a clear sense, it is simply not possible to exist outside a genealogy, as evidenced by the psychological, spiritual, and physical trauma of tribal "relocations," which involve the severing of affiliational ties with the nonhuman world.[32] Banishment, which required severing affiliational ties with the human world as well, was regarded as at least the equivalent of a death sentence. It was a punishment infrequently inflicted, and reserved only for those cases where the traditional forms of conflict resolution, typically based on the "physical and spiritual need for members of a family to work together and aid in one another's well-being," had failed.[33]

Genealogies need not, and for indigenous peoples typically do not, confine themselves to the human. Because they relate origins, they address themselves to specific places and to the nonhuman beings inhabiting them. So genealogies map affiliations spatially as well, placing individuals and families in relation to one another, and locating them in – by connecting them to – the earth. Insofar as everything has an origin, everything (human and nonhuman) has a genealogy which situates it relationally in time – linking those who have been with those yet to be, as well as in space – linking everything to a particular place and to everything in that place. In this sense, genealogies are stories of temporal and spatial belonging. They relate how a person or a people belongs in a particular time and place, how the nonhuman things in that place have come to belong there, and how all of these belong to one another.

The significance of human ties of affiliation with the nonhuman world is symbolically captured in language and in practice among many indigenous cultures. It can be seen in the Mayan custom of burying a newborn's umbilical cord in the parents' house "in the hope that when the baby

31 N. Scott Momaday, "Native American Attitudes to the Environment," in Walter Holden Capps and Ernst F. Tonsing (eds.), *Seeing with the Native Eye: Essays on Native American Religion* (New York: Harper, 1976): 84.

32 "Dislocations" would be a more accurate term to describe the wrenching, the pulling out of joint, that is involved in removals of indigenous peoples from the land to which they belong.

33 Manu Meyer, "To Set Right – Ho'oponopono: A Native Hawaiian Way of Peacemaking," *Compleat Law* (Fall 1995): 30; see also Philmer Bluehouse, "The Ceremony of Making Peace," *Native Americas* (Fall 1996): 54; David Wilkins, "Exiling One's Kin: Banishment in Indian Country," *News from Indian Country* (June 1997): 17A.

reaches adulthood he or she will understand the importance of home and the dependence on land."[34] Or in the analogous Diné practice:

> We perform many different things when a child is born so the child will be familiar with the spiritual beings of the area. At birth the woman offers the afterbirth to a young tree and buries the child's umbilical cord in Mother Earth. These things create spiritual ties between us and the land.[35]

It is reflected in the Maori word for land, *whenua*, which also means placenta, and in *hapu*, which means both pregnant and extended family or subtribe. "The expression 'te u kai po' refers to the area where you were brought up, but it also means to be breast fed."[36] As Waerete Norman notes:

> The burying of whenua was also seen as helping to sustain the land. The practice of burial reflects the importance of tiaki whenua and tiaki taiao [caring for the land and environment] to ensure a future sustained by papatuanuku [earth mother]... Whenua and placenta is one and the same land.[37]

These practices reveal how crucial affiliational ties between the human and nonhuman are. As one senior Gumadji clan leader, Galarrwuy Yunupingu, observes, "Aboriginal belief systems based on affinity to land underpin Aboriginal existence."[38]

> We believe the land is all life. So it comes to us that we are part of the land and the land is part of us. It cannot be one or the other. We cannot be separated by anything or anybody.[39]

[34] Rigoberto Queme Chay, "The Corn Men Have Not Forgotten Their Ancient Gods," in Pablo Piancentini (ed. Inter-Press Service), *Story Earth: Native Voices on the Environment* (San Francisco, California: Mercury House, 1993): 27.

[35] "Affidavit of Kee Shay" ¶ 15, *at* 230, *Manybeads v. United States*, 730 F. Supp. 1515 (D. Ariz. 1989) (No. 88–410).

[36] Roma Mere Roberts *et al.*, "Kaitiakitanga: Maori Perspectives on Conservation," in *Pacific Conservation Biology: A Journal Devoted to Conservation and Land Management in the Pacific Region* (1995): 10.

[37] Waerete Norman, "*Tikanga Wahine* in a Changing World," (unpublished Ph.D. dissertation, University of Auckland, 2000): 136–7.

[38] Galarrwuy Yunupingu, "Introduction" in Galarrwuy Yunupingu (ed.), *Our Land is Our Life: Land Rights—Past, Present and Future* (St. Lucia, Queensland: University of Queensland Press, 1997): xv–xvi.

[39] Galarrwuy Yunupingu, "From the Bark Petition to Native Title," in Yunupingu, *Our Land is Our Life*: 2–3.

Such practices affirm the presence and persistence of genealogical bonds that link the human and nonhuman. They are expressions of human belonging, of the intimate relationship between a people and a land. Aboriginal activist Michael Dodson comments that "our . . . reason for existence is the land . . . We have grown the land up . . . Removed from our lands, we are literally removed from ourselves."[40] For Maori, too, "people belong to earth. Earth is not a possession of the people."[41]

If a people belongs to a land, and land inheres in a people, it cannot be alienated or disowned. It cannot be reduced to a commodity.[42] It cannot be replaced or done without. Haunani-Kay Trask notes that the Hawaiian language has two ways of showing possession. The "a" possessive indicates acquired status, and the "o" possessive indicates inherent status. Whereas most material objects take the "a" form, land – like one's body and one's parents – takes the "o" form. "Thus, in our way of speaking, land is inherent to the people; it is like our bodies and our parents. The people cannot exist without the land, and the land cannot exist without the people."[43] Buffalo Tiger (Miccosukee Seminole) makes a comparable point: "The land is a part of our body, and we are a part of the land."[44] Furthermore, he explains:

> It is the white man who buys land and puts a fence around it . . . It's hard for us to come to terms with the white man because our philosophy is so different. We think the land is there for everyone to use, the way our hand is there, a part of our own body.[45]

"We belong to the earth," as Cheyenne elder Henrietta Mann puts it, "as much as children belong to their mother or to their parents."[46] Similarly,

[40] Michael Dodson, "Land Rights and Social Justice," in ibid. 39, 41.

[41] Waerete Norman, "*Tikanga Wahine*," 136–7.

[42] As Vine Deloria notes:

> Within the western context we are always inclined to see land as a commodity and think first of its ownership; in contrast, the traditional Indian understanding of land focused on its use, and the duties people assume when they come to occupy it.

Vine Deloria, Jr., "Out of Chaos," in D.M. Dooling and Paul Jordan Smith (eds.) *I Become Part of It* (New York: Harper Collins, 1989): 216.

[43] Haunani-Kay Trask, *From a Native Daughter* (Monroe, Maine: Common Courage Press, 1993): 151–2.

[44] Peter Matthiessen, *Indian Country*, 4th edition (New York, New York: Penguin Books, 1984): 45.

[45] Ibid.

[46] "*Paha Sapa*: The Struggle for the Black Hills" (HBO television broadcast, Sept. 1993), re-released on videotape: "*Paha Sapa*: The Struggle for the Black Hills" (Mystic Fire Video,

for Maori, "land was not something that could be owned or traded. They did not seek to own or possess anything, but to belong. One belonged to a family that belonged to a hapu that belonged to a tribe. One did not own land. One belonged to the land."[47]

When possession or ownership is understood as an inherent, rather than an acquired, status, the term "belong" becomes especially apt. To belong to the land is to be attached or bound to it by birth, by allegiance, and by dependence. The resulting relationship of belonging may be characterized as one of intimacy, or better, of inherency. The land is involved in the constitution of a people. It characterizes them, as they do it:

> The relationship between the crocodile and myself and all my clansmen is a very special relationship . . . I see a crocodile as an animal that is part of me and I belong to him, he belongs to me. It's a commonness of land ownership. Everything that I have comes from the crocodile. Crocodile, he's the creator and the land giver to the Gumatj people . . . We have always treated crocodile in a way that it is part of a family.[48]

The land and living entities which make it up are not apart from, but a part of, the people. Nor is "the environment" something outside of, or surrounding, a people. The relation of belonging is ontologically basic.

With inherent possession, agency is sometimes held to be reciprocal – a people belongs to/owns the land, and the land belongs to/owns a people. Sometimes it is the inverse of that implied by acquired possession – although a people belongs to the land or the land owns a people, a people does not own the land nor does the land belong to a people. Several Maori commentators, for example, reject the notion of stewardship as a translation of the Maori term *kaitiaki* because of its connotations of guarding someone else's property: "Ownership of property . . . was a foreign concept . . . Thus the resources of the earth did not belong to man but rather, man belonged

1994). The quoted material was a statement made during the film by Henrietta Mann, a Cheyenne elder and former National Administrator of Native American Education.

47 Eddie Durie, "The Law and the Land," in Jock Phillips (ed.), *Te whenua, Te Iwi: The Land and the People* (Wellington, New Zealand: Allen & Unwin, 1987): 78.

48 Helen Watson (with the Yolngu community at Yirrkala) and David Wade Chambers, *Singing the Land, Signing the Land: A Portfolio of Exhibits* 26 (Geelong, Victoria: Deakin University, 1989) (quoting Galarrwuy Yunupingu in "Living with Crocodiles" (ABC television broadcast transcript)).

to the earth."[49] Dell Wihongi agrees: "It is wrong to think that we humans act as 'kaitiaki' guardians of nature . . . The earth kaitiaki's us."[50]

According to the recent Muriwhenua Land Report to the Waitangi Tribunal:

> Maori saw themselves as users of the land rather than its owners. While their use must equate with ownership for the purpose of English law, they saw themselves not as owning the land but as being owned by it. They were born out of it, for the land was Papatuanuku, the mother earth who conceived the ancestors of the Maori people . . . That land descends from ancestors is pivotal . . . The community's right to land . . . was by descent from the earth of that place.[51]

The report goes on to stress that the belief that land descends from the ancestors is central to an understanding of the Maori land-tenure system: "The community's right to land, in pure terms, was by descent from the earth of that place . . . Deceased forebears and generations to come had as much interest in the land as any current occupier."[52] Land allocations to outside individuals "were not an alienation of the land but the incorporation of the individuals . . . they augmented, not the recipient but the community[,] . . . for it was the recipient who was most obliged."[53]

Genealogically embedded individuals are thus bound, and answerable, to one another. At the most fundamental level, they are responsible for one another, ontologically and morally. Genealogical bonds, then, are normative bonds, generating moral responsibilities to the natural world and all the living beings which it sustains; they give rise to "reciprocal relations," which define "responsibilities . . . between humans and the ecosystem."[54] That the human and nonhuman worlds are bound by relations of reciprocity or correspondence has significant implications for appreciating

49 Maori Marsden and T.A. Henare, cited in Roberts *et al.*, " *Kaitiakitanga*," 14.

50 Ibid.

51 Waitangi Tribunal, "Muriwhenua Land Report" (1997): 23. Available at http://www.waitangi-tribunal.govt.nz/reports/.

52 Ibid., 24.

53 Ibid., 25. Thus, land sales were at odds with the Maori understanding of the relationship between land and people. Land transactions "were not about transferring property but about defining relationships between people. There appears to have been no Maori law of property transfer entirely divorced from continuing personal responsibilities between the parties." (Ibid., 4.)

54 Winona LaDuke, "Traditional Ecological Knowledge and Environmental Futures," *Colorado Journal of International Environmental Law and Policy*, 5 (1994): 128.

the role responsibilities of indigenous peoples. They are obligated to provide their lands with sustenance, to sustain them by means of practices and ceremonies (and whenever necessary, by protest and resistance), even as the land sustains them.

Respect, or the Wish-to-Be-Appreciated

Truganinny, the last of the Tasmanians, had seen the stuffed and mounted body of her husband and it was her dying wish that she be buried in the outback or at sea for she did not wish her body to be subjected to the same indignities. Upon her death she was nevertheless stuffed and mounted and put on display for over eighty years. – Paul Coe, Australian Aborigine Activist, 1972[55]

We have seen that the genealogical bonds or ties of affiliation joining human to human, and what is human to what is not, have both descriptive and normative aspects. Because genealogical bonds acknowledge relations of reciprocity, they entail mutual obligations and responsibilities. They recognize that beings are related and indebted to one another, and are to respond to one another in ways which respect that fact. We can turn now to the concept of respect, the central and perhaps single most widely shared moral principle among indigenous peoples. The Iroquois also refer to it as the "wish-to-be-appreciated," the "fundamental shared perception – the first principle – of existence. As long as everything is appreciated for what it does and what it shares to sustain the cycles of Creation, the world will be in balance and life will continue."[56] It actively informs a vast number of diverse practices, teachings, and beliefs regarding how the natural world and its constituent beings are to be treated.

If we heed the Iroquois account, respect seems best regarded as a matter of appreciating the inherent value[57] of some entity or activity – the value

55 Wendy Rose, "Epigraph to Truganinny," *The Halfbreed Chronicles and Other Poems* (Los Angeles, California: West End Press, 1985): 56.

56 Jose Barreiro, "The Search for Lessons," *Akwe:kon* (Summer 1992): 28.

57 The western philosophical contrast between intrinsic and instrumental value does not reflect well the sense of respect and disrespect commonly encountered in indigenous knowledge and value systems. Although disrespect as reduction to the purely instrumental may not be far off the mark, the notion of intrinsic value as what is valuable "in and of itself" seems markedly at odds with the sense of relatedness or affiliational ties discussed here. The latter may be better captured by a notion of inherent value, understood as the value that something has insofar as it inheres in, or belongs to, the natural world, and plays an integral role therein. Because its continued functioning is essential to the completeness and continuation of the whole, its value is not to be overridden or discounted. This places enormous importance on

which it has by virtue of the fact that it inheres in, or belongs to, the natural world. This involves realizing the vital role that it plays in sustaining the natural world, its processes and beings, its systems and cycles. "No part of the earth," Leslie Silko reminds us, "is expendable."[58] To realize that (and especially how) some entity is integral to the completeness and continuation of the whole, and to appreciate that its contribution to the natural world is indispensable, requires intimate knowledge and familiarity with it. Respect consists of a continuum of behaviors informed by such knowledge, and ranges from avoiding inappropriate treatment of something to responding to it in ways that actively maintain its ability to continue performing its vital function.

Knowledge or familiarity may come from prolonged, intimate contact with a being or a place. The Diné translation of "sense of place" is *ketl'ool*, which implies a rootedness in the Earth, a familiarity with one's surroundings "that breeds respect and symbiosis rather than contempt and exploitation."[59] Such familiarity extends, of course, to nonhuman beings. Kee Shay, protesting the removal of the Diné from Big Mountain, speaks of "the land where we are known":

> Here on our land we are familiar with the springs, rocks, mountains, hills, etc., they are familiar with us . . . Each day I come to know my relatives here a little better.[60]

Alternatively, the simple awareness of relatedness may ground respect. Among the Cree, for example, one of the main reasons for showing respect to nonhuman animals is that human and nonhuman animals are related, they "share the same Creator."[61] With the deepening of knowledge and respect that typically comes with increased familiarity, the relationship

proper understanding of the nature of the role that something plays. The manner in which this respects the integrity and indispensability of the individual is well captured by the manner of keeping council traditional to many Native North American tribes, for whom the goal was to reach a consensus that all could accept on the basis of an attentive hearing of all positions present.

58 Leslie Marmon Silko, *Yellow Woman*, 94.

59 Steve Semken, "Keyah: A Geological Sense of Place," in Diné College Instructor's Guide (1997): 2. (Unpublished).

60 "Affidavit of Kee Shay," ¶ 13, at 230.9.

61 Fikret Berkes, "Environmental Philosophy of the Chisasibi Cree People of James Bay," in Milton M.R. Freeman & Ludwig N. Carbyn (eds.), *Traditional Knowledge and Renewable Resource Management in Northern Regions* (Occasional Publication #23, Boreal Institute for Northern Studies, University of Alberta, Edmonton, Alberta, 1988): 13.

between human and nonhuman animals may change. As one Cree hunter observes:

> There is a saying that "the land would feel unfamiliar or uneasy with you if you are a stranger there." Such a person may have poor luck at first, but later on the game will get to know him."[62]

That relationship will be damaged by any action, intentional or otherwise, of disrespect:

> My brother was trapping otter. He had left his trap in the water a bit too long . . . He had caused the fur to spoil, and knew that this was a crime against the animals . . . He thought it would take perhaps three years before the otter will decide to come back to his trap again.[63]

The hunter in this last case has treated the otter inappropriately, dismissing or degrading its value. He thereby diminishes the significance of the otter's contribution and demeans its role in preserving the natural order. Reciprocity has been neglected; the hunter has failed to meet his fiduciary responsibilities – both to the otter and to those for whom the otter has sacrificed itself: "A hunter always speaks as if the animals are in control of the hunt. The success of the hunt depends on the animals . . . Hunters have to show respect to the animals."[64] Respect involves avoiding acts that degrade or ignore the integral value of the game. It also involves performing acts that reflect and sustain that value.

Given the affiliational ties that bind humans to the nonhuman, to the land and all of its constituent beings, respect is the most fitting and revealing moral response. It requires constant attentiveness to the value of something or someone, appreciation of the fact that that individual has its own unique contribution to make which is vital to the natural order, awareness of the constraints and limitations which characterize and contextualize it, and gratitude for all of this. None of this is possible without careful thought and observation, so that one can come to better understand what its function or contribution is, what conditions are needed to permit its continuation, how not to interfere with it, and how best to enable it. This is to suggest that respect is as much a cognitive virtue as it is a moral virtue.

62 Ibid., 11.
63 Ibid.
64 Ibid., 10.

For many indigenous cultures, knowing and valuing are integrated activities. As interdependent processes, they implicate and mutually inform one another. This is something that traditional storytelling and teaching emphasize: "[I]f knowledge is not conditioned by respect, it cannot be had, and conversely there can be no respect where there is no knowledge."[65]

Maori weaving offers an illustrative example of the richness of the indigenous understanding of respect. According to one well-known weaver, Erenora Puketapu-Hetet,

> We have a responsibility to this life force.[66] It is important to me as a weaver that I respect the *mauri* (life force) of what I am working with. Once I have taken flax from where it belongs, I must give another dimension to its life force so that it is still a thing of beauty.[67]

The weaver must respect the materials used. One aspect of this respect consists in knowing where the materials come from and how they will be used; another lies in ensuring that the materials are put to proper use. As John Patterson comments, "Everything has a *mauri* which must be respected. If the *mauri* of a forest or river is not respected it will not flourish, it will lose its vitality and fruitfulness."[68] Ensuring that that life force is respected and that the forest or river is able to continue to fulfill its vital role in the natural order is part of Maori *kaitiaki* (guardian) responsibilities:

> *Kaitiaki* must ensure that the *mauri* or life force of their *taonga* [treasures] is healthy and strong. A *taonga* whose life force has been depleted . . . presents a major task for the *kaitiaki* . . . They must do all in their power to restore the *mauri* of the *taonga* to its original strength.[69]

One obvious way to fail to appreciate the value of something is to distort or diminish its value. The treatment of the bodies of Truganinny and her husband, described earlier in this chapter, is a particularly egregious

[65] Laurie Anne Whitt, "Indigenous Peoples and the Cultural Politics of Knowledge," in Michael K. Green (ed.), *Issues in Native American Cultural Identity* (New York: Peter Lang, 1995): 241.
[66] Erenora Puketapu-Hetet, *Maori Weaving with Erenora Puketapu-Hetet* (Auckland, New Zealand: Pitman, 1989): 5.
[67] Erenora Puketapu-Hetet, "Te Atiawa," in D. Nicholas (ed.), *Seven Maori Artists: Interviews* (Wellington, New Zealand: V.R.Ward, 1980): 40. (Emphasis added.)
[68] John Patterson, *Exploring Maori Values* (Palmerston North, New Zealand: The Dunmore Press, 1992): 23.
[69] Roberts, "Kaitiakitanga," 23.

instance of disrespect, but there are others deserving of mention. The relation of belonging or inherent possession which binds a people to a land is at odds with the process of alienation and acquisition that accompanies commodification. Aboriginal writer Liz Johnson makes this point directly: "The land is our old people and those of us who are still here today are of that same land. When I take a handful of dirt and say "This is ME," it's true, the same as it was true when my early forefathers said it."[70] And land, as the Maori would say, has its own *mauri*, or life force.[71] It is not a commodity whose value is determined by the marketplace. It is heritage. It is life itself. In his study of European and American Indian ways of inhabiting New England ecosystems, William Cronon argues that, more than anything else, what distinguished English and Indian concepts of ownership was the treatment of land and property as tradeable commodities.[72] Whereas the indigenous inhabitants construed the right of ownership as the right to use the land "as an ecological cornucopia, not to possess it as a tradeable commodity,"[73] for the colonists

> what was sold was not a bundle of usufruct rights, applying to a range of different "territories," but the land itself. . . [,] an abstract area with fixed bounds . . . Once the land was bounded in this way, a host of ecological changes followed almost inevitably.[74]

70 Liz Johnson, "Cultural Revitalization," *Identity* 4, No. 2 (1981): 13.

71 See Ranginui Walker, "The Relevance of Maori Myth and Tradition," in Michael King (ed.), *Te Ao Hurihuri* (Auckland, New Zealand: Reed Publishing, 1992): 171.

72 See William Cronon, *Changes in the Land: Indians, Colonists, and Ecology of New England* (New York, New York: Farrar, Straus & Giroux, 1983): 75.

73 Ibid., 67.

74 Ibid., 68. Cronon observes that Indian usufruct rights were inherently non-exclusive and that transactions involving them "had more to do with sharing possession than alienating it." (Ibid.) This divergence between western and indigenous legal concepts led repeatedly to much misunderstanding and to the expropriation of native lands, in North America and elsewhere. It figured, for example, in Australian High Court Justice Blackburn's 1970 decision in the *Milpirrum* case. As Helen Watson-Verran argues, Justice Blackburn acknowledged that the Yolngu claimants had "established the existence of a subtle and powerful knowledge system, recognizable as a system of law," one which linked clans to one another and to the land. (Helen Watson-Verran, "Re-Imagining Land Title and Ownership, in *Science in Society Working Papers: Working Disparate Knowledge Systems Together,* Vol. 2, No. 5 (Geelong, Victoria: Deakin University School of Social Inquiry, 1994): 74.) Yet, Justice Blackburn contended that it "did not provide for any proprietary interest in the clans in any part of the areas claimed . . . [and] . . . it seems easier on the evidence, to say that the clan belongs to the land than that the land belongs to the clan." (Ibid.) His "evidence" was, in fact, a different conception of land ownership, which turned on rights of exclusion.

One reason for the fierce resistance of indigenous peoples to the varied forms of contemporary biocolonialism is that it commodifies, privatizes, and commercializes both knowledge of the natural world and genetic life forms themselves. To convert life forms into intellectual property is to distort their value, to alter their contribution to the natural order. The commodification of both knowledge and genetic resources entailed by biocolonialism results in the abandonment of crucial moral responsibilities to future generations.[75] The Zuni, for example, have formulated a Cultural Resources Advisory Team to provide guidance concerning Zuni genetic resources. It has declared that Zuni seeds "should not be sold or given to outsiders for profit, resale, breeding or trademarketing."[76] The reason is that if Zuni seeds are transformed into a commodity and sold, the Zuni will no longer know how the seeds will be used. Because they will no longer be under Zuni control, their abuse cannot be prevented. To convert their seeds into commodities would mean that the Zuni would no longer be able to discharge their moral responsibility to ensure that these gifts are not abused.[77]

Indigenous recognition that the process of commodification may distort something's value and significance, and result in a failure to meet one's custodial responsibilities regarding it, is widespread. It is not limited to the commodification of genetic materials, but includes the commodification of knowledge as well. Consider the Maori account of this. The third of the three baskets of knowledge, which form the basis of traditional Maori epistemology, contains all knowledge of the natural world (agriculture, medicine, astronomy, fishing, crafts, etc.). Such knowledge is considered *tapu* – sacred and set apart, or removed from profane use. It is treated with

[75] See Laurie Anne Whitt, "Biocolonialism and the Commodification of Knowledge," *Science as Culture*, Vol. 7, No. 1 (1998): 33.

[76] Daniela Soleri and David A. Cleveland, "Gifts from the Creator: Intellectual Property Rights and Folk Crop Varieties," in Tom Greaves (ed.), *Intellectual Property Rights for Indigenous Peoples* (Oklahoma City, Oklahoma: Society for Applied Anthropology, 1994): 34.

[77] Most recently, in 2004, the Little Traverse Bay Band of Odawa Indians passed a tribal code to protect genetic material by expressly prohibiting the patenting of organisms. The latter is held to be of danger to the Tribe's health, welfare, and economic security because it "threatens the loss of biodiversity by limiting access to genetic variants through enforcement of proprietary rights and encouraging the spread of a single variant of an organism in place of other natural variations." (Little Traverse Bay Band of Odawa Indians, Waganakising Odawak Tribal Code, Title IV, ch. 10, Act Prohibiting the Patenting of Organisms, 2004). For similar examples, see Debra Harry and Le'a Malia Kanehe, "Indigenous Land and Property Rights: Asserting Sovereignty over Cultural Property: Moving Towards Protection of Genetic Material and Indigenous Knowledge," *Seattle Journal of Social Justice* Vol. 5 (2006).

special respect because it is also endowed with *mana* or power. As a gift from the gods, it is not to be passed on lightly. Above all, knowledge that is *tapu* must never be transformed into a commodity:

> [O]ur elders never allow us to sell any knowledge of anything Maori that is really tapu. To them it is priceless. Money can never buy knowledge and when they teach they will tell people: "This knowledge I am passing over to you must never be sold."[78]

One is responsible for such knowledge and for how it will be used, or misused.

Knowledge, Inherent Value, and Landkeeping

Respect, then, consists in appreciating something's inherent value, the value which it has by virtue of the fact that it inheres in, or belongs to, the natural world. To treat something with respect involves knowledge – minimally, the knowledge that it plays an integral role in sustaining the natural order. To know more than this, to know something of what that role is and how it plays out, to know its limitations and constraints as well as its possibilities, positions one to be more respectful toward it, i.e., better situated to avoid behaviors that will diminish it and to adopt those which will enable its continued functioning. To come to know such things is to know better just how something inheres in, or belongs to, the natural order. But how does one come to know such things? How does one learn? And when one does (to return, finally, to Ammoneta Sequoyah and Alice Benally) is it possible to separate that knowledge from what is, and where it is, known?

Knowing is a reciprocal activity. To know the forests and lakes of a place is to be known by that place. "Here on our land," Kee Shay explains, "we are familiar with the springs, rocks, mountains, hills, etc . . . . They are familiar with us."[79] But, she continues:

> We do not just know these places but the spiritual beings at these places . . . We cannot use [the healing powers of] herbs in a foreign area where we do not know the spiritual beings, they would not hear us.[80]

[78] N. Pewhairangi, "Learning and Tapu," in Michael King (ed.), *Te Ao Hurihuri Aspects of Maoritanga* (Auckland, New Zealand: Reed Publishing, 1992): 11.
[79] "Affidavit of Kee Shay," 230.
[80] Ibid., 227, 230.

Hearing and listening, speaking and communicating are at the heart of the process of knowing. This is apparent in many traditional stories, and remains very much a vital aspect of many indigenous knowledge systems. According to one Cree hunter:

> The Cree say, "all creatures are watching you. They know everything you are doing. Animals are aware of your activities." In the past, animals talked to people. In a sense, there is still communication between animals and hunters . . . The hunter tries to think what the bear is thinking. Their minds touch. The hunter and the bear have parallel knowledge, and they share that knowledge. So in a sense they communicate.[81]

And there are stories in many indigenous cultures about how humans and nonhumans were once fluent in one another's languages: "Our brothers, the bears and the wolves and the eagles, are Indians. They are Natives, as we are. At one time we spoke their language; at one time we conversed, a long time ago."[82]

It is by remembering and listening to stories that one learns; they are vehicles for knowing and respecting the natural world. In discussing First Nations law and how it has been handed down to the present, Anishinabe law professor John Borrows contends that First Nations law originates

> in the political, economic, spiritual and social values expressed through the teachings and behavior of knowledgeable and respected individuals and elders. These principles are discovered in the rich stories, ceremonies, and traditions within First Nations. These stories contain the law in First Nations communities as they represent the accumulated wisdom and experience of First Nations conflict resolution.[83]

Using the legal case method, Borrows retells a traditional tale to demonstrate how the Elders of the Anishinabe Nation use it to define environmental responsibilities and to stress that there is "a compact between humans and their surroundings which must be considered when humans make governmental decisions about themselves and their neighbors."[84] He then

[81] Berkes, "Environmental," 10.

[82] Oren Lyons, "Our Mother Earth," in Dooling and Smith, *I Become Part of It*, 272.

[83] John Borrows, "Living Between Water and Rocks: First Nations, Environmental Planning and Democracy," *University of Toronto Law Journal*, 47 (1997): 454.

[84] Ibid., 457.

applies the decision in this case to a contemporary controversy over land use in Ontario. Lumbee law professor Robert A. Williams makes a similar point regarding the values which inform American Indian views of environmental justice. They are typically reinforced by narratives

> which seek to invoke our imaginative capacities to see the social, physical and spiritual worlds we inhabit as connected and interdependent. Through such stories and their interrelated themes of harmony and humility, we are taught a system of values which induces a profound attitude of respect for the forces which give life to the complex world of which we are but a small part.[85]

Stories, thus, are vital components of indigenous knowledge and value systems. They are themselves generated from the land, and so are inseparable from it. Leslie Silko maintains that Laguna Pueblo stories are so much a part of the ancestral lands "that it is almost impossible for future generations to lose them":

> [T]here is a story connected with every place, every object in the landscape. Dennis Brutus has talked about the "yet unborn" as well as "those from the past," and how we are still all in this place, and language – the storytelling – is our way of passing through or being with them, of being together again.[86]

Storytelling is a form of conversing with the natural world, part of the way in which things come to be known. It transmits important information about the nature of that world, its beings, and processes. Stories are a means of relating knowledge and of correlating behavior. They show how "those from the past" are bound to the land, to those from the present, and to those "yet unborn," and how those from the present should conduct themselves in light of this.

Insofar as stories often relate accounts of humans listening, speaking, and communicating with the nonhuman, they in turn emphasize the importance to indigenous knowledge systems of converse with (in the full etymological sense of "to live or keep company with") the natural world

[85] Robert A. Williams, Jr., "Large Binocular Telescopes, Red Squirrel Pinatas, and Apache Mountains: Decolonizing Environmental Law in a Multicultural World," *West Virginia Law Review*, 96 (1995): 1135.

[86] Leslie Silko, *Yellow Woman*, 59.

and its constituent beings. Joseph Bruchac relates an Abenaki story[87] in which hunters travel to the island known as Gluskabe. Gluskabe grants the wish of one of them to be a good hunter, so as to provide for his family and people, by offering him a pouch. The hunter opens it, but finds nothing inside:

> Yet as he sat there, holding the open pouch, there came into his mind a great understanding. He realized the ways he must proceed to hunt animals. He began to understand how to prepare himself for a hunt and how to show the animals respect so that they would always allow him to hunt. It seemed he could hear someone speaking to him, more than one person. Then he realized what he was hearing. He was hearing the voices of the animals themselves, telling him about their ways.[88]

Andean agriculture testifies to a similar view by placing conversing and dialogue at the center of the process of mutual nurturance between humans and the nonhuman world: "We have great faith in what nature transmits to us . . . [I]t is the voice of nature itself which announces to us the manner in which we must plant our crops."[89] The potency and significance of conversing with the natural world is also evident within Maori stories about ancestors claiming territory, naming landmarks after parts of their bodies, and leaving these names behind: "[M]ost of the names evoke ancestral histories. A child would often be taught a particular account *in that place*, so that the place and its knowledge were one."[90] Tribal understanding, as Mere Roberts and Peter Wills observe, is thereby "locked together . . . with the entities themselves so that a place and its knowledge could not be separated."[91] One result of this is that the land itself serves as the repository of knowledge and that place names function as

[87] See Joseph Bruchac, "Gluskabe and the Four Wishes" in Dooling and Smith, *I Become Part of It*, 56–7.

[88] Ibid.

[89] Frédérique Apffel-Marglin, "Development or Decolonization in the Andes?," in Frédérique Apffel-Marglin and Julio Valladolid Rivera, *Regeneration in the Andes* (quoting Grimaldo Rengifo Vasquez): 10.

[90] Anne Salmond, "Theoretical Landscapes: On Cross-Cultural Conceptions of Knowledge," in D. Parkin (ed.), *Semantic Anthropology* (London: Academic Press, 1982): 85.

[91] Roma Mere Roberts and Peter R. Wills, "Understanding Maori Epistemology: A Scientific Perspective," in Helmut Wautischer (ed.), *Tribal Epistemologies: Essays in the Philosophy of Anthropology* (Brookfield, Vermont: Ashgate, 1998): 49.

> mnemonic devices whereby the narrative related to that particular place, and its meaning, can be recalled. Recounting the narrative at that very location enables the knowledge associated with the name to be experienced; to be felt as well as heard.[92]

It is in this sense that, as suggested earlier in this chapter, indigenous knowledge of the natural world is presentational. The presence of the natural world is a condition for the very possibility of knowledge. Knowledge is located in the world as much as it is located in a people or a person; it is part of what relates the human and nonhuman. It is also thoroughly contextualized: Specific knowledge requires specific places whereby it can be recalled and experienced.

Thus, Ammoneta Sequoyah's knowledge (Exhibit Five) cannot be severed from the natural world and stored elsewhere (in libraries or data banks) for latter "consumption." He is deeply aware that if his knowledge of medicinal herbs is to continue then the plants must remain in their familiar places, where he may continue to exercise his custodial responsibilities toward them. His knowledge depends on his continued appreciation of their inherent value, of how they belong to, contribute to, and function within, the natural order. Kee Shay and Mae Tso, in the face of impending "removal" from their ancestral homelands on Big Mountain (Exhibit Six), share a comparable awareness: "It is here we know how to use the herbs, how to bring out the healing powers of the herbs by calling to the spiritual beings in the herbs."[93]

> These sacred plants and herbs only grow in certain areas on the land. They can only be gathered from locations which our ancestors and medicine men have instructed us are sacred sites . . . We know the sacred plants of the area and they know us. If we went to another area of land, we would not know the spiritual beings and they would not help us.[94]

[92] Ibid., 55. Indeed, when Roberts and her Maori colleagues presented their paper on Maori Kaitiakitangi ("the act of guardianship"), the response of some First Nations members in the audience was "astonishment that we should attempt to teach such knowledge in a situation (university lecture theatre) completely removed from the place or the land in which the knowledge itself was embedded." (Roma Mere Roberts, "Indigenous Knowledge and Western Science: Perspectives from the Pacific," in Collected Papers No. 1, *Centre for Pacific Studies*, University of Auckland (May 1998): 66.)

[93] "Affidavit of Kee Shay," ¶ 6, 227.

[94] "Affidavit of Mae Tso," *Manybeads v. United States*, 730 F. Supp. 1515 (D. Ariz. 1989) (No. 88–410): ¶ 35, at 328.

Kee Shay also expresses the sense in which for her and her people forced relocation is dislocation – the disruption of the natural order and the severing of the affiliational ties that bind the people to the land. To sever those ties is to sever the knowledge embedded in them, and to abandon one's role responsibilities as guardian of that portion of the natural world. It is to estrange, if not destroy, an entire knowledge and value system:

> When the white man talks of relocation he talks of finding a new place to live, a new job, a new place to pray to his God . . . The white man can practice his religion anywhere, he does not know the earth. The Diné are different, the land is sacred to us, we cannot practice our religion elsewhere, only on the land where we are known . . . It is like your family . . . You could not leave your relatives if they were sick – it is in this way that we must stay with this land, our relative.[95]

[95] "Affidavit of Kee Shay," ¶ 10, at 228–9. The removal of some 12,000 Diné under a 1974 federal law is popularly portrayed as a Diné/Hopi land dispute, but it is in fact tied to mining interests. See Bill Weinbert, "Requiem for Big Mountain: The Road to Relocation Is Unrelenting," *Native Americas* (Fall 1997): 30.

3

Value-Neutrality and Value-Bifurcation

The Cultural Politics of Science

Exhibit Seven. Excerpt from testimony by Luca Cavalli-Sforza, population geneticist and principal proponent of the Human Genome Diversity Project (HGDP) at the 1993 Hearing on the HGDP before the U.S. Senate Committee on Governmental Affairs:

> *Senator Akaka:* Preservation of genetic data of near-extinct populations is an important issue that I believe warrants further examination. Would you say that a primary component of your proposed study is the collection of genetic samples from cultures that are vanishing? Why does this project need to be done now? Why the urgency?
>
> *Dr. Cavalli-Sforza:* We are observing, because of economic development of Third World countries, an enormous increase in migration, and also disappearance of populations living in peripheral locations, and very frequently marginal conditions . . . If we want to reconstruct populations history, and understand under what conditions certain diseases became prevalent in a population, we have to study these things now, before complete confusion.[1]

Exhibit Eight. Excerpt from testimony provided at a 1993 meeting of the United Nations Commission on Sustainable Development by Victoria Tauli-Corpuz indigenous representative:

> After being subjected to ethnocide and genocide for 500 years (which is why we are endangered), the alternative is for our DNA to be collected and stored. This is just a more sophisticated version of how the remains of our ancestors are collected and stored in museums and

[1] United States Senate, "Human Genome Diversity Project: Hearing before the Committee on Governmental Affairs." (Washington, DC: U.S. Government Printing Office, 1993): 39.

> scientific institutions. Why don't they address the causes of our being endangered instead of spending $20 million for five years to collect and store us in cold laboratories. If this money will be used instead to provide us basic social services and promote our rights as indigenous peoples, then our biodiversity will be protected.[2]

Cavalli-Sforza and Tauli-Corpuz are agreed on one thing: Genetic diversity is worth preserving. To do so, Cavalli-Sforza and other proponents of the HGDP propose that scientists take samples from the bearers of such diversity[3] before they "vanish," and deposit these in data banks as a genetic "fund" for future research. For Tauli-Corpuz and other indigenist critics of the HGDP, the ethically and politically appropriate means to preserve genetic diversity is to ensure that its bearers themselves survive.

The political role of science – the ways in which it supports and sustains the complex systems of practices that constitute the oppression of indigenous peoples – figures prominently in indigenist critiques of biocolonialism. These critiques directly challenge the neopositivist ideology which sustains and provides the justificatory rhetoric for much of western science policy and practice. An ideology of science may be regarded as a cluster of convictions about the nature, significance, and practice of science.[4] These convictions tend to be implicit, rather than explicit, and are passed on largely through education and professionalization.[5] The ideology of contemporary imperial science relies heavily on both assertions, and assumptions, of value-neutrality to legitimate extractive biocolonialism.

[2] Victoria Tauli-Corpuz, "We Are Part of Biodiversity. Respect Our Rights," *Third World Resurgence*, 36 (1993): 26.

[3] More exactly, this project targets "the smaller differences that characterize differences among ethnic groups or populations" rather than "the very large differences that exist among people within ethnic groups or populations" (U.S. Senate, 3). However, as Jonathan Marks notes, this is a mistaken focus if understanding the extent and nature of human genetic diversity is the object, for the "knowledge that most human genetic variation is polymorphic rather than polytypic, should make it more important to preserve many samples from relatively fewer groups, than to preserve few samples from many groups." (*Human Biodiversity: Genes, Race and History* (Hawthorne, New York: Aldine de Gruyter, 1995): 175).

[4] See Andrew McLaughlin's analogous discussion of ideologies of nature (*Regarding Nature* (Albany, New York: State University of New York Press, 1993): 6–10), which I have drawn upon here.

[5] This last is true of science as it is practiced with the dominant culture, although even there professionalization is a relatively recent phenomenon. Western science is, however, only one form that knowledge of the natural world has taken.

Value-Neutrality and the Pure/Applied Science Distinction

One of the most firmly entrenched commitments of western science is to value-neutrality. Value-neutrality is a familiar, widely acknowledged thesis about the practice and ideology of western science, especially in its positivist and neopositivist formations. At its simplest, it is the claim (or assumption) that science is value free, unburdened by "external" ethical and political values. Science (or science proper) enjoys a certain axiological immunity, and is unaffected by the values – ethical, social, political, and cultural – which admittedly shape those who do science. Helen Longino describes value-neutrality as a "functional myth" and a consequence of a more general view regarding the independence of science from its social context. It serves to

> clear the way, conceptually, for the elaboration of a particular approach to a set of phenomena once that approach has attracted the consensus of a significant portion of the relevant scientific community.[6]

The crucial filter, cleansing science of its "external" or "non-epistemic" values, is the scientific method, the singularity, uniformity, and immutability of which has been challenged even by mainstream philosophy of science.[7]

As even the most ardent defenders of value-neutrality grant that political and moral values enter into the uses of science, the thesis of value-neutrality rests on a distinction between pure and applied science (or science and technology), the tenuous nature of which is increasingly admitted. In his comprehensive study of the thesis of value-neutrality, historian Robert Proctor observes:

> The image of pure science in the modern West is associated with a hierarchy from pure to applied, from theory to practice. And yet the myth confronts a reality: science throughout the modern world is recognized as a vital part of industrial and military production.

[6] Helen Longino, *Science as Social Knowledge* (Princeton, New Jersey: Princeton University Press, 1990): 225.

[7] See Larry Laudan, *Science and Values* (Berkeley, California: University of California Press, 1984). However, more recent and radical observations regarding the extreme porousness of this value filter have not been well received by mainstream science. See Paul R. Gross and Norman Levitt, *Higher Superstition: The Academic Left and Its Quarrel With Science* (Baltimore, Maryland: Johns Hopkins University Press, 1997).

> Science is planned, and increasingly so. Priorities are established and goals are set. When monies are given, there are expectations of returns.[8]

Given the relationship between western science and industry, the role of industry in academia, and the constraints on research reliant on government or corporate funding, it is difficult if not impossible "to separate a passive, disinterested 'science' from a transformative, engaged 'technology' ":

> In the modern industrial laboratory discoveries are sought in areas of anticipated applicability; the establishment of biotechnology firms to explore recombinant deoxyribonucleic acid ("DNA") techniques is a recent example of industries sponsoring "basic research" with the expectation of applying the knowledge gained to medicine or agriculture.[9]

Because values of multiple sorts manifestly do enter into the uses which humans make of science, this supporting distinction[10] separating pure from applied science, the production of scientific knowledge from its use, or simply science from technology, is crucial. When conjoined to the thesis of value-neutrality, the pure/applied science distinction enables the claim that science itself, unlike its use, is neutral and not subject to moral evaluation. So just as National Rifle Association supporters contend that guns don't kill, people do, scientists can avail themselves of a comparable claim about the products of their research activities.

Not surprisingly, the importance of distinguishing between a value-neutral science and its value-laden use increased after Hiroshima and Nagasaki. However, the tenuousness of such a distinction is increasingly plain. Currently, biotechnology is a "commercialized science" – a $410 billion industry with its own Washington lobby, the Biotechnology Industry Organization.[11] According to Sir Walter Bodmer, former president of the

[8] Robert N. Proctor, *Value-Free Science?: Purity and Power in Modern Knowledge* (Cambridge, Massachusetts: Harvard University Press, 1991): 4.

[9] Ibid., 3.

[10] This is really a host of supporting distinctions which I will not attempt to distinguish here because they tend to function in similar ways in the rhetoric of research justification with which I am concerned.

[11] This amount is as of 31 December 2005. See the Biotechnology Industry Organization's "Biotechnology Industry Facts," available at http://bio.org/speeches/pubs/er/statistics.asp.

Human Genome Organization, "the issue [of ownership] is at the heart of everything we do."[12] Controversy over patenting the human genome has riddled both the Human Genome Project (HGP) and the HGDP since their beginnings. Despite this, the patenting of human DNA has been formally supported by scientists in the International Human Genome Organization.[13] The HGP has been a catalyzing social, political, and economic force, rapidly creating a variety of new social relationships, such as venture capital–funded start-up companies initiated by university professors[14] and entrepreneurs. These developments demonstrate well that modern western science "is a strategic enterprise in which the acquisition of knowledge is an investment that is only made in the expectation of some return."[15] Moreover, scientists themselves are increasingly investing in their own research. As one prominent biologist and science critic, Richard Lewontin, has noted, "No prominent molecular biologist of my acquaintance is without a financial stake in the biotechnology business."[16]

If the process of acquiring and conveying knowledge (paradigmatically, knowledge of the natural world) is held to be value free according to the thesis of value-neutrality, a knowledge product that fails in this is regarded as deviant, an errant departure from the epistemological ideal and from Truth itself which is, of course, also value free. The natural world is, in Alexandre Koyré's term "devalorized." As one historian of positivism comments, science is neutral "because nature itself is neutral . . . devoid of value . . . (this) ideal of value-neutrality is not a single notion, but has arisen in the course of protracted struggles over the place that science should have

[12] Michael Waldouz and Hilary Stout, *The Wall Street Journal*, 17 April 1992, 1.

[13] They only oppose cases of partial patenting or patenting when the biological function of the gene sequence is unknown. (See Phil Bereano, Message posted to *Native-L* on 31 October 1995. Available online at: http://nativenet.uthscsa.edu/archive/nl/9511/0014.html.)

[14] According to Martin Kenney (*Biotechnology: The University-Industrial Complex* (New Haven, Connecticut: Yale University Press, 1986),

> the pervasive role of professors in managing and directing the startups is unique in the annals of business history . . . Biotechnology, a science that is capable of being commercialized, has been totally dependent on university research. In no other fledgling industry have university scientists played such an all-encompassing role. (4)

[15] Dirk Stemerding and Jaap Jelsma, "Compensatory Ethics for the Human Genome Diversity Project," *Science as Culture* 5:24 (1996): 336.

[16] Richard C. Lewontin, "The Dream of the Human Genome," *The New York Review of Books* (May 28, 1992): 37.

in society."[17] Thus knowledge claims in this tradition are independent of context or perspective, of "personal, social and cultural values . . . (of) group or individual preferences about what ought to be."[18] Nor are they socially or historically situated. Recent critics describe this as "the view from nowhere" generated by those who can afford the luxury of "the dream from everywhere."[19] They contend that situated knowers "cannot perform the abdications of responsibility that orthodox positivism's value-neutral 'god-trick' would allow, cannot . . . remove themselves from view as distinctively embodied, located epistemic agents."[20]

The delusory nature of value-neutrality has recently been noted even by the National Academy of Sciences, which argues that science is value-laden, that values are central and ineliminable in scientific research. This includes not only "internal" or epistemological values (such as accuracy, simplicity, fertility, scope, etc.) but "external" ones as well, including the philosophical, religious, cultural, political, and economic.[21] Similarly, in a 1995 "Report of the Subcommittee on Bioethics and Population Genetics," the International Bioethics Committee of the United Nations Educational, Scientific and Cultural Organization (UNESCO) rejected the thesis of value-neutrality:

> Scientists are not immune from the usual array of assumptions, dislikes, biases and prejudices that beset the wider community. Unfortunately, scientists have at various times in history believed themselves to be working in a value free domain, gathering the pure crystals of data and indeed trumping other human values and concerns in their

17 Robert Proctor, *Value-Free Science?*, 262, 263. I owe much, in my discussion here, to Proctor's lucid and riveting account of the history and politics of positivism.

18 Helen Longino, *Science as Social Knowledge*, 4.

19 See Sandra Harding, *Whose Science? Whose Knowledge?* (Ithaca, New York: Cornell University Press, 1991) and Susan Bordo, *The Flight to Objectivity* (Albany, New York: State University of New York Press, 1987). In Donna Haraway's account of situated knowledges and knowers, such attempts to adopt "the view from nowhere" are described as "the god-trick." See Donna Haraway, "Situated Knowledges" in Donna Haraway, *Simians, Cyborgs, and Women: The Reinvention of Nature* (New York, New York: Routledge 1989).

20 Lorraine Code, *Ecological Thinking: The Politics of Epistemic Location* (New York, New York: Oxford University Press, 2006): 267. Code is alluding here to Haraway's "the god-trick," ibid.

21 National Academy of Sciences (NAS), "Methods and Values in Science," in Sandra Harding (ed.), *The 'Racial' Economy of Science: Toward A Democratic Future* (Bloomington, Indiana: Indiana University Press, 1993): 341–3. While the latter such values, the NAS observes, can and have harmed science, they can and do contribute positively to it too and are necessary parts of scientific practice. The danger lies in not detecting, or identifying, them.

> pursuit of ever higher degrees of scientific knowledge. As Alasdair MacIntyre . . . has observed, it is a mistake, albeit "a pertinacious and long-lived one," to imagine that an "observer can confront a fact face-to-face without any theoretical interpretation interposing itself." But while philosophers of science may now be largely agreed that "this was an error," it is still a temptation for scientists to imagine that you can stare a fact in the face and view it just as a fact.[22]

Although science has never been insulated, as positivism imagined, from the circumstances of its making or the contexts in which it arises, the economic affiliations and sociocultural embeddedness of contemporary technoscience reveal just how spurious such an imagining is: "the structures and effects of institutions and forms of patronage that underwrite and enable laboratory research and the circulation/application of scientific knowledge . . . count among conditions that make knowledge possible."[23]

A corollary to value-neutrality is the denial of any significant relations or mutual influences between cognitive and evaluative processes. This is best captured by Poincaré's argument that science is immune to moral critique. Ethics and science have their own domains which "do not interpenetrate . . . they can never conflict since they can never meet. There can no more be immoral science than there can be scientific morals."[24] A fact/value duality is thereby embraced. On the one hand, there are facts – claims about what is the case, and on the other hand, values – claims about what ought to be the case. To attempt to move from one to the other is to commit a logical fallacy. Indigenous views that our cognitive rapport with the world is simultaneously a moral one, and that there is an important sense in which knowing and valuing arise together, would be seen to founder on this "is/ought" dichotomy. As Robert Proctor states: "At one level, value-neutrality is defended as a consequence of an ontological dualism between the true and the good. In the twentieth century formulation, propositions about "what ought to be" can never be derived from

22 UNESCO, "Report of Subcommittee on Bioethics and Population Genetics of the UNESCO International Bioethics Committee" (15 November 1995). Available online at: http://portal.unesco.org/shs/en/files/2303/10596456491populationCIB3_en.pdf/population CIB3_en.pd. This report discussed the HGDP and was unusual in that it had significant indigenous input.

23 Lorraine Code, *Ecological Thinking*, 265.

24 Henri Poincaré, *The Value of Science* (New York: Dover Publications, 1905): 12.

propositions about "what is"; facts cannot be derived from values."[25] Moral and scientific discourse are thus severed. Moreover, within one influential strain of positivist thought – logical positivism – all propositions (including the ethical and political) not susceptible to empirical verification were rendered literally meaningless.[26]

Coupled with this has been a persistent tendency, within the Anglo-American analytic philosophical tradition, to reduce all knowledge to propositional knowledge, to only what is expressible in propositions: "all knowledge of objects is knowledge of truths of propositions about these objects."[27] Knowledge is characteristically transmitted in a propositional (usually written) form. In principle, this type of transmission makes knowledge readily accessible, public, or open to all.[28] Learning and teaching such knowledge does not require the presence, or mediation, of another person. One learns by comprehending what is asserted in propositions, and for this a book will do. There is a corresponding tendency to reject claims to knowledge that one is unable to express in words. Knowledge emerges primarily as an acquisitive process, as a matter of "the acquisition of true propositions about the world."[29]

Although Karl Popper takes credit for having "killed" logical positivism,[30] value-neutrality and the broader legacy of positivism persist in a variety of different, sometimes muted or mutated, forms. Within science studies and the philosophy of science, for example, one finds it in the debate between internalists and externalists over the role of political, social, and cultural variables in accounts of theory change. It even emerges among otherwise staunch critics of positivism, such as Barry Barnes and the

25 Proctor, *Value-Free Science?*, 7.

26 This followed from the adoption of a verificationist criterion of meaning. See A.J. Ayer, *Language, Truth and Logic* (Oxford: Oxford University Press, 1936).

27 Richard Rorty, "Intuition," in Paul Edwards (ed.), *The Encyclopedia of Philosophy*, Vol. IV (New York: MacMillan, 1967): 210.

28 Although, as Lorraine Code points out "even the punctiform "S-knows-that-*p*" knowledge claims of exemplary status in orthodox Anglo-American epistemology can be articulated, heard, and enacted only by knowers inculcated into a form of life – a habitus and ethos – where conditions for their articulation and acknowledgement are already in place." *Ecological Thinking*, ix.

29 Richard E. Palmer, "Toward A Postmodern Interpretive Self-Awareness," *The Journal of Religion*, 55:3 (1975): 320.

30 He did so in "Who Killed Logical Positivism?" in Karl Popper, *Unended Quest* (La Salle, Illinois: Open Court, 1982).

followers of the influential Edinburgh school's "strong programme" in the sociology of science. As one commentator observes: "Those who announce that science is 'socially constructed' often do so from a neutralist vantage point that rivals the narrowest positivist empiricism of the 1950s."[31] Barnes's principle of the "sociological equivalence of belief systems" embraces a radical relativism according to which no belief is worse, or less worthy, than any other. The evaluations one may find in science, he maintains, are "not of great importance, and . . . (are) eliminable."[32] Consequently, he is prepared to say, "It would be incongruous to 'expose' the writings (of the late nineteenth-century eugenicists) as 'racist,' since this set of conceptions fitted naturally and securely in the taken for granted world of the time."[33]

The most vigorous defense of value-neutrality has come from economics – a field in which questions of value, of why things have the worth that they do, are central. Ironically, the economists most deeply involved in policy making have most emphatically declared their value-neutrality. Milton Friedman for instance, contends that positive economics is "in principle independent of any particular ethical position or normative judgements."[34] Yet as Proctor observes, "Something is obviously awry if advocates of conservative, Chicago School economics can portray their work as "value-neutral." How has value-neutrality come to occupy such a special place in economic theory?"[35]

Proctor's answer is that it has been an invaluable ideological weapon in debates over distributive justice. The emergence of the new subjective theory of value was central in the rise of modern economics. It allowed value to be seen "as a purely individual phenomenon, dependent on nothing but individual whim or personal preference,"[36] on the pleasure an

[31] Proctor, *Value-Free Science?*, 223.

[32] Barry Barnes, *Scientific Knowledge and Sociological Theory* (London: Routledge & Kegan Paul, 1974): 127.

[33] Barnes, *Scientific Knowledge*, 145. Barnes's comment leaves one apoplectic. For whom exactly did such conceptions 'fit naturally and securely'? Who was prepared to take a racist world 'for granted'? The answer, presumably, is those whose interests were served by theories of eugenics and biological determinism. Then as now that is a minority, although a powerful minority, of humanity.

[34] Milton Friedman, *Essays in Positive Economics* (Chicago, Illinois: University of Chicago Press., 1953): 4.

[35] Robert Proctor, *Value-Free Science?*, 183.

[36] Ibid.

object brings to the consumer. Challenges raised by Marxists and utilitarians regarding value redistribution could thereby be countered, effectively discouraging "certain structural and ideological questions . . . from becoming the objects of discourse":

> If preferences are ultimately subjective, then how can anyone really ever know how preferences should be compared? The marginalist principle of subjective value was a brilliant refutation of Mill's argument for redistribution; it also served as a persuasive counterpoint to welfarist arguments that state support for pensions, health care, and so forth would serve the social good.[37]

Knowing and valuing, then, tend to be conceptualized as discreet, autonomous, and closed processes within the dominant system of knowledge. The commitment to value-neutrality and the attendant failure to appreciate the important sense in which epistemology and ethics are implicated in, and by, one another stands in marked contrast to indigenous views discussed in Chapter 2. It also has been instrumental in shaping the diverse practices of cultural imperialism examined in Chapter 1.

Consider, for example, the archaeologist's portrayal in Exhibit Two (see Chapter 1) of the desecration of Indian graves as a "real clash" between knowledge and value, between "science and religion" – a concerted effort to shut down the science of archaeology. Are there any moral limits to archaeological inquiry? Any ethical and ideological assumptions embedded within it? Does it reflect oppressive relations of power between dominant and indigenous cultures? These questions cannot coherently be formulated across the chasm of the "is/ought to be" divide. Yet it is only the sacred sites and burial grounds of Native America that are regularly subjected to archaeological study in the United States. When the Tennessee Valley Authority caused the excavation of a large number of graves, the remains of more than one thousand Indian graves were stored in boxes for scientific study, whereas those of persons of other races were reburied with suitable respect for religious beliefs. The scientific value of these materials was the only justification for their excavation.[38] As one tribal leader

[37] Ibid., 187, 200.

[38] Dean C. Higginbotham, "Native Americans Versus Archaeologists: The Legal Issues," *American Indian Law Review*, Vol. 10 (1982): 100–1.

recently protested in testimony before the U.S. Senate Select Committee on Indian Affairs:

> What other racial group in this country has been forced to endure the sacrilege of watching the remains of . . . relatives ripped from their burial sites and displayed to satisfy a totally unfathomable and morbid sense of scientific curiosity? . . . Archaeological significance (is) the death knell for many sacred sites . . . Initial decisions to dig up and shelve are made by those predisposed to digging and shelving. The propriety of the decision, if questioned, is subjected to peer review by others already predisposed to digging and shelving.[39]

Similarly, in Exhibit Seven, Dr. Cavalli-Sforza's effort to justify the urgency of the HGDP's collection of genetic data appeals only to what he sees as the impending loss for scientific knowledge if isolated indigenous populations vanish. The assumption that their disappearance is inevitable is unquestioned. As Tauli-Corpuz makes clear in Exhibit Eight, Cavalli-Sforza fails utterly to see any continuity between his research project and the historical legacy of political and scientific abuses which indigenous peoples have endured.

It is also instructive to place the marketing of American Indian spirituality (Exhibit One), and the whole collection of profitable practices that constitute cultural imperialism, within the context of value-neutrality and fact/value duality. Such epistemological commitments provide those engaged in such practices with an effective (and self-deceptive) means of hanging on to what has been stolen "while separating themselves from the *way* in which it was stolen."[40] It is, after all, just so much value-neutral social scientific knowledge (albeit knowledge of indigenous spirituality) that they are acquiring. That this has been a matter of actual acquisition, of purchase, is significant. When value is regarded as a function of the pleasure an object brings to the person who consumes it (as it is within positive economics[41]), the way is smoothed for the appropriation, remaking, and sale of indigenous spirituality – of sacred objects, ceremonies,

39 "Statement of Pat Lefthand," *Improvement of the American Indian Religious Freedom Act: Hearings Before the Senate Select Committee on Indian Affairs*, United States Senate on S. 2250, 100th Congress, 2nd Session 217 (1988): 27.

40 Renato Rosaldo, *Culture and Truth* (Boston, MA: Beacon Press, 1993): 70.

41 Positive economics, according to John Neville Keynes, deals with "what is." Normative economics deals with "what ought to be." See Proctor, *Value-Free Science?* 182–3.

and knowledge. Sweat lodges, pipe ceremonies, sun dances, and vision quests all have a price tag attached to them, and are placed for sale in the marketplace, their value reduced to and determined by the pleasure they bring to their consumers, to those who, as Donna Haraway so aptly puts it, in the "cannibalistic western logic that readily constructs other cultural possibilities as resources for western needs and action . . . seek . . . a solution to the forms of alienation built into western scientific and social practice.[42]

Indigenism, Value-Bifurcation, and Boundary-Work

The thesis of value-neutrality and the pure/applied science distinction lie at the heart of the positivist and neopositivist understanding of science. As such, they have been discussed extensively in the literature of science studies. Largely overlooked, however, is a third ideological commitment – to value-bifurcation – which plays a crucial role in the rhetoric of research justification. A well-entrenched practice within western philosophical traditions, value-bifurcation demarcates and sharply distinguishes the realm of ethics from that of politics. The bifurcated nature of the distinction is central to it. Ethics and politics are held to differ in kind, not just degree. Politics, it is said, "is social and collective, while ethics only pertains to the behavior of individuals."[43] The bifurcated nature of the distinction is crucial to it:

> Beginning with Aristotle, philosophers have noticed that there is a logical juncture where ethics finds its limits and politics begins. That turning point comes when we move beyond questions of individual conduct to consider the nature of human collectivities and our membership in them.[44]

When deployed in the practice of science, value-bifurcation effectively channels normative criticism by deflecting it away from the political and issues of power, and by simultaneously restricting normative critique to a cosmetic or surface ethics. The result is what might best be described as an apolitical ethics of science. The role of power in ethics is either completely disregarded or it is channeled into narrowly envisioned accounts

[42] Donna Haraway, *Primate Visions* (London: Routledge, Chapman & Hall, Inc., 1989): 247.
[43] Elizabeth Grosz, *Sexual Subversions* (Sydney, Australia: Allen & Unwin, 1989): xvii.
[44] Langdon Winner, "The Social and Professional Responsibility of Engineers," in Deborah Johnson, *Ethical Issues in Engineering* (Old Tappan, New Jersey: Prentice-Hall, 1991): 379–80.

of informed consent and the violation of individual autonomy.[45] At best, particular practices are deemed morally wrong whereas the relations of power responsible for them – which are themselves morally reprehensible and which must be challenged if such practices are to be effectively countered – are overlooked. It has also sometimes led to an amoral politics of science[46] including a tendency to emphasize science "policy" and to displace the politics of science. That politics and power do indeed figure in the origins and development of science, in scientific knowledge production is overlooked, if not dismissed. As Jean-Pierre Berlan comments in his discussion of biopatents, "Because we do not confront these questions politically, we turn to ethics."[47]

Although most characteristic of the Anglo-American philosophical tradition, the practice of value-bifurcation has left its mark even in fields with radical, oppositional commitments. In cultural studies, for example, it is apparent in the tendency of cultural theorists to emphasize one or the other of two seemingly divergent problem contexts. On the one hand, there have been efforts to examine and critique practices of subject formation, generating questions regarding the ways in which the individual is inserted into social positions. On the other hand, in contrast to such microlevel concerns, cultural theorists have also focused on the macrolevel, addressing primarily the forces operative in social, political, and economic formations. Although culture itself has "come to designate a problematic of mediation which attempts to link . . . practices of subject formation and the analysis of power or hegemony in the social formation," the middle or mediating ground between the processes of subject, and of social, formation has been neglected. In particular, there has been a failure to explicitly theorize the concept of community within cultural studies.[48]

45 Analogous results follow for the field of engineering. Langdon Winner touches on this, although he does not allude directly to the matter of value-bifurcation. See Winner, ibid.

46 This is evident in the works of critics of positivism, such as Barry Barnes. See Barnes, *Scientific Knowledge*.

47 Jean-Pierre Berlan, "The Commodification of Life," *Monthly Review*, 41 (1989): 26.

48 See Martin Allor, "In Private Practices: Rearticulating the Subject/Audience Nexus," *Discourse Social/Social Discourse* 2 (1989). We cannot fully understand the processes of subject formation without reference to the context in which they occur – typically communities – and to the ways in which communities shape, and reciprocally are shaped by, the individuals who inhabit and who conduct their lives within them. Nor can we have a rich grasp of the effectivity of forces operative in the larger social formation without considering how they are mediated by communities. Because it is typically within and through communities that individuals

For their part, a number of feminists have also neglected, or pointedly abandoned, the notion of community.[49] By contrast, many indigenist theorists have not. Indeed, indigenist critiques and activism draw vitally on the notion of community, which is conceptually and experientially central to indigenous knowledge systems. Interestingly, when discussion of community is taken up within the analytic philosophical tradition (only comparatively recently, within communitarian critiques of traditional liberal theories), we often find the same failure to address issues of power. As Sue Sherwin has noted: "communitarian theories . . . are committed to protecting and preserving community values, without evaluating their status in the hierarchies of oppression. They privilege the status quo. . . ."[50]

The conjunction of value-bifurcation with value-neutrality and the pure/applied science distinction thus sets in play a normative dynamics which offers powerful rhetorical protection, significantly enhancing the force and effectiveness of assertions that the production of scientific knowledge, unlike its use, is value-free. Science is shielded from direct involvement in moral and political debate. Charges that specific initiatives of western science such as the HGDP involve material oppression and conceptual domination are muted or dismissed because they embed these initiatives within the political, historical, social, cultural, and economic contexts which shape them and which they help shape.

No mere "academic" matter, this development has been of strategic, pragmatic benefit to western science, ensuring that the dynamics of power which mediate scientific practice, and most notably scientific knowledge

experience and resist the oppressive forces which intrude on their lives, the failure of radical critics to theorize community in turn contributes to the evisceration of criticism at the level of praxis. The prospect that communities themselves are generative of unique and distinctive forces not reducible to those operative in the larger social formation, forces which may serve to buffer and/or exacerbate existing relations of power and dominance, is also overlooked. See Laurie Anne Whitt and Jennifer Daryl Slack, "Communities, Environments and Cultural Studies," *Cultural Studies*, 8 (1994): 5.

49 This has, however, begun to change. In her most recent book, *Ecological Thinking*, Lorraine Code takes her earlier work to task for being "caught within an ethos of liberal individualism" and as relying "on an excessively benign conception of community." She now embraces a view in which community "is a sine qua non for the production, circulation, and acknowledgement of claims to know" and which is infused with awareness of "the effects of geographical-ecological-material locations and of hierarchical social orders that enable, structure, and/or thwart practices of establishing, contesting, verifying, and justifying knowledge claims." (viii)

50 Susan Sherwin, *No Longer Patient: Feminist Ethics and Health Care* (Philadelphia, Pennsylvania: Temple University Press, 1992): 54.

production, are ignored. Both ethics and politics are moved out of the space of knowledge production, while a depoliticized ethics is reserved for assessing knowledge use. The result, as we will see, is a rhetoric of pursuit or research justification which ensures that favored projects proceed unimpeded by substantive criticism. Normative critiques impact scientific knowledge production only when favorable; when unfavorable, they are deflected or disengaged, unable to bear upon knowledge production. This serves as an effective means of managing normative criticism: Only so much of a certain kind directed in a particular way to specific areas is allowed.

Conjoining value-neutrality with value-bifurcation also facilitates dismissal of radical critiques of biocolonialism and of western science generally. It mutes charges of material oppression and conceptual domination by shielding science from direct involvement in moral and political debate. When ethics and politics are moved out of the space of knowledge production, and a depoliticized ethics is reserved for assessing knowledge use, the cultural politics of science becomes so much ideological fluff. The commitment to value-neutrality and value-bifurcation is central to what sociologist of science Thomas Gieryn refers to as *boundary-work*, the attribution of selected characteristics to science, to its method, its practitioners, or to the knowledge which it produces "for purposes of constructing a social boundary that distinguishes some intellectual activity as non-science."[51] Such boundary-work establishes science's cultural authority – "the probability that particular definitions of reality . . . will prevail as valid and true,"[52] and secures science's cognitive authority among "other cultural practices offering different accounts of reality,"[53] as well as among the cognitive practices of other cultures, such as those addressed in Chapter 2. Indeed, science "is next to being *the* source of cognitive authority: anyone who would be widely believed and trusted as an interpreter of nature needs a license from the scientific community."[54]

[51] Thomas F. Gieryn, "Boundary-Work in Professional Ideologies of Science," *American Sociological Review*, 48 (December 1983): 782.
[52] Paul Starr, *The Social Transformation of American Medicine* (New York: Basic Books, 1982): 13.
[53] Thomas F. Gieryn, "Boundaries of Science," in Sheila Jasanoff *et al.* (eds.), *Handbook of Science and Technology Studies* (Thousand Oaks, California: Sage, 1995): 405.
[54] Barry Barnes and David Edge (eds.), *Science in Context: Readings in the Sociology of Science* (Cambridge, Massachusetts: MIT Press, 1982): 2.

Much of western science's credibility, as well as its cultural and cognitive authority, derives from scientists' efforts to exclude values from their space – "a bit of boundary-work" Gieryn notes "never sufficiently convincing to prevent incessant challenges."[55] By reducing political values to ideological biases, and ethical values to subjective inclinations, western science is able to present itself as neither ideological nor particular, that is, "western." Objectivity and universality are elevated as desiderata and preconditions of any science. Neither of these commitments is merely "academic." They are of strategic, pragmatic benefit to the western knowledge system, enabling it – especially in the form of science – to dismiss knowledge of the natural world formulated within indigenous knowledge systems and to ignore the dynamics of power that mediate relations between western and non-western cultures. Both of the latter ease the process of, and enhance the prospects for, imperial science in the service of corporate and/or national interests.

The history of the encounter of western science and indigenous peoples has been devastating, and it is being updated and reproduced daily. The thriving multibillion dollar partnership between the biosciences and the biotechnology industry, for example, directly impacts and often targets indigenous peoples.[56] Indigenous resistance to these developments is growing, forceful, and effective. It demonstrates the promise of an already vital indigenist theoretical perspective which analyzes the political role of science with special attention to how it impacts indigenous peoples. As a theoretical position and as political practice, indigenism has been discussed by various indigenous activists and scholars, but it has yet to figure actively or prominently in (predominantly non-indigenous) western radical agendas and social justice movements. Even many politically left organizations, and the conferences they convene, fail to attend to indigenous issues, often supposing they can be classified under "Third World" concerns. Yet this not only fails to accommodate indigenous struggles in the industrialized nations, it also ignores the fact that, for many indigenous peoples, their most immediate oppression is at the hands of the nation-state within whose boundaries they have been determined to lie.

[55] Thomas Gieryn, "Boundaries of Science," 423.

[56] See Jack Kloppenburg, Jr., "No Hunting! Scientific Poaching and Global Biodiversity," *Z Magazine* (Sept. 1990): 104–8.

Indigenism advances critiques of the dynamics of power, and the shifting power relations, that enable the continued oppression of indigenous peoples. It stresses the existence, effectiveness, and potential of indigenous agency in resisting oppression and in formulating concrete proposals for securing justice.[57] Justice, however, cannot be adequately addressed in the abstract; "the actual forces that undermine it, as well as those that support it"[58] must be examined, if justice is to be secured. Hence, indigenist critiques of science do not rely on the myopic ethics produced by the conjunction of value-neutrality and value-bifurcation; it is not enough to assert merely that a particular practice is morally wrong and ought not continue. The relations of power responsible for it, which are themselves morally reprehensible, must be challenged if the practice is to be effectively countered. Like other initiatives of western science, the HGDP (examined in Part II) is embedded within political, historical, social, cultural, and economic contexts which shape it and which it helps shape. Indigenism conjoins contextualized critique of the oppression of indigenous peoples with concrete proposals for realizing justice, and with recognition of the existence, effectiveness, and potential of indigenous agency.

To resist value-bifurcation and secure both a politically enriched ethics and an ethically informed politics, every critique must consider "which questions get asked and which are ignored . . . whose interests are affected by the decisions that have been made and who has the power to control the agenda."[59] Indigenists also address how a specific practice, project, or institution impacts indigenous peoples' cultures and lands. To morally evaluate specific initiatives of biotechnoscience involves establishing moral criteria to determine whether and how such initiatives should be undertaken; it also involves making political judgments.[60] These judgments are made

[57] Ronald Niezen refers to it as "[t]he international movement that aspires to promote and protect the rights of the world's "first peoples." It has arisen "out of the shared experiences of marginalized groups facing the negative impacts of resource extraction and economic modernization and . . . the social convergence and homogenization that these ambitions tend to bring about." *The Origins of Indigenism: Human Rights and the Politics of Identity* (Berkeley, California: University of California Press, 2003): 4, 9.

[58] Sherwin, *No Longer Patient*, 55.

[59] Ibid., 4.

[60] See ibid., 51.

whether one supports or attacks the initiative, and irrespective of one's role in it.

Knowledge, Power, and Science

The three convictions about the nature and practice of science discussed in this chapter inform the dominant knowledge system's response to fundamental questions about knowledge, such as: How does one know? What counts as knowledge? What role does power play within this knowledge system? They are part of the ideology of science, which, Roy MacLeod argues, spins the role of western science in conquest as no more than a contingent one. If science is "benevolent, apolitical and value-neutral" and its extension is a value-free aid to material progress and civilization, then science has only an incidental role to play in empire, and the "civilizing, improving advantages of new knowledge, in moral and material progress, surely cannot be questioned."[61]

However, MacLeod contends, there are flaws in this reasoning: ". . . the bonds forged through science are indissolubly linked to political development. Through science comes a language (conveniently the language of the mother country); through this language . . . comes control."[62] Numerous scholars have traced the historical connection among colonialism, science, and capitalist expansion. Nationalizing science in the interests of capitalist and colonialist expansion, Zeshan Kahn argues, made it possible for "corporate scientific advancement to proceed under the guise of a patriotic calling rather than the self-interests of a capitalist elite."

> The contemporary fears of indigenous people may not seem so fantastic when these historical patterns return in a contemporary form. Although the military conquests of colonial days may be over, economic imperialism is viewed by many as thriving, generally through the appropriation of natural resources that are later turned into sizable profits for these "imperialist" companies. If nations endorse their corporate self-interests over the fears of exploitation raised by indigenous peoples, the patterns of historical economic imperialism and

61 Roy MacLeod, "On Visiting the 'Moving Metropolis': Reflections on the Architecture of Imperial Science," *Historical Records of Australian Science*, 5:3 (1982): 1.

62 Ibid.

> colonialism resurface. Assuming a nation does nothing to restrict corporate involvement with a "scientific" expedition, the transnational corporation still becomes the neo-colonizer.[63]

By allowing access to and exportation of data, biocolonialism concentrates knowledge about a people and their environment in the hands of an imperial power.[64] Such knowledge, irrespective of the intentions of its collectors, is not only a potential weapon, but also a means of control, facilitating the manipulation of a people by that power. It thereby exacerbates well-entrenched injustices, contributing "to the asymmetric patterns [of distribution] already existing in the world."[65]

Many indigenous peoples have long recognized that knowledge and power implicate one another. Some recent research in the philosophy of science and science studies has also stressed that questions of knowledge and power "do not belong to distinct domains of inquiry, and that answering each requires sustained attention to the other."[66] It seeks to demonstrate that and how "scientific knowledge and political order come into being together."[67] This research has focused, in Michel Foucault's words, on "the process by which knowledge functions as a form of power and disseminates the effects of power."[68] Indigenist responses to biocolonialism and especially the Diversity Project have addressed just this issue,

[63] Zeshan Q. Kahn, "Colonialism Revisited: Insights into the Human Genome Diversity Project" *Journal of Law and Social Challenges*, 3 (1999): 116.

[64] Some would challenge this on the grounds that publicly available knowledge cannot be concentrated in anyone's hands. (See Dennis Karjala, "Biotech Patents and Indigenous Peoples," *Minnesota Journal of Law and Science*, 7 (2006): 488). As a practical matter, however, the fact that knowledge, particularly specialized knowledge, is publicly available does not prevent its concentration. Indeed, much knowledge that is technically "publicly available" is neither widely dispersed nor accessible when it is. (For better or worse, knowledge of modal logic is concentrated in the hands of modal logicians, despite its public availability.) Moreover, in cases such as that of the Guajajara (Exhibit Three, Chapter 1), one of the consequences of biocolonialism plainly is "that the source peoples can no longer use their traditional knowledge in their traditional ways." (Ibid.)

[65] Irving Louis Horowitz, *The Rise and Fall of Project Camelot* (Cambridge, Massachusetts: MIT Press, 1967): 299.

[66] Joseph Rouse, "The Dynamics of Power and Knowledge in Science," *The Journal of Philosophy*, 88 (1991): 665.

[67] Jenny Reardon, *Race to the Finish: Identity and Governance in an Age of Genomics* (Princeton, New Jersey: Princeton University Press, 2005): 8.

[68] Michel Foucault, *Power/Knowledge: Selected Interviews and Other Writings, 1972–1977* (New York: Pantheon Books, 1980): 69.

so vital to understanding the political dynamics mediating indigenous and western knowledge systems. This chapter concludes by reviewing some of this recent work on knowledge and power in western science, which helps to illuminate certain processes that are at work in biocolonialism.

Philosopher Joseph Rouse has developed a detailed alternative to the conventional understanding of the role of knowledge and power within western science.[69] It addresses important aspects of power relations, and of the production and assessment of knowledge to which the standard account fails to do justice. Rouse points out that, although knowledge and power have both been regarded as things which agents acquire, possess, and use, they have also been taken to constitute analytically distinct domains of human inquiry. The domain of knowledge includes representations, whereas the domain of power consists of human actions. These two domains are usually seen to interact in a particular way: "power may suppress knowledge, or distort it ideologically; it may also provide resources needed to achieve or accelerate knowledge acquisition, which in turn may augment power."[70] According to his alternative account, the details of which do not concern us here, knowledge and power are not distinct domains of things, but rather

> interconnected ways of posing questions to and concerns about the same domain . . . They represent different ways of configuring and interrogating a wide range of our engagements with the world and each other . . . (and) neither is adequately addressed without serious attention to the other.[71]

Rouse relies upon Thomas Wartenberg's account of power as a particular type of ongoing social process which is "continually being reconstituted and/or altered by means of the actions and understandings of social agents."[72] In addition to being dynamic, power is also situated; the role of "peripheral social others" is crucial in understanding power relationships. One agent has power over another as the result of the social field within which they are both situated.

69 See ibid. and Joseph Rouse, *Knowledge and Power: Toward a Political Philosophy of Science* (Ithaca, New York: Cornell University Press, 1987).
70 Rouse, "The Dynamics of Power," 658.
71 Ibid.
72 Thomas Wartenberg, *The Forms of Power: From Domination to Transformation* (Philadelphia, Pennsylvania: Temple University Press, 1990): 164.

On this account, a relationship between two agents is a power relationship because, and only insofar as, others will normally respond to them by aligning themselves with the dominant agent's actions. Power, thus, is always mediated by what Wartenberg calls a "social alignment"; through the actions of many peripheral agents, the connection between the dominant agent's actions and the denial or fulfillment of the subordinate agent's wishes is established or enforced. On this view, the social world "becomes an array of overlapping social alignments oriented by ongoing struggles of domination and resistance, within which agents and their actions are situated."[73] Within the context of biocolonialism such social alignments are clearly at work. They include transnational corporations, scientists and technicians, the legal systems and political policies of various nation-states, international legal regimes, nongovernmental organizations of various sorts, alliances of farmers and peasants, indigenous organizations, communities, and activists. We will see all of these groups engaged directly in the struggle over the HGDP in the following two chapters.

Although Wartenberg restricts the domain of power to this social world, Rouse expands it to elements of the natural world because power relations not only require keeping other human agents in line, but also depend on a reliable alignment of the physical environment. The construction and extension of scientific laboratories or "microworlds" shape and transform not only the social but the natural world – materials, things, processes, and practices. Thus, he contends that power cannot legitimately be withheld from the "natural world" and confined to the "social world."[74] To illustrate the argument, he shows how "genes" emerge as an object of possible discourse

> through accumulations of capabilities and insights in specific contexts (e.g. laboratories with their own projects, protocols and materials, but also experimental systems such as pisum, drosophila, maize and bacteriophage). These cannot be extended to other locations without complex and subtle mutual adaptations.[75]

Among these are the standardization, simplification, and adaptation of laboratory practices and equipment, and the knowledge they embody.

[73] Rouse, "The Dynamics of Power," 659.

[74] It is worth noting, parenthetically, that this approach has some limited analogy to the indigenous conception of power, in which the natural world is also vitally implicated.

[75] Rouse, "The Dynamics of Power," 660.

The material and conceptual working environment to which they are extended also requires modification. To take something as knowledge, Rouse suggests, is to project it as a resource for ongoing activity, be this future research or "applications."

Rouse's account of knowledge and power in science can be put to valuable use in understanding just how much was at stake for indigenous peoples in the debate over the HGDP. The Project's goal was to collect and analyze DNA samples from diverse, predominantly indigenous, populations and "to develop databases and resources that could be used to investigate new questions in the future."[76] The "wealth of information harbored in the DNA of aboriginal peoples"[77] would be transferred to databases that were openly intended to function, in Rouse's terms, as resources for ongoing research activity (although Project organizers specifically denied any intention of developing applications).[78]

The database microworlds, in which this genetic information was to be preserved, would be located regionally as well as centrally. Although it is not likely that they would be situated on the actual lands of the indigenous peoples who would serve as the source of the genetic material, they would certainly impact these communities by transforming the relations of power between them and their surrounding nation-states. The laboratory microworlds on which the Project would rely would likely affect indigenous peoples and lands for two reasons. One is that the Project actively discouraged a "bleed and run" scenario. Another is that training in genetic research was being offered as an incentive to establish the regional HGDP committees that would do the sampling. Thus, the promise of training in such techniques as growing white blood cells, preparing DNA, and analyzing DNA markers using the polymerase chain reaction was seen as "luring many developing countries to participate in the HGDP."[79] As one

[76] National Science Foundation, "Pilot Projects for a Human Genome Diversity Project: Special Competition" (1996). File nsf96112. Available online at: http://www.nsf.gov.

[77] Leslie Roberts, "A Genetic Survey of Vanishing Peoples," *Science*, 252 (1991): 1614–17.

[78] Surprisingly, given historical precedent and the economic and political realities of securing funding for such research, they also question its likelihood: "Although very unlikely, it is nevertheless possible that the results of the HGD Project" will lead to commercial applications. (Human Genome Diversity Project, "FAQ," 1996. Available online at: http://www.stanford.edu/group/morrinst/hgdp.faq.html.

[79] Patricia Kahn, "Genetic Diversity Project Tries Again," *Science*, 266 (1994): 720–2.

molecular biologist in Nairobi noted, "The new biology must find its way into Africa . . . this is a way of doing it."[80]

Members of the sampled indigenous populations were exceedingly unlikely to be members of the regional committees. Anthropologists who worked among them and who secured their trust would certainly be. In fact, they clearly constituted an acknowledged and crucial part of the social alignment mediating power in this case, having generated the initial list of the 722 populations deemed "most worthy" of genetic study. Indeed, it was acknowledged that the populations ultimately sampled would turn on the availability of anthropologists with ties to them. "Isolated and indigenous peoples participate with ethnologists because they trust them," reports one anthropologist and proponent of the Project.[81]

Many indigenous peoples have a long history of struggle with and domination by the nation-states in which they are situated, and which would be well represented on these committees. Such committees would decide, among other things, "what scientific questions to emphasize, which populations to approach, and how to adapt the ethics rules to local conditions and cultures."[82] The HGDP would significantly impact the social, material, and conceptual environments of indigenous peoples, sustaining and enhancing existing unequal relations of power. Indigenous people were acutely aware of this and of the kinds of tensions and disputes it would exacerbate, or initiate, within their communities.

This transformation of the social and natural worlds is a manifestation of power. Charges of biocolonialism might best be seen in this light. Rather than the theft and settling of indigenous lands, the colonization at issue involves, in part, their transformation through the wholesale exportation of the microworlds of western science onto them. Genetic information would be extracted from indigenous peoples, processed in these microworlds, made available for use and eventually purchase, regardless of whatever measures the Project organizers might take to prevent the latter outcome. The current social alignments, the current relations of power between dominant western and subordinated indigenous cultures,

80 Ibid., 722.
81 John Moore, cited in Anna Maria Gillis, "Getting a Picture of Human Diversity," *Bioscience*, 44:1 (1994): 9.
82 Ibid.

would be reinforced and strengthened by the Diversity Project, as the array of interest groups that constitute and enable western technoscience (corporations, governments, institutions, organizations, entrepreneurs, and scientists) responded in ways coherently aligned with the dominant agents' actions.

By conceiving knowledge and power as interwoven processes rather than distinct domains, Rouse's account replaces a neopositivist ideology with one in which the value-laden nature of scientific research – and of knowledge production as well as of knowledge use – is manifest. It insists on the contextualization of research projects like the HGDP within their social, cultural, and political settings: "Human genetic diversity simply cannot become an object of study absent social and moral choices about what we want to know and who we want to become."[83] The oppressive relations of power that have historically structured dominant–indigenous interactions are not somehow magically suspended when scientific research is planned and executed. As we will see in Part II, the debate surrounding the HGDP offers a vivid example of both how these relations of power shape contemporary research and of how the normative dynamics of value-bifurcation work to conceal this.

[83] Jenny Reardon, *Race to the Finish*, 8.

PART II

THE HUMAN GENOME DIVERSITY PROJECT: A CASE STUDY

We move now to a case study which exemplifies the ideology of the new imperial science in practice, as well as the sustained attack upon it that is being mounted by indigenist critics of biocolonialism. In 1988, the Human Genome Organization (HUGO) began a massive multibillion dollar effort to map and sequence the human genome known as the Human Genome Project (HGP). Because the HGP did not consider population-level variation, population geneticists would suggest a collateral study. On the eve of the Columbus Quincentenary, several leading geneticists proposed the Human Genome Diversity Project (HGDP). In an article in *Genomics* entitled "Call for a Worldwide Survey of Human Genetic Diversity: A Vanishing Opportunity for the Human Genome Project," they asserted: "The Human Genome Project can now grasp a vanishing opportunity to preserve the record of our genetic heritage . . . The genetic diversity of people now living harbors the clues to the evolution of our species, but the gate to preserve these clues is closing rapidly."[1] At an estimated cost of $25 million, the Diversity Project was formally brought under the auspices of HUGO in January 1994 when an international executive committee was formed to oversee HUGO's relations with the Project.

The stated goal of the HGDP, at least initially, was to collect, analyze, and preserve for future study DNA from diverse populations in order to understand human variation, and to learn more about human origins,

[1] L. Luca Cavalli-Sforza *et al.*, "Call for a Worldwide Survey of Human Genetic Diversity: A Vanishing Opportunity for the Human Genome Project," *Genomics*, 11 (1991): 490.

evolution, and ancient migration patterns.[2] "Isolated" human populations were of most interest, and those specifically mentioned were all indigenous. Anthropologists, archaeologists, and linguists gathered to draw up an initial list of the 722 populations considered most worthy of genetic study by having their cell lines immortalized. "This is just 50 people trying to represent the world," one said.[3] The gate to this study is "closing rapidly" because these "Isolates of Historic Interest"[4] are "vanishing," "rapidly disappearing," or "in danger of dying out or being assimilated."[5] The visual images accompanying the articles are telling. An anonymous individual from the Arawete tribe is captioned as a "vanishing resource," and a sidebar entitled "A Few of the Chosen" includes images of Yanomami and Chukchi people with the caption "They made the list."[6] Indigenous peoples have dubbed it the "vampire project."[7]

This effort to discern the microphylogeny of human populations before population "contact," (symbolically taken to have begun in 1492) has been criticized on conceptual and methodological grounds.[8] Biologist and anthropologist Jonathan Marks, for example, claims that the HGDP confuses cultural with biological categories. Its goal, he observes, is "guided by an archaic idea: the establishment of the ultimate genetic phylogeny of human groups," which obliges its advocates "to maintain that non-European human populations are generally 'pure,' and have been spared the vagaries of history, of contact, and of gene flow – assumptions that

[2] As noted later in this chapter, although the Diversity Project began principally as a history project, it rhetorically reconstructed itself as a medical research project.

[3] Leslie Roberts, "Genetic Diversity Project: Anthropologists Climb (Gingerly) on Board," *Science*, 258 (20 November 1992): 1301.

[4] Jenna Roberts, "Global Project Underway to Sample Genetic Diversity," *Nature*, 361 (1993): 675.

[5] For this language, see Roberts, ibid., 33 as well as Leslie Roberts, "A Genetic Survey of Vanishing Peoples," *Science*, 252 (21 June 1991): 1617 and Leslie Roberts, "How to Sample the World's Genetic Diversity," *Science*, 257 (28 August 1992): 1205.

[6] Jenna Roberts, "Global Project," 33; Leslie Roberts, "A Genetic Survey," 1617; Leslie Roberts, "How to Sample," 1204.

[7] John Liddle, quoted in David Nason, "Tickner Warns Over Aboriginal Gene Sampling," *The Australian* (Jan. 25, 1994): 3.

[8] I address these only briefly here. For more discussion, see Margaret Lock, "Editorial: Interrogating the Human Genome Diversity Project," *Social Science & Medicine*, 39 (1994): 605; Jonathan Marks, "Commentary: The Human Genome Diversity Project," *Anthropological News*, April 1995: 72; Jonathan Marks, *Human Biodiversity: Genes, Race, and History* (Hawthorne, New York: Aldine de Gruyter, 1995): 176–80.

are certainly gratuitous."[9] Thus it perpetrates the erroneous assumption "that only Europeans were socially cosmopolitan, and other peoples were generally isolated and pristine – that Europeans had history, and others did not."[10] To suppose that population contact "suddenly began in 1492 or later, and to project a pseudo-history onto human population biology, are unlikely to be optimal intellectual strategies for studying the genetic variation in our species."[11]

The debate over the Diversity Project vividly illustrates the conjunction of the pure/applied science distinction, the thesis of value-neutrality, and the practice of value-bifurcation. The rhetoric of research justification which they enable, and how they work together to deflect substantive ethical and political critiques of science, is examined in Chapter 4. That such critiques may yet be effectively and forcefully made is especially apparent in the debate between the Diversity Project's proponents and its indigenist opponents. Chapter 5 addresses the nature and force of these critiques, as well as what is at stake in them.

[9] Marks, *Human Biodiversity*, 175.
[10] Ibid., 177.
[11] Ibid., 178.

4

The Rhetoric of Research Justification

An article in the journal *Science* presented the following rationale for pursuing the Human Genome Diversity Project (HGDP): "Indigenous peoples are disappearing across the globe . . . As they vanish, they are taking with them a wealth of information buried in their genes about human origins, evolution, and diversity . . . each (population) offers "a window into the past" . . . a unique glimpse into the gene pool of our ancestors . . . Already, there are indications of the wealth of information harbored in the DNA of aboriginal peoples."[1] According to its advocates, the HGDP proposed to increase knowledge of human genetic diversity by preserving for future researchers the genetic materials responsible for that diversity. Ensuring the survival of the human sources of those genetic materials was not a scientific priority. Some of the Project's supporters may have regarded the latter as a social priority, although arguments from them to this effect are elusive. Indeed there is a decided sense of inevitability in the talk of "vanishing" that fueled the urgency of the research enterprise. In the words of geneticist Francis Collins, "I do think the urgency is a compelling argument . . . populations are not going to be there indefinitely for us to decide at some future date we would like to sample them."[2]

Preserving human genetic materials for future study is seen as a scientific priority; they are crucial resources for scientific knowledge production. Whereas the use of knowledge of genetic diversity is subject to ethical and political critique, its production (the story goes) is not. Conversely, preserving the human sources of the desired genetic materials is not and

[1] Leslie Roberts, "A Genetic Survey," 1614.

[2] United States Senate, "Human Genome Diversity Project: Hearing before the Committee on Governmental Affairs," Washington, DC: U.S. Government Printing Office, 1993: 23.

cannot be a scientific priority because, as a matter of ethics and politics, it is not (seen to be) a matter of science. Even though knowledge production such as that proposed by the HGDP has substantive ethical and political dimensions, there is a rhetoric of research justification in play which serves to obscure them. This rhetoric relies crucially upon the conjunction of the three commitments of neopositivist science examined in Chapter 3: value-neutrality, the pure/applied science distinction, and value-bifurcation.

The Normative Dynamics of Value-Bifurcation

The rhetoric which obscures the political workings of research initiatives like the HGDP is not unique to them. It played a comparable role in earlier debates over the HGP. Indeed, the key rhetorical strategies were developed in that debate. Given this, and the explicit tie made by the Diversity Project's proponents between it and the HGP, it will be helpful to consider the latter closely and in tandem with the HGDP. Advocates of both the HGP and the HGDP have relied upon value-bifurcation to support these bioscience initiatives as well as to defend them against their critics. The response typically made when serious normative concerns regarding these projects were raised is illustrative. In 1989, the European Economic Community (EEC) considered proposals for the establishment of a research program in human genetics. Objections from the European parliament prompted the EEC to withdraw, modify, and resubmit the initial proposal. The "planned scientific content of the programme"[3] remained unchanged. Only "the intentions and consequences of the programme"[4] were revisited. In the new version of the proposal, the name was changed from "Predictive Medicine" to "Human Genome Analysis."[5] It also called for "in-depth discussions of the ethical, social and legal aspects of human genome analysis" in order to identify any "possible misuses."[6] Although there were many political aspects to be addressed, there is no

[3] Debora MacKenzie, "European Commission Tables New Proposals on Genome Research," *New Scientist* (25 November 1989): 24.

[4] Bo Andreassen Rix, "Should Ethical Concerns Regulate Science?: The European Experience With the Human Genome Project," *Bioethics*, 5:3 (1991): 255.

[5] For discussions of this, see Robert Cook-Deegan, *The Gene Wars* (New York: W.W. Norton & Company, 1994); MacKenzie, "European Commission"; and Dirk Stemerding and Jaap Jelsma, "Compensatory Ethics for the Human Genome Diversity Project," *Science as Culture*, 5:24 (1996).

[6] MacKenzie, "European Commission," 24.

inclusion of them in this charge. Moreover, by reserving discussion of ethics for the uses (more exactly, misuses) of the knowledge gained, the ethical (and political) considerations involved in producing that knowledge in the first place were sidestepped and silenced. As Dirk Stemerding and Jaap Jelsma observe, ethics was "moved from the space of knowledge production to a separate space of special committees and programmes."[7]

This is an initial, key move in the normative dynamics of value-bifurcation, and in making it, the EEC took for granted a pure/applied science distinction, separating "science as a quest for pure knowledge" from "society as a body which has to 'identify the limits' beyond which applications of this knowledge would become unacceptable."[8] Having removed ethics from the space of knowledge production, the proposal invites the articulation of "bioethical principles" that will facilitate the regulation of "the eventual uses of genetic analysis."[9] Some uses of genetic knowledge are declared "unacceptable developments" which must be "precluded," such as hereditary genetic modifications and the use of genetic analysis for monitoring individuals.[10] As in the United States, where the discussion of ethics was reserved for a special program, known as ELSI (Ethical, Legal and Social Implications – once again, note the absence of Political Implications), the "ethics" had been attended to and the science could proceed. The ELSI Branch of the HGP would devote its attention "to the consequences of having increased ability to obtain genetic information on individuals"[11] and how to avoid any subsequent genetic discrimination against them. It was created "to define these [ethical, legal, and social] issues and to develop initial policy options to address them."[12] The ethico-political question which ELSI was not charged with addressing is whether such knowledge should be produced in the first place.

It is instructive to see just what becomes of normative issues in knowledge production after value-bifurcation has done its work. After noting that estimates of the cost of the U.S. HGP alone were for some $3 billion over a 15-year period, ethicist Thomas Murray observes that the appropriateness

7 Stemerding and Jelsma, "Compensatory Ethics," 348. My thinking on these matters is deeply indebted to their article.
8 Ibid., 338.
9 MacKenzie, "European Commission," 24.
10 Ibid.
11 United States Senate, "Human Genome Diversity Project," 8.
12 Ibid., 10.

of this "is largely a matter of science policy rather than ethics."[13] Science policy, on this reading, appears to be a purely prudential matter: "Even if it is not the wisest way to spend research resources, that would not make it unethical."[14] The oddity of this is increased by his admission that the most significant challenge the HGP raises may well "have to do with the way we understand ourselves, our nature and significance, and our connections with our ancestors and descendants."[15] Surely the pursuit of a project with implications of this magnitude is a matter for ethical and political concern?

A similar pattern of reasoning and rhetoric is discernible in the debate over the HGDP. The pure/applied science distinction is invoked, ethical issues are reserved for the latter, management of them is handed over to a special ethics committee, and political issues are largely (if not very successfully) displaced. The New Zealand Health Research Council, for instance, organized a conference with the promising title "Whose Genes Are They Anyway?" Yet in the draft "Consensus Report" that emerged from it, the philosophers and scientists present asserted that:

> The spirit of science is independent of commercial, political and religious interests.
>
> The application of knowledge derived from science should be for human good and open for public scrutiny.[16]

Moreover, in an article assessing the ethical implications of the HGDP, we find:

> Knowledge in and of itself is not immoral; however the potential for adverse effects from the acquisition and utilization of this knowledge has contributed to this moral dilemma.[17]

[13] Thomas H. Murray, "Ethical Issues in Human Genome Research," in Kristin Shrader-Frechette and Laura Westra (eds.), *Technology and Values* (Lanham, Maryland: Rowman & Littlefield, 1997): 416.

[14] Ibid. Indeed to suggest, as many critics of both the HGP and HGDP have done, that such expenditures are ethically questionable is, according to Murray, to succumb to "the profligate manner in which epithets such as unethical and immoral are used to tarnish a person or enterprise we do not like." (Ibid.)

[15] Ibid., 426.

[16] Warren Tate, "A Report on the HRC Consensus Development Conference," *Centre for Gene Research Newsletter* (August 1995). This was available online at http://biochem.otago.ac.nz:800/cgr/cgrnews.html, but the issue has been deleted from the site. However, a copy is on file with the author.

[17] Elizabeth Clay McPherson, "Ethical Implications of the Human Genome Diversity Project," *Nursing Connections*, 8:1 (1995): 42.

The dynamics of value-bifurcation which served the HGP figured prominently in justifying the HGDP. Francis Collins, of the National Center for Human Genome Research, suggested that "the experience gained through setting up the Human Genome Project applies to the Diversity Project,"[18] and proposed that the National Research Council (NRC) review it to determine "how to handle the very thorny ethical issues"[19] it raises. The problem, of course, was that one of the "thorniest" of all was whether there should *be* such a project. The NRC did conduct a review, and this was not among the questions raised. In fact, before the NRC's review was even completed, the National Science Foundation (NSF) had circulated a call for "Pilot Projects for a Human Genome Diversity Project."[20]

Such value-bifurcation encourages a curious normative strabismus. When values are bifurcated, all that is left of the ethics of science is an applied, or cosmetic, ethics, and all that is left of the politics of science is policy, or regulation. Both reductions are invaluable to a rhetoric of research justification and to the management of normative critique. The former ensures that issues of power in ethics are restricted to concerns for autonomy and informed consent, if not neglected entirely. The latter encourages a persistent preoccupation with science policy and legal or regulatory issues.

Loane Skene, for example, a member of the Law Reform Commission of Victoria (Australia), comments that ethicists are concerned "not so much with the ethics or morality of mapping the human genome but rather with the use that will be made of that knowledge."[21] She then concludes that:

> the most effective method of regulating the problems that may arise from the human genome project is to concentrate, not on the research involved in the project, but rather on the uses that may be made of the information gained from it.[22]

18 United States Senate, "Human Genome Diversity Project," 8.

19 Ibid., 9.

20 NSF, "Pilot Projects for a Human Genome Diversity Project: Special Competition," file nsf96112 (1996) available via the NSF homepage, http://www.nsf.gov. Note that the NRC posted its "Study on the Proposed Human Genome Diversity Project: Request for Input and Notice of Public Meetings" to the e-mail news list *Native-L* on June 16, 1996. Available online at: http://nativenet.uthscsa.edu/archive/nl/9606/0078.html.

21 Loane Skene, "Mapping the Human Genome: Some Thoughts for Those Who Say 'There Should Be a Law on It,'" *Bioethics*, 5:3 (1991): 245.

22 Ibid., 248.

This involves, she suggests, regulating

> *indirectly* . . . because the results of the research might be used for a particular purpose, or because there has been a breach of a law or some other regulatory provision that incidentally applies to the activity in question.[23]

Examples would be laws concerning informed consent and patent law – both issues which figure centrally, and analogously, in the HGDP debate. The development of a Materials Transfer Agreement and a Database Access Agreement in response to indigenous concerns about commercial exploitation is a case in point. Objections raised against knowledge production were "re-routed" and managed at the level of application. Although the chance that HGDP research would lead to commercially valuable products is, according to its proponents, "very remote . . . our current planning anticipates that this unlikely event is not impossible."[24] The Agreements are intended "to ensure that, should the cell lines have commercial values, the benefits will flow back to the sampled populations."[25] Possible commercial uses of the research are acknowledged but "in essence, the HGDP is trying to rid *itself* of the moral implications of profiting from collected biological material" while "washing its hands clean of the possible uses of its research."[26]

The reduction of ethics to an applied, cosmetic ethics is described by Stemerding and Jelsma as yielding a "compensatory ethics" or a "politics of compensation," which

> seeks to control the implications of scientific and technological developments only through compensatory measures that should prevent undesirable effects of new knowledge and technologies.[27]

[23] Ibid., 244–5. The tendency to seek rationales for existing practices without substantively modifying or challenging them, is evident in this article as well. Skene's final comment is that there is already in place substantial "legislation and administrative machinery that is . . . relevant to the matters in question." (Ibid., 248.)

[24] Luca Cavalli-Sforza and Henry T. Greely, Message posted to *Native-L* on 8 July 1993. Available online at: http://nativenet.uthscsa.edu/archive/nl/9307/0046.html.

[25] Ibid.

[26] Marina L. Whelan, "What, if Any, are the Ethical Obligations of the U.S. Patent Office? A Closer Look at the Biological Sampling of Indigenous Groups," *Duke Law and Technology Review* (2006): 22.

[27] Stemerding and Jelsma, "Compensatory Ethics," 346–7.

Ethics becomes a "supplementary activity,"[28] concerned only with the implications of specific technoscience projects for society. By reserving a space for ethics in knowledge application and removing it from knowledge production, and by creating committees such as ELSI and its European counterpart ESLA (ethical, social and legal aspects) specifically charged with examining the implications of the knowledge being gained, concerns about the HGP could be rhetorically managed, and research could proceed apace. As Garver and Garver observe, "the U.S. Human Genome Project established an . . . (ELSI) programme so that these anxieties can be addressed and answered while the scientific research is being processed."[29] Political issues could be ignored or displaced, reduced to policy and regulatory concerns, and the real issues of power could be avoided. Ethics (and politics) were not regarded as central in knowledge production:

> Rather than viewing ethics as integral to the conceptualization of research, many participants argued that the science needed to be worked out first; ethical protocols to accommodate the science could follow. Science, for example, could define the subjects from whom informed consent should be gained. Ethical protocols could then be written to help researchers gain this consent in an ethical manner. Such an approach by-passed questions about the role the informed consent process itself would play in defining subjects (in this case, groups), questions that proved of enormous importance to many of the indigenous groups in North America and Australia that the Project hoped to sample.[30]

How likely is it that applied ethics will offer substantive value criticism of bioscience and of initiatives like the HGP and the HGDP? Not very, if certain, primarily feminist, analyses of applied ethics are accurate. Cheryl Noble has pointed out that applied ethics tends to endorse the status quo, and thereby justify (if not facilitate) existing social practices because it appeals to principles that are essentially "only highly abstract descriptions of norms already embodied in those practices."[31] Sue Sherwin also notes that "the apparatus of technical theory is invoked to defend or, at

[28] Ibid., 348.

[29] Kenneth L. Garver and Bettylee Garver, "The Human Genome Project and Eugenic Concerns," *American Journal of Human Genetics*, 54 (1994): 149.

[30] Reardon, *Race to the Finish*, 161.

[31] Cheryl Noble, "Ethics and Experts," *Hastings Center Report*, 12:3 (1982): 9.

most, modestly reform existing practices."[32] Ethics committees no less than professional conferences, textbooks, and journals of applied ethics, are "chiefly occupied with establishing an ethical rationale for existing practices within the field."[33]

As an instance, one recent article assessing the ethics of the HGP proposes a "preventive ethics," then quickly comments that to do so "is not to be against the HGP. It is simply to argue for a preventive ethics which will allow maximum benefit from the project."[34] Some ways of accommodating ethical concerns are little more than appearance, or cosmetics. Entities such as ELSI and the Ethics Subcommittee of the HGDP may do little more than provide moral window dressing and apologetics.[35] An ethics committee, as Okanagan activist Jeannette Armstrong has stated regarding the HGDP, may serve as little more than "a P.R. operation for the project."[36] Good public relations are not incidental to such projects because public funding must be secured. It is more readily secured when "ethics" figures as part of a project's aim. Consider the goal of the Canadian genome project, which is to

> comprise a coherent, collaborative activity in mapping and sequencing of genomes, both human and nonhuman; the collection and

[32] Sue Sherwin, *No Longer Patient* (Philadelphia, Pennsylvania: Temple University Press, 1992): 87.

[33] Ibid.

[34] Margo Vicedo, "The Human Genome Project: Towards an Analysis of the Empirical, Ethical, and Conceptual Issues Involved," *Biology and Philosophy*, 7 (1992): 262.

[35] Sherwin's comments regarding the medical field are apt here:

> the very willingness of the medical establishment to absorb bioethics into their credentials for membership raises suspicions. By such actions, the profession is able to demonstrate its serious interest in moral matters, and this explicit professional concern in medical ethics encourages the public to maintain its trust in physicians' judgment. When intolerable abuses of that trust become public, damage control is usually initiated through a renewed professional commitment to moral education and enforcing ethical standards. Physicians are not required to engage in deep soul-searching or to address any significant challenges to their traditional ways of organizing health-care delivery. (Sherwin, *No Longer Patient*, 86)

[36] Cited in Beth Burrows, "Life, Liberty, and the Pursuit of Patents," *The Boycott Quarterly*, 2:1 (1994): 53. Judith Swazey points out that the ELSI component of the project provides "an opportunity for the scientist-shapers of the project to affirm, 'Look how ethical and socially responsible we are being,'" and worries that it will be treated by scientists and clinicians as "politically necessary but basically irrelevant appendages to the 'real work' of the Genome Project." (Judith Swazey, "Those Who Forget Their History: Lessons From the Recent Past for the Human Genome Quest," in George Annas and S. Elias (eds.), *Gene-Mapping* (Oxford, UK: Oxford University Press, 1992): 46.)

> distribution of data; the training of human resources; the development and transfer of associated technologies; and the evaluation of associated ethical, legal, and social issues.[37]

Moving to the European context, we find this:

> All of the proposed measures, e.g. protection of genetic information, evaluation of ethical, social and legal aspects and the setting up of a committee on these issues have been integrated into the programme.[38]

The conclusion to be drawn here is *not* that ethics committees are undesirable. There are few political or practical alternatives to working with, if not within, them. However, as tangible institutional responses to value-neutrality and value-bifurcation, their susceptibility to co-optation, rhetorical manipulation, and the selective "management" of normative critique is pronounced. The thirty-three-page report of an early ethics workshop is instructive.[39] Only questions regarding *how* the Diversity Project should proceed are discussed. Significant misgivings are raised about the conduct of the Diversity Project, but no one raises the question of *whether* or *why* it should proceed. Note too that the NSF's call for pilot projects went out *before* the National Research Council completed its 1996 Study on the Proposed Human Genome Diversity Project, which was intended to assess ethical, legal, and social issues, scientific value, etc. This underscores the extent of the failure to regard, and to address as an ethical issue, whether the Diversity Project *should* proceed. As John Galtung has argued, "a major aspect of scientific colonialism is the idea of unlimited access to data of any kind, just as the colonial power felt it had the right to lay its hand on any product of commercial value in the territory."[40] The dividing hand of value-bifurcation ensures that certain normative issues are never raised.

Rhetoric, Knowledge Production, and the Pure/Applied Science Distinction

Pure and applied research is thoroughly interwoven in both initiatives of bioscience discussed here. Appeals to medical applications, the reality of

[37] C.R. Scriver, cited in Robert Cook-Deegan, *The Gene Wars*, 204–5.

[38] Rix, "Should Ethical Concerns Regulate Science?", 255.

[39] See the "Summary of Planning Workshop 3(B): Ethical and Human Right Implications, Human Genome Diversity Project" (Bethesda, Maryland: HGDP Organizing Committee, 1993).

[40] Johan Galtung, "After Camelot," in Horowitz, *The Rise and Fall of Project Camelot*, 300.

commercialization in the case of the HGP, and its threat in the case of the HGDP all attest to this. Medical genetics and the development of medical technology have been described as "important supplemental projects"[41] of the HGP, and indeed, that project was barely underway before, "in a rapid blurring of big science and big business,"[42] it became enormously profitable for certain of its participants. As early as 1994, the HGP "had already created its first millionaires,"[43] as many scientists began gene patenting in earnest.

Critics have noted that the Diversity Project's self-characterization went "through a metamorphosis, starting life as a history project and moving on to be described as a medical research project in its most recent incarnation."[44] Although the initial official goal of the HGDP was to collect and analyze DNA samples from diverse populations and "to develop databases and resources that could be used to investigate new questions in the future,"[45] the samples might, the Frequently Asked Questions (FAQ) stated, "help lead to identification of genetic factors in some human diseases and eventually to ways to treat or prevent those diseases."[46] Although "possible biomedical applications,"[47] were alluded to, this argument was somewhat muted in the actual public debate. There are reasons for this. If medical applications had been a central goal of the Project, it would have had to collect data it had no plans to collect, including "phenotypes or life-history data to accompany the genetic material they plan to warehouse."[48] The appeal to medical applications sits very uncomfortably next to the oft-repeated disavowal of the likelihood of commercial applications resulting from the Project, with the attendant question of who would profit:

[41] United States Senate, "Human Genome Diversity Project," 11–12.

[42] Lawrence M. Fischer, "Mining the Genome: Big Science as Big Business," *The New York Times*, 30 January 1994, Section 1: 1.

[43] Ibid. Some scientists, however, have voiced ethical and professional reservations about their colleagues reaping private profit from government-sponsored research. In a revealing analogy, one geneticist (who asked to remain anonymous), commented, "This is a quick and dirty grab – like the wild West, where everyone was trying to stake a claim. It's basically people with a lot of human genome money trying to cash in." (Ibid.)

[44] "Letter from Pat Mooney and Edward Hammond, of Rural Advancement Foundation International (RAFI), to Concerned Readers regarding U.S. Patent on Hagahai Persons' Cell Line" (26 October 1995). Available online at: http://nativenet.uthscsa.edu/archive/nl/9510/0310.html.

[45] Human Genome Diversity Project, FAQ (1996). Available online at: http://www.leland.stanford.edu/group/moprrinst/HGDP.html.

[46] Ibid.

[47] NRC, "Study on the Proposed Human Genome Diversity Project."

[48] Marks, "Commentary," 72.

"the proposed [Diversity Project] is not and will not be a commercial venture. It is thought the chance that this research will lead to the devlopment [sic] of commercially valuable products is very remote."[49] This interweaving of knowledge production and knowledge application was tied in large part to the need to secure funding. As Senator Akaka insisted in the Senate Hearings on the HGDP, although the Project

> promises to answer many social and anthropological questions about mankind . . . Federal funding for such a project must be based on the potential for yielding tangible benefits for medical science.[50]

Despite this, the demarcation of knowledge from its use plays a central role in the justificatory rhetoric which attends these bioscience projects. Stemerding and Jelsma observe that the EEC "emphatically distinguished" the HGP's principal goal – "acquisition of 'ever more precise knowledge of the human genome'" – from "future decisions aimed at the application of this knowledge."[51] HGP advocates also emphasized the pure/applied science distinction. According to one leading British molecular biologist, Sydney Brenner, discussion of the project must be separated into two parts, "one concerning the acquisition of the knowledge, the other its application."[52] "Knowledge itself can, at worst, be only neutral," he explains, and "everything else that will stem from the knowledge, good or bad, will take place outside the laboratory in the social realm."[53]

What is happening here? According to Stemerding and Jelsma, the pure/applied science distinction itself is evoked then erased:

> in shaping human genome science and creating a human genome project, the distinction between knowledge and its applications . . . is constantly blurred. Yet, in discussion of the ethical implications of the project, the distinction is deliberately maintained and generally accepted as self-evident, not only by policy makers, but also by scientists and those reflecting on the project's ethical implications.[54]

[49] Cavalli-Sforza and Greely, "Message of 8 July 1993."
[50] United States Senate, "Human Genome Diversity Project," 21.
[51] Stemerding and Jelsma, "Compensatory Ethics," 336.
[52] Sydney Brenner, "Old Ethics for New Issues," *Science and Public Affairs* (August 1991): 35.
[53] Ibid.
[54] Stemerding and Jelsma, "Compensatory Ethics," 337.

The result of such conceptual sleight-of-hand, Stemerding and Jelsma contend, is that "anticipations of ethical, social and legal implications" were seen as needed "not in assessing the desirability of the genome programme itself, but in identifying limits to its future applications."[55]

Yet perhaps something rather different is going on. To be successful, any rhetoric of research justification relies on two things: It must mount effective counterarguments, in rebuttal of a project's critics, and it must advance supporting arguments that make a positive case for initiating or continuing research. In the rhetorical strategy employed by advocates of the HGP and the HGDP, the pure/applied science distinction is invoked very differently in counterarguments than in supporting arguments. In counterarguments, the distinction serves as a kind of protective normative buffer. A negative moral evaluation of the uses or results of scientific knowledge is not allowed to reflect back on, or impede, the acquisition of that knowledge. By contrast, in arguments to justify the HGP, the distinction serves more as a facilitating normative transducer. That is, a positive moral evaluation of the uses or results of scientific knowledge is to count as reason for acquiring that knowledge. Potential knowledge application (applied science) cannot tell against knowledge production (pure science) in the counterarguments, but it can and does when it comes to supporting arguments.

If this account is correct, the pure/applied distinction itself remains in place, and what changes is its normative porousness. Arguments of support are able to get through; arguments in opposition are not. This move is undefended and, indeed, seems indefensible. It tends, however, to be rhetorically effective; the diversionary effect of this strategy is powerful. In the case of the HGP:

> Given that the potential applications of ever increasing genetic knowledge were to be scrutinized, the programme in which this knowledge is produced was no longer questioned in parliament.[56]

Robert Cook-Deegan observes that the way for final approval was cleared upon the "explicit inclusion of a program to consider the ethical, social, and legal aspects (ESLA) of genome research."[57] Similarly, Francis Collins,

[55] Ibid., 336.

[56] Stemerding and Jelsma, "Compensatory Ethics," 336.

[57] Cook-Deegan, *The Gene Wars*, 202.

after noting the ELSI precedent set by the HGP, recommends that the HGDP

> as it is organized and funded, develop mechanisms to address the ethical and legal challenges that the project will encounter . . . [and] that an advisory group be established to monitor the research and the use of the information it generates.[58]

In the context of value-neutrality and value-bifurcation, this porous distinction between pure and applied genomic science allows normative evaluations of a project to be selectively routed past knowledge production to knowledge application, depending on whether they support or oppose the bioscience initiative in question. It also allows the role of politics to be sidestepped altogether. The payoff of such a rhetorical strategy is that the terms of the debate are effectively defined, if not altered. The issue becomes not *whether* but *how* a given project will proceed. Thus, although "the implications of the human genome project are a point of serious concern" to be addressed by an ELSI or an ESLA,

> there is no question that the project should continue. That is, ethical issues arise not in decisions about *creating* this knowledge, but only in its *use*.[59]

The fact that the NSF's call for HGDP Pilot Projects was issued prior to the completion of the NRC's assessment of ethical, legal, and social issues is telling: Scientific knowledge production moves ahead after normative objections have been contained for study at the level of knowledge use. So too is the summary report of the first major workshop addressing the HGDP's ethical implications.[60] In some 33 pages, only questions regarding how the HGDP should proceed are discussed. Although serious doubts were expressed about various aspects of the conduct of the Project, the issue of whether there should be such a project was never part of their collective reflections.

58 United States Senate, "Human Genome Diversity Project," 10–11.

59 Stemerding and Jelsma, "Compensatory Ethics," 347.

60 Henry Greely, HGDP, "Summary Document" Report of the International Planning Workshop (9–12 September 1993). Available online at: http://www.stanford.edu/group/morrinst/hgdp/summary93.html.

The success of this rhetorical move is painfully apparent when ethicists themselves take up the theme. Margo Vicedo opens an article on the HGP by declaring:

> The project to map and sequence the different genes of an organism is not new. The novelty of this task is the creation of an interdisciplinary and multinational enterprise to obtain all the data about the chemical constitution of our genome and to establish a common language to unify our knowledge. When criticisms are raised about the HGP, therefore, they should be directed at the way in which the program is to be developed . . . It is not a question of *whether* the project should be carried out, but of *how* it should be done.[61]

The term "therefore" is extremely puzzling and disturbing here. The fact that something has been "going on" does not morally justify its continuance. Nor is it clear why a change in scale would be morally insignificant.

Thus James Watson contends that the HGP should not only move ahead, but with full speed ahead. Given the severity of genetic diseases, there are "strong ethical reasons to obtain this genetic knowledge as fast as possible and with all our might."[62] The justifications are as diverse as the moral goods to which they appeal. Pursuit of the HGP will result in progress, Watson maintains: "this is the first time in 10,000 years of civilization that humans have had the capacity to upgrade their quality of life."[63] It will yield truth and advance knowledge: It provides, in Watson's famous comment, "the ultimate tool for understanding ourselves at the molecular level . . . We used to think our fate was in the stars. Now we know, in large measure, our fate is in our genes."[64] The sequence of human DNA, according to Renato Dulbecco, is "the reality of our species and everything that happens in the world depends on those sequences."[65] Moreover, Daniel Koshland asserts, it will solve significant social problems:

61 Vicedo, "The Human Genome Project," 255.
62 James D. Watson, "The Human Genome Project: Past, Present and Future," *Science*, 248 (1990): 46.
63 Cited in Swazey, "Those Who Forget Their History," 47.
64 Cited in L. Jaroff, "The Gene Hunt," *Time* (20 March 1989): 63, 67.
65 Renato Dulbecco, "A Turning Point in Cancer Research: Sequencing the Human Genome," *Science*, 231 (1986): 1056.

> The homeless problem is tractable. One third of homeless are mentally ill – some say 50%. These are the ones who will most benefit from the Genome Project.[66]

Analogous rhetoric is used to support the HGDP. Speed metaphors are invoked repeatedly. Scientists, "racing against the clock,"[67] have "little time to waste"[68] because

> indigenous people are disappearing across the globe . . . (and) as they vanish, they are taking with them a wealth of information buried in their genes about human origins, evolution and diversity.[69]

The gate to study is said to be "closing rapidly"[70] because the indigenous sources of the desired genetic materials are "vanishing," "rapidly disappearing," and "in danger of dying out or being assimilated."[71] (This speed rhetoric, and the tendency to speak as though indigenous peoples had nearly disappeared from the face of the earth, "recalled the all too-familiar ideologies of the Vanishing Indian . . . and served to permanently situate the HGDP within the particularly American colonial and racial discourses of the nineteenth century that constituted that Indian."[72]) Diverse justifications are advanced. Its main value lies "in its enormous potential for illuminating our understanding of human history and identity."[73] However, it will also create "a unique bridge between science and the humanities . . . [and] make a significant contribution to the elimination of racism."[74]

As with the HGP, this rhetoric of research justification travels a one-way moral assessment street. The potential good that may come out of the HGDP in terms of knowledge gained is seen as adequate reason for pursuing it, whereas potential harm is not seen as adequate reason for abandonment. Innovation, Stemerding and Jelsma point out, "is generally expected to have positive results, so any decision to forego these results is

66 Cited in Jon Beckwith, "A Historical View of Social Responsibility in Genetics," *BioScience*, 43:5 (1993): 330.
67 Leslie Roberts, "A Genetic Survey," 1614.
68 Roberts, "How to Sample," 1204.
69 Roberts, "A Genetic Survey," 1614.
70 Cavalli-Sforza, "Call for A Worldwide Survey," 490.
71 For numerous instances of this sort of language, see the articles by L. Roberts, "A Genetic Survey," "How to Sample," and "Genetic Diversity Project."
72 Joanne Barker, "The Human Genome Diversity Project," *Cultural Studies*, 18:4 (2004): 585.
73 HGDP, "Summary of Planning Workshop."
74 Ibid.

considered immoral."[75] It is not that the potential good of these projects is seen as outweighing the potential harm. It is that potential harms are never allowed to tell against the conduct of the research itself. Indeed, the term "harm" is itself carefully avoided in the NRC's request for input on their Study of the HGDP. After asking what respondents regard as the "major potential benefits" to society of such a project, they then ask what "concerns" it raises, and what "potential benefits and risks" the project would pose for indigenous populations.[76]

The selective porosity of the pure/applied science distinction in rhetoric that would justify these projects is also evident in the comments of Mary-Claire King to the Senate Hearing on the HGDP. She mentions her lab's work in identifying "families of children who were kidnapped and whose parents were killed by military forces in Argentina during the Dirty War," in an effort to win support for genome research. Yet as one commentator observes,

> this is just the flip side of the police state abuses of DNA identification that she and other HGDP advocates disavow as unconnected to their "basic science" interests.[77]

When normative critiques are able to impact knowledge production only in one direction (when favorable to these projects), and unable to impede knowledge production (when unfavorable), the skids are indeed well greased.

The Rhetoric of Pursuit

The debate over the HGDP offers a unique opportunity to study the rhetoric of research pursuit. It also provides a particularly vivid illustration of how the three commitments of neopositivist science examined in this, and in the previous, chapter work together to deflect substantive ethical and political critiques of science, as well as of how such critiques may yet be effectively and forcefully made. The issue was, at the time, also one of considerable ethical and political immediacy. Compared to the HGP,

[75] Stemerding and Jelsma, "Compensatory Ethics," 345.
[76] NRC, "Study on the Proposed Human Genome Diversity Project."
[77] A point made by an anonymous referee of the journal *Perspectives on Science: Historical, Philosophical, Social.*

the HGDP had yet to pick up full speed. The fact that, as a rhetoric of research justification for the HGDP, its success was marginal, and indeed ultimately failed, only augments its interest.

Recall that the HGDP was presented by several leading geneticists as "A Vanishing Opportunity for the Human Genome Project."[78] Its stated goal, at this stage, was "to preserve the record of our genetic heritage" by collecting, analyzing, and preserving for future study DNA from diverse, largely indigenous, populations in order to understand human variation and to learn more about human origins, evolution, and ancient migration patterns. However, as critics have noted, the HGDP's self-characterization went "through a metamorphosis."[79] This rhetorical reconstruction of the HGDP was in response to powerful and sustained normative critiques originating, in large part, from the proposed (indigenous) subjects of research themselves[80] – the HGDP's so-called "Isolates of Historic Interest."[81] Over a two- to three-year period, this opposition increased in extent and intensity, and the HGDP reconstructed its mission in response to it, all the while seeking support from various funding agencies. According to one report, the controversy "scared U.S. funding agencies and forced the project organizers to rethink their approach."[82] This process of rhetorical reconstruction demonstrates how the normative dynamics of value-bifurcation shape and distort research initiatives in bioscience.

Consider first the evolution of the HGDP's justificatory rhetoric. Initially, it tied itself closely to the HGP, presenting itself as a "vanishing opportunity" for that research initiative. The link lay in the fact that a major

[78] Cavalli-Sforza, "Call for a Worldwide Survey." This article was preceded by an article by L. Roberts, entitled "A Genetic Survey of Vanishing Peoples."

[79] RAFI, "Stealing Indigenous Genes." *Abya Yala News*, 7:2 (1994): 10.

[80] These include The World Council of Indigenous Peoples' Resolution on the Human Genome Diversity Project; the Declaration of Indigenous Peoples of the Western Hemisphere Regarding the Human Genome Diversity Project; the National Congress of American Indians; the UN Working Group on Indigenous Populations, 10th Session; Geneva Intellectual Property Rights (IPR) Workshop; South and Meso American Indian Information Center; the Third World Network's Call For A Campaign Against the HGDP; Pan American Health Organization Resolution; the Karioca Declaration; the Mataatua Declaration; the Maori Congress; the Guaymi General Congress; Asian Consultation on the Protection and Conservation of Indigenous Peoples' Knowledge; the Philippine Support Group/Cordillera People's Alliance; the Onandaga Council of Chiefs; among others. For the text of some of these, see the Indigenous Peoples Council on Biocolonialism (IPCB) Web site, www.ipcb.org.

[81] Jenna Roberts, "Global Project Under Way," *Nature*, 361 (1993): 675.

[82] Patricia Kahn, "Genetic Diversity Project Tries Again," *Science*, 266 (4 November 1994): 720.

goal of the HGP "is to create biological tools that will permit access to any region of the human genome."[83] One major reason for doing this is to better understand genetic diversity: "It would be tragically ironic if, during the same decade that biological tools for understanding our species were created, major opportunities for applying them were squandered."[84] Another population geneticist, Kenneth Kidd, noted that, by 1984, new molecular tools became available that promised to transform their field. The irony was that the populations that he and Cavalli-Sforza most wanted to study were "disappearing." They decided that they needed to collect and preserve DNA samples from indigenous peoples immediately. However, they usually had to resort to asking anthropologist friends to collect samples for them because funding was a problem: "Both Luca (Cavalli-Sforza) and I have been frustrated by the difficulty of getting grants for this kind of work."[85]

"Having the tools" is certainly one reason scientists may want to undertake a research project, yet its status in this instance seems to be elevated from a necessary to a sufficient condition for justifying research pursuit; in other words, knowledge production, or pure science, should be undertaken for its own sake because there are scientists who can, and want to, undertake it. Geneticist Kenneth Weiss, for example, alludes to

> the sad need we face in today's science to devote large fractions of our time to seeking funds, and to try to justify the expenditure. I think our country should again make room for scientific inquiry that is justified because it is interesting – that is what drew most of us to our careers in the first place.[86]

It is not, however, what draws funding to research projects, and this "pure science" research justification evaporates fairly quickly as a supporting argument for the Project[87] – all the more so because it is a liability

83 Cavalli-Sforza, "Call for A Worldwide Survey," 490.

84 Ibid.

85 Leslie Roberts, "A Genetic Survey of Vanishing Peoples," 1616.

86 United States Senate, "Human Genome Diversity Project," 44.

87 There is an occasional frank acknowledgement that the HGDP "is a proposal seeking a direction" (United States Senate 1993, 6) and that scientists are unsure just what knowledge they are seeking to advance by collecting this genetic information. Biologist Robert Sokal comments that "Fifty years from now, we'll have completely new technology to ask questions we cannot ask today . . . The important thing is to keep those (DNA) cell lines alive." Cited in Robert L. Smith, "DNA Probe Angers the Endangered," *Syracuse Post Standard* (September 9,

when it comes to formulating counterarguments. Its presence increases the HGDP's vulnerability to the charges of critics, such as those of Maori activist and scholar Aroha Mead, that it represents the interests of a minority of privileged academics,[88] an exclusive group of western professionals, "possibly at the expense of the unity and survival of indigenous communities struggling to remain intact"[89] after a legacy of genocide, assimilation, and oppression. Indeed, it forces the whole issue of a political reordering of priorities and a more socially just allocation of scarce resources to the fore. Genetic research, Debra Harry contends, "is not a priority . . . They've come to take our blood and tissues for their interests, not for ours."[90]

1993). According to New Zealand biochemist Warren Tate, reporting to the Center for Gene Research News regarding events at the 1995 "Whose Genes Are They Anyway?" conference:

> I came away from the conference with one or two lessons. Firstly, scientists must speak out amongst themselves to lobby against initiatives which they see are wrong . . . Such an example at the conference was the Human Genome Diversity Project . . . The project involves collecting samples from 500 of the world's 8000 populations or so and establishing genetic information on a data base – for what? So scientists can think up good projects to use the information apparently . . . an end point of establishing a data base for future good ideas made me somewhat uncomfortable (oops we have applied these principles in our own research!)

88 Some anthropologists have mentioned the potential benefit to their field. HGDP critic Jonathan Marks sardonically observes that "One of the strongest arguments in support of the HGDP is that it could represent a pot of 'free money' for anthropologists" (Marks, "Commentary," 72). Project proponent John Moore comments that not only will they "be deluged" with data from the Project "if all goes well," but this has the potential to unify the badly divided discipline, "to bring the fields of anthropology back together again." (John Moore, "Putting Anthropology Back Together Again," *American Anthropologist*, 96:4 (1994): 941). *Science* writer Leslie Roberts has stated, "ultimately which populations are sampled will depend on finding anthropologists who want to study them" (Leslie Roberts, "Genetic Diversity Project," 1301). Of course, the database itself is avowedly intended to benefit the scientific community, as a source and resource for new research projects.

89 Aroha Mead, "Letter from Aroha Mead, Director, International Association of the Mataatua Declaration, to Dr. Darrell Macer, Sub-Committee on Population Genetics," United Nations Educational, Scientific and Cultural Organization (UNESCO) International Bioethics Committee, UNESCO-Bioethics & Human Population Research (July 29, 1995). Available at: http://nativenet.uthscsa.edu/archive/nl/9510/0350.html.

90 Declan Butler, "Genetic diversity proposal fails to impress international ethics panel," *Nature*, 377 (5 October 1995): 373. A Northern Paiute activist and scholar, Debra Harry, is the Executive Director of the IPCB, an organization devoted to helping indigenous peoples protect their genetic resources, knowledge, and rights from the harmful aspects of biotechnology. (The Web address is www.ipcb.org.) See her essay, "Acts of Self-Determination and Self-Defense: Indigenous Peoples' Responses to Biocolonialism," in Sheldon Krimsky and Peter Shorett (eds.), *Rights and Liberties in the Biotech Age: Why We Need a Genetic Bill of Rights* (Lanham, Maryland: Rowman & Littlefield, 2005) Her documentary film on biocolonialism, "The Leech and the Earthworm," is available on the IPCB Web site.

Such political objections directed against knowledge production[91] are later re-routed to bear on knowledge use. The rhetoric of justification extended is transformed in the HGDP's FAQ. The interests it represents are pointedly described more inclusively:

> We believe that most will agree that one or more of several uses of the DNA samples justify pursuing this project now and with vigor . . . One goal of the Project is to find out what the people sampled would like to learn from the genetic data and then try to answer those questions as well.[92]

Instead of assuming any responsibility for re-ordering the priorities that shape knowledge production, the FAQ bows to the current status quo as inevitable and deflects the political critique. To the question "Couldn't that money be better spent?" the response is:

> Perhaps, but there is no reason to believe that it would be . . . there is no reason to believe that those funds, if not spent on the Human Genome Diversity Project, would be better spent on relieving poverty. More likely they would be spent on another scientific project.[93]

Besides, "$5 million per year . . . would not go far toward solving those problems, even in North America."[94] There can be no clash of priorities if preserving genetic diversity is the proper purview of science and preserving the bearers of such diversity is not – the result secured by the conjoined forces of value-neutrality and value-bifurcation. Working within "frameworks that separated science from politics"[95] in an area of research – human genetic variation – that has been steeped in politics since its origins, the Project's proponents would never genuinely engage the issues raised by the Project's critics, for whom political questions are "fundamental to the

91 It is worth emphasizing that these objections are themselves raised in a particular context and are directed against a specific case of knowledge production – the HGDP. Any facile, hasty generalization of them to *all* cases of scientific knowledge production would be just that.
92 Human Genome Diversity Project FAQ.
93 Ibid.
94 Ibid. What are the implications of the observation that $5 million a year wouldn't make enough of a difference anyway? Perhaps that no proposal to address important, systemic social problems should be taken seriously unless it is clear that there is enough funding (how much is that?) to make a difference? Or that $5 million could be cut from existing social programs because it does "not go far toward solving those problems"?
95 Reardon, *Race to the Finish*, 155.

formulation of research agendas."[96] Seeing themselves as "good, anti-racist scientists," they were puzzled and dismayed by "critics' charges that they were furthering colonialism."[97]

The "tie" to the HGP would also be decisively loosened, and there were repeated assertions that the HGDP is not part of the HGP. Their frequency and emphasis suggest that this is more than a matter of simply clarifying similar acronyms: "It is important to realize that these are two separate and distinct undertakings with markedly different goals (and funding . . . and histories.)" Why was it increasingly important to communicate this? One reason was the need to secure funding independent of the HGP. From 1991 through 1994, HGDP advocates were heavily invested in the search for support beyond that provided for a series of Planning Workshops. However, such a distinction was also needed to counter the mounting criticisms, addressed at length in the next chapter.

96 Ibid., 164.
97 Ibid., 158.

5

Indigenist Critiques of Biocolonialism

We are not opposed to sharing with humanity. What we oppose is being exploited when our poverty is not resolved.
– José Acosta[1]

At the June 1993 session of the United Nations Commission on Sustainable Development, indigenous representatives described the Human Genome Diversity Project (HGDP) as "very alarming": "We are calling for a stop to the Human Genome Diversity Project which is basically an appropriation of our lives and being as indigenous peoples."[2] They also raised concerns about patenting and commercial exploitation: "How soon will it be before they apply for IPRs [Intellectual Property Rights] to these genes and sell them for a profit?"[3] That same year, a workshop on the "Ethical and Human Rights Implications" of the HGDP convened, during which it was suggested that sampling begin "with the least politically risky groups . . . If the Project does not proceed carefully and properly, it could spoil the last good opportunity to obtain some of this data."[4] What were "proper procedures?" Paul Weiss, an anthropologist, proposed the following strategy, according to the summary report:

[1] "Who Owns Life? Patenting Human Genes," World Media Foundation Television Broadcast, *Living on Earth*, transcript (May 13, 1994): 14.

[2] Victoria Tauli-Corpuz, "We Are Part of Biodiversity. Respect Our Rights," *Third World Resurgence*, 36 (1993): 26.

[3] Ibid., 26. A copy of the "Declaration of Indigenous Peoples of the Western Hemisphere Regarding the Human Genome Diversity Project," signed on 19 February 1995 by numerous indigenous organizations. Available online at: www.ipcb.org.

[4] Henry Greely, HGDP, "Summary Document" Report of the International Planning Workshop (9–12 September 1993). Available online at: http://www.stanford.edu/group/morrinst/hgdp/summary93.html.

> "Immortalization" can be a very sensitive term and should be avoided when talking about the intended creation of cell lines. (Someone suggested using "transformation," the standard European practice.) Whether to tell people what you intend to do, as a technical matter, is a difficult question.[5]

As one favorable article in the journal *Nature* understated: "the [Diversity Project] has insufficiently anticipated the inevitable objections to it."[6] Numerous critiques in numerous fora were advanced throughout the 1990s, contesting what has been described in previous chapters as the legacy of value-neutrality and value-bifurcation: the deflection of normative criticism away from the production of scientific knowledge and its restriction to dilemmas of knowledge application; the reduction of ethics to a supplementary, or compensatory activity, tacked on to the uses of science, and focused exclusively on developing measures to mitigate undesirable effects; and the attendant displacement of reflection on how relations of power factor practically and morally into both. These critiques were a means of revealing and resisting the implications of biocolonialist practices for indigenous peoples, cultures, and resources. They openly and repeatedly undermined the effort of Diversity Project proponents to abstract, isolate, and immunize the Project from history. As Mick Dodson noted, in its early incarnation, the Diversity Project described threatened peoples as " 'Isolates of Historic Interest' or 'IHIs' . . . not peoples who have been abused and violated to the point of extinction; not peoples who are in desperate need of respect and support to survive in their integrity; but 'Isolates of Historic Interest.' "[7]

Contesting the Diversity Project

The controversy over the HGDP raised crucial issues about the role of power in the formulation, pursuit, and justification of western scientific research. A main venue for much of the debate it provoked was a listserve, where a virtual struggle was waged. Administered by Gary Trujillo from

5 Paul Weiss, as cited in ibid., 6.

6 Jenna Roberts, "Global Project Underway to Sample Genetic Diversity," *Nature*, 361 (1993): 675.

7 Michael Dodson, "Social Justice for Indigenous Peoples," The third David Unaipon Lecture (October 1993). Available online at: http://catalogue.nla.gov.au/Record/1453330.

Texas A&M University, *Native-L* was a high-volume forum dealing with indigenous issues across the world. The depth and force of indigenous opposition to the Diversity Project apparently took many by surprise. "I don't think it initially crossed anyone's mind that [the Diversity Project] would be controversial," one supporter notes.[8] Such surprise stems from a failure to contextualize the Diversity Project, to situate it in the broader cultural politics in which practices of western science – especially those impacting indigenous peoples – are, and have historically been, steeped. Indigenist critics are attentive to this. Historically informed and politically aware, they are filled with the hard lessons learned from prior encounters with western science and acutely conscious of social and power relations. Okanagan activist Jeannette Armstrong, for example, preceded her discussion of the Diversity Project by reviewing how indigenous genetic resources have been exploited in the name of pharmaceutical science.[9] Debra Harry, director of the Indigenous Peoples Council on Biocolonialism, and Aroha Te Pareake Mead, the Foreign Policy Convenor and Deputy Convenor of the Maori Congress, also situated it in the cultural politics governing the interaction of western science and indigenous peoples, as did many other indigenist critics.[10]

By contrast, Diversity Project proponents tended to proceed as though it were possible to remove and insulate the Diversity Project from history and politics. The hand-washing comment of the frustrated geneticist that "We are scientists not politicians" is typical, and has been met with a trenchant response: "As if opening the veins of indigenous peoples of the world might not constitute a significantly political act."[11] The skirting of moral issues and political realities was striking in the Diversity Project's Frequently Asked Questions (FAQ), which stated that if sampling was too long delayed, some human (i.e., indigenous) groups might disappear as

8 Patricia Kahn, "Genetic Diversity Project Tries Again," *Science*, 266 (1994): 720.

9 See Jeannette Armstrong, "Global Trade Targets Indigenous Gene Lines," *National Catholic Reporter*, 27 (January 11–12, 1995).

10 See generally Debra Harry, "The Human Genome Diversity Project," *Abya Yala News*, 8 (1994): 8; Aroha Mead, "Letter from Aroha Mead, Director, International Association of the Mataatua Declaration, to Dr. Darrell Macer, Sub-Committee on Population Genetics," United Nations Educational, Scientific and Cultural Organization (UNESCO) International Bioethics Committee, UNESCO-Bioethics & Human Population Research, (July 29, 1995). Available online at: http://nativenet.uthscsa.edu/archive/nl/9510/0350.html.

11 Jonathan Marks, "Commentary: The Human Genome Diversity Project," *Anthropological News* (April 1995): 72.

discrete populations "usually through urbanization or other forces leading to the loss of their language or the other characteristics that identify them as a separate group."[12] This convenient, politically numb, dismissal of the many ways in which oppression historically has impacted, and continues to impact, the survival and well-being of indigenous peoples is the rule rather than the exception in the writings of Diversity Project proponents. "Nowhere in the [Diversity Project] literature," Aroha Mead asserts, "Have I ever sighted acknowledgement of the extent and effects of the first wave of colonization . . . have they even thought about political distinctions or, in pursuit of a 'pure scientific goal,' are they ignoring the social, political, economic, cultural realities?"[13]

The "inevitability" of the Project went unquestioned in the HGDP literature, the discussion always being "framed in an assumption that the Diversity Project is inevitable and its critics had best join the parade or lose any opportunity to improve its operation."[14] Over the course of the decade, the HGDP rolled relentlessly on, despite massive, emphatic, and reiterated objections from the major indigenous organizations at the international, national, and local levels. At a heated meeting in Guatemala, Henry Greely – the Stanford Law Professor who chaired the Ethics subcommittee of the North American HGDP – admitted to his critics

> that the West and western science had done terrible things to indigenous peoples, but . . . that our project was different – that we were trying to do things right . . . I encouraged them to become involved in order to help us insure that the Project did not harm their interests.[15]

He acknowledged indigenous peoples' deep weariness of being studied but did not skip a beat in his support of it. The Diversity Project's indigenist critics were not at all convinced "that a worldwide campaign to collect

[12] Human Genome Diversity Project, "FAQ" (1996). Available online at: http://www.stanford.edu/group/morrinst/hgdp/faq.html.

[13] Mead, "Letter from Aroha Mead."

[14] Pat Mooney and Edward Hammond, "Letter from Pat Mooney and Edward Hammond, of RAFI, to Concerned Readers regarding U.S. Patent on Hagahai Persons' Cell Line" (October 25, 1995) http://aises.uthscsa.edu/natnet/archive/nl/9510/0310.html.

[15] Henry Greely, "Letter from Hank Henry Greely, North America HGDP Ethics Committee Chair, to Ken, HGDP Visits Guatemala" (December 16, 1993 trip report). This is no longer available on the former Rural Advancement Foundation International (RAFI) Web site. A copy is on file with the author.

indigenous human cell lines is inevitable."[16] The HGDP itself was derailed as a result of their opposition, but the ultimate, long-term success of such resistance remains to be seen.[17]

Planned or Under Way?

One of the more striking features of the public debates between HGDP critiques and Henry Greely and other HGDP advocates was the

[16] Ibid.

[17] The exact status, however, of the HGDP currently remains in question, as is confirmed by two recent studies. Joanne Barker, for example, notes that although the HGDP was seriously impeded by the National Research Council (NRC) report, and although its proponents insist it has discontinued,

> its website is still operating, with frequent updates, suggesting that the HGDP may not be formalized as such but its participants are still moving on with their plans. The Indigenous People's Coalition on Biocolonialism . . . has been informed on numerous occasions in recent years that indigenous communities in North America have been approached by HGDP participants. (Joanne Barker, "The Human Genome Diversity Project," *Cultural Studies*, 18:4 (2004): 598)

The HGDP is listed on the Web site of the Morrison Institute for Population and Research Studies at Stanford University (www.stanford.edu/group/morrinst/hgdp.html).

Jenny Reardon draws attention to the hidden, if not secret, nature of ongoing research in human genetic variation:

> Much genomic research on human diversity moves forward today in private companies or in an ad hoc way, accompanied by little or no debate. This should be cause for great concern . . . one organizer describes . . . a "morphed" Human Genome Diversity Project. Although this proponent of the initiative was willing to tell me of its existence, he was unwilling to provide any details. He justified his silence by stating the project had very little money, and it was still too early in the planning phase to say anything about it. (Personal correspondence with author, November 2003). (*Race to the Finish: Identity and Governance in an Age of Genomics* (Princeton, New Jersey: Princeton University Press, 2005): 166, 208)

She adds that for genetic variation research to proceed "without a broad-ranging societal debate about race, identity and authority . . . threatens to reproduce structures of race and racism that we seek to transform and overcome in domains other than the scientific." (166)

The Indigenous Peoples Council on Biocolonialism (IPCB) lists the many respects in which the National Geographic Society's Genographic Project would seem to be the, or at least a, successor project to the HGDP: "The main significant difference is that the Genographic Project has secured private funding, and thus does not have to undergo the same depth of public scrutiny. The absence of federal oversight raises the level of risk, leaving indigenous peoples with fewer mechanisms for accountability." (Debra Harry and Le'a Malia Kanehe, "Genetic Research: Collecting Blood to Preserve Culture?", *Cultural Survival Quarterly*, Issue 29.4 (January 6, 2006). See also the Web site for IPCB at www.ipcb.org.) The Genographic Project intends to collect 100,000 indigenous DNA samples, hoping to reconstruct ancient migrations. See Amy Harmon, "DNA Gatherers Hit Snag: Tribes Don't Trust Them," *The New York Times*, 10 December 2006.

latter's constant reiteration that the HGDP "remains in its planning stages."[18] Although the Human Genome Project (HGP), in 1994, had been functioning for a number of years and had significant funding, the HGDP, it was emphasized, was not underway. It "is a PROPOSAL," Greely emphasized.[19] A series of qualifiers threads its way through these reassurances, however: "the Project is *still largely* in the planning stage";[20] "*In most of the world*... it remains entirely in the planning stage";[21] "The Project is not collecting any samples (*except possibly a few* in Europe, through the European regional committee)";[22] "the HGDP is a regionally organized project that remains entirely in the planning stages *in most of the world*."[23] (Emphases added.)

What is to be made of these hedged denials regarding the status of the HGDP? There are at least two rhetorical possibilities the nature and marked divergence of which reveals how value-bifurcation undermines robust normative critiques of proposed research projects. From the perspective of HGDP advocates, the need to secure funding while avoiding misrepresentation necessitated simultaneous claims that, although there was some limited work in progress, the HGDP itself was still a proposal and not under way. On the one hand, the HGDP *as such* had been neither authorized nor funded and, because funds were being sought precisely to initiate it, it could not be presented as already under way. On the other hand, selected work *was* under way that was either intended to contribute to the project or would eventually fall under it. For instance, the 1994 Annual Report of one lab (Julia Bodmer's, a member of the HGDP International Executive Committee) notes: "As a contribution to both the 12th International Histocompatibility Workshop Anthropology Study and the Human Genome Diversity Project we have collected 160 samples from

[18] Henry Greely, "Message posted to *Native-L* on 6 May 1994." Available online at: http://nativenet.uthscsa.edu/archive/nl/9405/0055.html .

[19] Henry Greely, "Message posted to *Native-L* on 25 October 1993." Available online at: http://nativenet.uthscsa.edu/archive/nl/9310/0325.html.

[20] Henry Greely, "Message posted to *Native-L* on 2 February 1994." Available online at: http://nativenet.uthscsa.edu/archive/nl/9402/0020.html.

[21] Henry Greely, "Message posted to *Native-L* on 26 October 1995." Available online at: http://nativenet.uthscsa.edu/archive/nl/9510/0319.html.

[22] Henry Greely, "Message posted to *Native-L* on 25 October 1993." Available online at: http://nativenet.uthscsa.edu/archive/nl/9310/0325.html.

[23] Henry Greely, Message posted to *Native-L* on 20 October 1995. Available online at: http://nativenet.uthscsa.edu/archive/nl/9510/0225.html.

individuals indigenous to the Orkney Islands."[24] In the following year's Annual Report, mention is made that "The anthropology study will be used as a pilot study for the Human Genome Diversity Project."[25] Moreover, because the existence of such ongoing funded research might well have enhanced the case for the fundability of the HGDP, the prudent advocate might have been disinclined to overlook it. As one commentator points out: "the exigencies of seeking funding require putting the best possible face on it."[26]

However, the danger was that this strategy might also derail assessment of the ethico-political issues which figure in research justification, allowing knowledge production to proceed without the benefit of normative critique. Indeed, this was the very danger courted when the National Science Foundation (NSF) issued its call for Pilot HGDPs before the National Research Council's (NRC's) appraisal of its normative implications was concluded. The worthiness of a proposed (pilot or otherwise) research project like the HGDP must not be assumed simply because limited work had been funded and was already under way. Some supporters, for example, defended it as involving a mere change of scale: "the work doesn't constitute anything fundamentally new," it is "merely a way to organize" the collecting of samples that has been going on for years.[27] The moral conclusion that such reasoning invites – that, therefore, the HGDP is morally innocuous and more a matter of bureaucratic efficiency than anything else – is an obvious non sequitur. Morally suspect research doesn't cease being objectionable simply because it becomes better organized. Indeed, in the case of the HGDP, the contrary would seem to be true. As anthropologist Jonathan Marks observes, this would be "a large-scale, publicly visible, and highly funded 'Project' "[28] that not only permits, but encourages, a sample collection which is already morally problematic.

The adamant, but qualified, insistence of Greely and others that the HGDP was not really (or not very extensively) underway had a very different rhetorical force for HGDP critics, for whom it appeared as a gesture of

24 "The Human Tissue Trade," *Rafi Communiqué* (Jan/Feb. 1997). Available online in the ETC archives at: http://www.etcgroup.org/en/archives.htm.

25 Ibid.

26 Noted by an anonymous referee of the journal *Perspectives on Science: Historical, Philosophical and Social.*

27 Joan Gutin, "End of the rainbow," *Discover*, 15:11 (1994): 72.

28 Marks, "Commentary," 72.

mollification that served to weaken the force of their objections (nothing is happening yet, so why worry?) and by doing so to ease the funding process. These objections were political as well as ethical in nature, directed against the HGDP as a proposed program of knowledge acquisition. Above all, the HGDP was being critiqued as yet another manifestation of biocolonialism, one that seemed particularly oblivious to political critique. As John Liddle, director of the Central Australian Aboriginal Congress, contended:

> If the Vampire Project goes ahead and patents are put on genetic material from Aboriginal people, this would be legalized theft. Over the last 200 years, non-Aboriginal people have taken our land, language, culture and health – even our children. Now they want to take the genetic material which makes us Aboriginal people as well.[29]

As already noted, resistance to the HGDP was so pronounced that many of its supporters were startled.[30] This opposition ranged from concerns over the likelihood of commercialization, biopatenting, and continued exploitation of indigenous peoples, to the various impacts such knowledge acquisition might have on indigenous communities. The latter include internal disruption caused by controversies over sampling as well as by the clash of worldviews, and the danger to indigenous communities posed by the involvement in the HGDP of surrounding – typically hostile – nation-states,[31] as well as by the threat of genetic manipulation and of indiscriminate access to the HGDP database. Nilo Cayuqueo, Director of the South and Meso American Indian Information Center (SAIIC), alludes to a number of these in his response to Greely:

> The information you gather about our genetic make-up will be readily available to governments, foundations and corporations. For the past 500 years, these institutions have waged an unbridled war of oppression and genocide against our people. The implications are

[29] D. Nason, "Tickner warns over Aboriginal gene sampling," *The Australian* (25 January 1994): 3.

[30] Patricia Kahn, "Genetic Diversity Project Tries Again," *Science*, 266:5186 (1994): 720.

[31] Aroha Mead stated the concern here well:

> Many states actively oppress indigenous communities. What mechanisms are in place to ensure that States do not use the HGDP to substantiate biases and objectives of government to undermine indigenous self-determination? If the HGDP relies on government funding, it almost guarantees a bias towards sponsoring government objectives which historically are counter-productive to indigenous objectives. (Mead, "Letter")

> potentially devastating for indigenous people all over the world... How are we going to be able to control these institutions from patenting and thereby owning the rights to our genetic material enabling them to make profits from our own blood?[32]

Along with many others, SAIIC called for a halt to the HGDP "until all of the moral, ethical, socio-economic, physical and political implications have been thoroughly discussed, understood and approved by indigenous peoples."[33] Their objections were plainly directed against proceeding with such knowledge acquisition.

By insisting that the HGDP was still pending and not under way, such normative critiques – which would otherwise threaten to impede the acquisition of knowledge in the first place – might be rhetorically deflected. The porous filter of the pure/applied science distinction could be put to work. As earlier with the HGP, "anticipations of ethical, social and legal implications" would take their place not "in assessing the desirability" of the HGDP itself, "but in identifying limits to its future applications."[34] Greely set the agenda for his Ethics Subcommittee as follows: "the creation of model protocol, discussing ethical, legal and practical issues in collecting DNA, and a workshop on the best methods to protect the rights of sampled populations in the collected DNA."[35] Because, he acknowledges, commercialization would be hard to exclude, materials transfer and database access agreements would be set in place to minimize it. The draft model protocol outlines the ethical issues that those engaged in DNA sampling for the HGDP will encounter. The longest section deals with informed consent procedures; one of the shortest is addressed to questions of ownership and control.[36] Thus although the negative critiques would be contained, and managed at the level of knowledge application, positive assessments of what would be gained from the HGDP would still go through, reflecting favorably upon the case for knowledge acquisition. Substantive political and ethical critiques of the HGDP would be diverted from the acquisition

32 SAIIC, "Message posted to *Native-L* on 9 November 1993." Available online at: http://nativenet.uthscsa.edu/archive/nl/9311/0069.html.

33 Ibid.

34 Dirk Stemerding and Jaap Jelsma, "Compensatory Ethics for the Human Genome Diversity Project," *Science as Culture*, 5:24 (1996): 336.

35 Greely, "Message of 6 May 1994."

36 See Henry T. Greely, "Proposed Model Ethical Protocol for Collecting DNA Samples," *Houston Law Review*, 33 (1997): 1469.

of such knowledge to its use, and would there be treated via document and committee as a matter of regulation (contractual agreements) and procedures for obtaining informed consent (the Protocol).

Racism or Representation?

In its later incarnations, the Diversity Project adopted a rhetoric of justification which attempted to obscure even the fact that those who would be sampled were predominantly indigenous. In response to indigenous opposition and the need to secure funding, supporters modified their arguments and rhetoric. Potential biomedical applications played a greater role. Although, if biomedical applications were indeed to be developed, then the two groups most likely to profit would be the corporations (which would market the therapeutic products) as well as those individuals with the diseases in question able to afford the genetic therapy or pharmaceuticals required. Members of sampled indigenous populations would be most unlikely to be among the latter.

Among the HGDP's "important practical uses" was "the application of the data to the study of disease"; the HGDP was held to be "an essential basis for genetic epidemiology."[37] Most notably perhaps is the fact that the HGDP began to characterize itself as a counter to racism. (Not surprisingly, the United Nations Educational, Scientific and Cultural Organization's [UNESCO's] International Bioethics Committee – which refused to endorse the HGDP – described this claim as the "most debatable" made by its proponents, arguing that "the prejudice that gives rise to racist and eugenic attitudes tends to pervert scientific results to its own ends."[38]) It did this by presenting itself as wanting to understand the diversity and unity of the entire human species or the whole "human

[37] Greely, "Summary Document." Philip Bereano argues that, if saving lives through medical advances were truly the goal the dominant society is seeking, then it would be funding efforts to reduce infant mortality instead. But

> that this issue is . . . essentially one of power, is illustrated by the fact that the vast majority of . . . infant deaths . . . occur in ghettos, barrios and reservations to women who do not have nearly the same power to influence Congressional investment choices as do academic biologists and Wall Street venture capitalists. (Philip Bereano,"Message posted to *Native-L* on 31 October 1995." Available online at: http://nativenet.uthscsa.edu/archive/nl/9511/0014.html.)

[38] Declan Butler, "Genetic diversity proposal fails to impress international ethics panel," *Nature*, 377 (5 October 1995): 373.

family."[39] According to the FAQ, the scientists involved with the HGDP were

> concerned that most human genome research concentrates only on persons from the major ethnic groups in the industrialized countries. Indigenous groups are not being served – and this deliberately ignores their importance as members of the human species.[40]

The HGDP then was necessary for moral reasons. In fact, failure to pursue it would be morally suspect, according to geneticist Kenneth Kidd: "We're not trying to exploit people; we're trying to include them. It's racist to avoid the totality of humans."[41] Cavalli-Sforza commented that "I know that a race gene does not exist. And that's what the project will show."[42] Greely, meanwhile, observed:

> We can acknowledge the diversity of our species only by studying that diversity, not by pretending that an American genome is "the" human genome . . . studying the diversity should help us see better how closely related all humanity is – that we are, in literal fact, an extended family.[43]

To reinforce this supporting argument, and to counter charges of racism, the HGDP also reconstructed its subjects. The initial call referred to "isolated human populations" and "indigenous populations of great interest."[44] Those populations specifically mentioned were all indigenous, as were those listed on the HGDP's list of more than 700 groups to be prioritized in sampling. The second HGDP workshop at Penn State spoke of

> "Isolates of Historic Interest" because they represent groups that should be sampled before they disappear as integral units so that their role in human history can be preserved.[45]

[39] Henry Greely, "Message posted to *Native-L* on 6 May 1994." Available online at: http://nativenet.uthscsa.edu/archive/nl/9405/0055.html.

[40] Human Genome Diversity Project, "FAQ" (1996). Available online at: http://www.stanford.edu/group/morrinst/hgdp/faq.html.

[41] Kahn, "Genetic Diversity Project," 721.

[42] Gutin, "End of the Rainbow," 74.

[43] Henry Greely, "Message posted to *Native-L* on 12 October 1993." Available online at: http://nativenet.uthscsa.edu/archive/nl/9310/0173.html.

[44] Luca Cavalli-Sforza, A. C. Wilson, C. R. Cantor, R. M. Cook-Deegan, and M. C. King, "Call for A Worldwide Survey of Human Genetic Diversity: A Vanishing Opportunity for the Human Genome Project," *Genomics*, 11 (1991): 490.

[45] RAFI, "Stealing Indigenous Genes," *Abya Yala News*, 7:2 (1994): 10.

However, as the HGDP came under increasing attack for "targeting" indigenous populations, it offered reassurances that, despite reports, it was "not an effort to collect samples from isolated populations in danger of disappearing (but) intends to take a representative sample of all human populations... No group is necessarily excluded."[46] Greely denied that the HGDP is "ABOUT indigenous populations, or, even worse, 'disappearing' indigenous populations. The Project is sampling the genetic diversity of ALL of humanity."[47] However, although it was true that HGDP scientists never "excluded" any particular group(s), it is also true that indigenous peoples were the focus and scientific "interest" of the HGDP. It was precisely the HGP's failure to include such groups that motivated the HGDP in the first place. This rhetorical move, like the others we have examined, is an effort to depoliticize and contain normative critiques within the facilitating space provided by applied ethics. It is flanked by a simultaneous effort to recruit: The former Isolates of Historic Interest and the HGDP are no longer "subjects" of "scientists" but "participating populations" involved in a "partnership."[48]

The emphasis and wording of the Diversity Project's goals were altered. Not only, its proponents insisted, would it increase knowledge in valuable ways, it would do so in one particular way. The Diversity Project seeks to understand the diversity and unity of the entire human species or family. Without it,

> science will characterize "the" human genome, with its historical and medical implications, largely in terms of what is known from a small sample of people of European ancestry... At a time when we are increasingly concerned with preserving information about the diversity of the many species with which we share the Earth surely we cannot ignore the diversity of our own.[49]

Bodmer described it as a "cultural obligation of the Human Genome Project."[50] Ken Weiss, head of the North American Diversity Project, echoed his point: "If we don't go ahead with this... when the Human Genome Project is done, a Navajo, say, will look at those results and

[46] Human Genome Diversity Project, "FAQ."
[47] Greely, "Message posted to Native-L on 2 February 1994."
[48] Greely, "Proposed Model Ethical Protocol," 1469.
[49] Human Genome Diversity Project, "FAQ."
[50] Roberts, "A Genetic Survey," 1615.

ask, 'Why did they bother? How well does that represent me?' "[51] As one Diversity Project scientist angrily remarked of the indigenous opposition: "They should be grateful to us."[52] The Diversity Project, then, is allegedly necessary for moral reasons. It is, in fact, a weapon against racism: "We're not trying to exploit people; we're trying to include them. It's racist to avoid the totality of humans."[53] Just as the HGP was held to provide a solution to homelessness, the Diversity Project was now held to provide a solution to racism.[54]

Yet the Diversity Project is avowedly focused on population-based differences. One of its objectives is to locate "those relatively few genetic markers which are concentrated in specific ethnic groups due to random mutation or the interaction of biological and cultural adaptations in specific ecological niches."[55] Given the nature and scope of the possible abuses, concerns about them should have been taken seriously and faced directly, although that would have involved situating the Diversity Project on a continuum of scientific research from which it wanted to distance itself. Several Diversity Project scientists had pointed to their "established track records in human rights" to defend themselves from charges of racism. According to Marc Feldman, "All of us have worked throughout our lives in an antiracist framework. Our political credentials are in order."[56] All the more reason then to expect more by way of political awareness. But the pure motives, faultless intentions, and previous good works of all those involved are plainly beside the point. They will not alter the fact that such work is embedded in cultural politics, that it bears a considerable historical burden, and that it lends itself to appropriation and abuse by individuals, organizations, and

[51] Gutin, "End of the Rainbow," 72.

[52] This comment was made at a 1997 conference on genetics by a scientist working with one of the Diversity Project's main proponents.

[53] Patricia Kahn, "Genetic Diversity Project," 721.

[54] According to Daniel Koshland: "The homeless problem is tractable. One third of homeless are mentally ill – some say 50%. These are the ones who will most benefit from the Genome Project." Cited in Jon Beckwith, "Thinking of Biology: A Historical View of Social Responsibility in Genetics," *Bioscience*, 43 (1993): 330.

[55] Margaret Lock, "Editorial: Interrogating the Human Genome Diversity Project," *Social Science and Medicine*, 39 (1994): 604.

[56] Gutin, "End of the Rainbow," 73. Jenny Reardon speaks of a "mismatch between organizers' understanding of themselves as good, anti-racist scientists, and critics' charges that they were furthering colonialism and practicing bad science." She attributes these divergent perceptions partly to the failure of the proponents (scientists, policy makers, and ethicists) "to bring into a sharp focus the intertwined epistemic and political contexts in which biological science is now asked to operate." Reardon, *Race to the Finish*, 159.

governments. It is pointless to impute intent here (i.e., deliberate political co-optation by individual scientists and their supporters, or a conscious effort to rhetorically deflect "troublesome" normative critiques). Doubtless there are instances of that, but it is neither necessary nor productive to assume or argue it. Far more interesting – and worth resisting – is how such rhetoric operates in the absence of intent, through the convergence of interests, ideology, inadequate analyses, and institutional constraints.

The characterization of the Diversity Project as a solution to racism was coupled with reassurances that, despite assertions to the contrary, it was going to sample everyone, excluding no one.[57] As with Greely's denials, all that can be said about such reassurances is that they were painfully transparent instances of rhetorical spin. Their adamant, vocal rejection by indigenous peoples not only jeopardized the possibility of locating cooperative populations to sample, it badly damaged the Diversity Project's public image, and thereby the likelihood of funding. Such responses are an unconvincing rhetorical two-step: Retreat into vague, inoffensive generalities about the "whole human family" and hope no one notices that indigenous peoples are ninety-nine percent of the diversity sought; emphasize talk of unity in a project that will study difference, and hope that people will forget the sorry history of western science's obsession with racial, class, and gender differences. As Ruth Hubbard maintains,

> Basing differences between the so-called races or between women and men, as groups, in "genes" simply uses that status-laden word to legitimate ideological constructs . . . scientists have often made it appear as though differences in power between individuals or groups of people were inevitable and natural results of biological difference, and hence of genes.[58]

Contextualizing the HGDP

Biological explanations, as Dorothy Nelkin observes, "do political work, 'creating the rules for belonging and exclusion.'"[59] From the Late Enlightenment on, racial differences have been singled out as "crucial aspects of

[57] Human Genome Diversity Project, "FAQ."

[58] Ruth Hubbard, "Constructs of Genetic Differences: Races and Sex," in Robert F. Weir *et al.* (eds.), *Genes and Human Self-Knowledge: Historical and Philosophical Reflections on Modern Genetics* (Iowa City, Iowa: University of Iowa Press, 1994): 157.

[59] Nelkin, 122.

reality" by those studying human variation, and "an extensive discourse on racial inequality began to be elaborated."[60] In the nineteenth century, sex and gender differences began to be emphasized as well. The more egregious episodes in the history of the study of human variation are legion.

The early-twentieth-century eugenics movement advocated sterilization of the "genetically unfit" and influenced medical practice, policy formation, and legislation – including the 1924 Immigration Act, which restricted immigration from the allegedly "biologically inferior races" of Southern, Central, and Eastern Europe. Initially influential in the United States, it soon spread abroad – most especially to Nazi Germany.[61] Nineteenth-century craniometry was seen to prove Nordic superiority by assuming it. Its most renowned practitioner was an American, Samuel Morton, who used his massive collection of skulls to "illustrate" the inferiority of American Indians, among others.[62] The history of intelligence testing is riddled with efforts to find a genetic basis for presumed human differences. The early class-obsessed (and fraudulent) work of Cyril Burt had a lasting impact on British educational policy,[63] and the more recent race- and class-fixated efforts of *The Bell Curve*'s Herrnstein and Murray nurture the political agenda of the Far Right.[64] Following World War II, and largely as a reaction to the eugenics movement, human genetic variation research redefined the concept of race in terms of populations, a move that was "deeply political, cultural, intentional and interested":

> It was an explicit strategy by geneticists to distance "good" science from the inherently political, racist and genocidal ends that eugenics had been put to during the war by the Nazi government.[65]

60 Nancy Stepan, "Race and Gender: The Role of Analogy in Science," in Sandra Harding (ed.), *The Racial Economy of Science: Toward a Democratic Future* (Bloomington, Indiana: Indiana University Press, 1993); 360. See also Nancy Stepan, *The Idea of Race in Science: Great Britain 1800–1960* (London: MacMillan, 1982).

61 See Allan Chase, *The Legacy of Malthus: The Social Costs of the New Scientific Racism* (Champaign, Illinois: University of Illinois Press, 1977).

62 See Stephen Jay Gould, *The Mismeasure of Man* (New York, New York: WW Norton & Company, 1981). For a history of the relations between archaeology and indigenous North Americans, see James Riding In, "Without Ethics and Morality: A Historical Overview of Imperial Archaeology and American Indians," *Arizona State Law Journal*, 24:1 (1992).

63 See R. C. Lewontin *et al.*, *Not in Our Genes: Biology, Ideology, and Human Nature* (New York: Pantheon Books, 1984).

64 See Steven Fraser (ed.), *The Bell Curve Wars* (New York, New York: Basic Books, 1995).

65 Barker, 577, 578. For a good discussion of early efforts to account for human diversity, as well as of that of the HGDP, see Margaret Lock, "Genetic Diversity and the Politics of Difference," *Chicago-Kent Law Review*, 75 (1999).

There also has been an extensive, ongoing program of research into sex differences, notably in the areas of aggressivity, brain-hemispheric asymmetries, and mathematical/visuospatial ability, which reinforces long-standing unfounded assumptions about female "deficiencies."[66] Where race, class, and gender differences have not themselves been the focus of scientific research and medical practice, they have figured heavily in other ways. In the Tuskegee syphilis experiment, race and class enabled the dismissal of proper informed consent procedures.[67] Gender and ethnicity were crucial in similarly subverting informed consent by American Indian women indiscriminately sterilized by the Indian Health Service during the 1970s.[68]

This is the broader sociopolitical and historical context of research into human differences. It is the inheritance of the Diversity Project, however unwanted by, and at odds with the intentions of, its proponents. If they wished to disown it, they would have had to proceed very differently than they did. Rhetorical two-stepping like the above was exactly how not to proceed. It was an attempt to further shield the Diversity Project from moral and political critique. The indigenous status, and precarious state, of many desired subject populations was cloaked, and the term "human groups" substituted for "indigenous peoples." Project supporters stressed the openness and public nature of their planning, but this rhetoric hid and manipulated. It also added to the offensiveness of the charge that indigenous peoples misunderstood and overreacted to the Diversity Project. According to the report of the International Bioethics Committee, the World Council of Indigenous Peoples "mistakenly thought that the [Diversity Project] was aimed exclusively at sampling from endangered populations, which it should not be."[69] Indeed it should not have been, but not only did the reports in scientific journals describing the Diversity Project, as well as the scientists' statements cited in those reports, give this inescapable impression, but it remained the case that the populations which would

[66] See Ruth Bleier, "Sex Differences Research," in Ruth Bleier (ed.), *Feminist Approaches to Science* (Elmsford, New York: Pergamon Press, 1986).

[67] See James H. Jones, *Bad Blood: The Tuskegee Syphilis Experiment* (New York, New York: Free Press, 1981).

[68] See Charles R. England, "A Look at the Indian Health Service Policy of Sterilization, 1972–1976" (1997). Available online at: http://www.dickshovel.com/IHSSterPol.html.

[69] "Bioethics and Human Population Genetics Research" (November 15, 1995). Available online at: http://portal.unesco.org/shs/en/files/2303/10596456491populationCIB3_en.pdf/populationCIB3_en.pdf.

be approached, largely with the assistance of anthropologists, would be almost exclusively indigenous. The rhetoric of the Diversity Project simply masked that fact. Even the International Bioethics Commission report noted that opposition was "based upon more than misunderstandings . . . or antiscience attitudes, but 'is a clash of philosophy and cultural insight.' "[70]

Indigenists emphasized this last important point, but Diversity Project supporters had little to say in response. Aroha Mead observed that "many in the [Diversity Project] have the mistaken view that the reason for indigenous opposition . . . rests in lack of understanding of the Project's aspirations, and confusion over minor details."[71] The critiques were directed to something quite fundamental – to the clash of knowledge and value systems that lay at the heart of this controversy. Although Mead's discussion is framed in terms of Maori beliefs, it resonates with the basic commitments of many other indigenous peoples. The concept of the human gene on which the Diversity Project relies, she notes, is at odds with the indigenous understanding of what a human gene is, of what and whom it represents, of what and for whom its purpose is determined, and of who the "owner or guardian" of human genes is. For the Maori people, and many others, the human gene is genealogy. In Maori, "a gene" is translated as *iratangata* – "life spirit of mortals." More commonly *whakapapa* genealogy is used; it is the basis for Maori connecting with themselves and others.[72] Because a gene, or genome, is imbued with a life spirit that has been handed down by the ancestors and is passed on to future generations, it is not and cannot be the property of individuals. It is part of the heritage of families, communities, tribes, and entire indigenous nations. Mead stressed that

> the indigenous and western scientific philosophies differ on this fundamental point . . . it is the difference in understanding of the origin of humanity, the responsibility of individuals, and the safety of future generations which sits so firmly at the core of indigenous opposition to the [Diversity Project] . . . this type of research proposes to interfere in a highly sacred domain of indigenous history, survival and commitment to future generations.[73]

70 Butler, "Genetic Diversity Proposal," 373.
71 Mead, "Letter," 49. I draw freely here on Mead's discussion in this letter.
72 For more on this, see Roma Mere Roberts and Peter R. Wills, Understanding Maori Epistemology, in Helmut Wautischer (ed.), *Tribal Epistemologies* (Surrey, United Kingdom: Ashgate Publishing, 1998).
73 Ibid.

Debra Harry concurred: "We don't view our genes as protein actions ready to be interpreted; for us our genes are sacred."[74]

The only response Diversity Project proponents made to this was that no one would force any population to participate. If a particular group's understanding of the natural world conflicted with that embraced by the Diversity Project, it could refuse to give consent. Presumably, if it did consent, then the Diversity Project would not be responsible for any unfortunate impacts on that group's belief system. This myopic view of moral responsibility ignores how unequal relations of power compromise the (western) practice of informed consent,[75] and furthers scientific aspirations at the expense of indigenous peoples: "Given the isolation of many of the populations involved, their non-literacy, and lack of acquaintance with a cosmology grounded in molecular biology, obtaining informed consent will be a contrived exercise, which, aside from human rights issues, may have some unforeseen results."[76] It may also have undesirable but foreseeable results. Project proponents were well aware of indigenist concerns about the commercial exploitation of genetic materials. Intellectual property rights, one noted, have provoked some misunderstanding:

> The Project was viewed as similar to plant prospecting trips, that had enriched the genetic stock available to western seed or pharmaceutical companies, and ultimately their profits, without providing any benefit to the people who had nurtured and domesticated those plants.[77]

It is precisely this connection that indigenists emphasized by situating the Diversity Project along a continuum of previous and ongoing practices

[74] Butler, "Genetic Diversity Proposal," 373.

[75] This has happened on various occasions. Consider the U.S. Government Accountability Office's (GAO's) review of the consent procedures used by the Indian Health Service from 1972 through 1976, when extensive sterilization operations were performed on American Indian women across the United States. Charging that the procedures lacked the basic elements of informed consent, the GAO noted that the women were not adequately informed of the advantages and disadvantages of sterilization; the form only summarized the oral presentation; and the form omitted the usual information at the top of the page notifying the patient that federal benefits would not be taken away if they did not accept sterilization. See Michael Sullivan DeFine, "A History of Governmentally Coerced Sterilization: The Plight of the Native American Woman" (May 1, 1997). Available online at: http://www.geocities.com/CapitolHill/9118/mike2.html.

[76] Lock, "Editorial," 605.

[77] Greely, Message of October 12, 1993.

of cultural imperialism, in which the resources (spiritual, material, and genetic) of indigenous peoples have been seized and commercially exploited. To put the Diversity Project in perspective, Philip Bereano suggests,

> Note that a First World society which does not provide indigenous communities with even the rudiments of public sanitation, preventative medicine, or curative treatments . . . is going to ask these communities to give us something which may be beneficial for our health care. After having dominated most of the mineral and vegetative resources of indigenous peoples, we are now talking about turning on their very bodies as the ultimate resources to exploit.[78]

Why Patenting Is Not an Answer

Diversity Project advocates insisted that it was not a commercial enterprise, that it sought knowledge rather than profit (although it never agreed to refuse corporate funding). Some, however, admitted the possibility of commercialization and contended that patenting would provide "part of the answer [to biocolonization], not part of the problem."[79] They proposed that patenting be allowed only with prior informed consent. The participating population would decide its position on patenting. Materials transfer and database access agreements would be used to contractually bind parties who take information from the Diversity Project's repository and database and to ensure that they observe whatever restrictions the population wanted; all of this would then be incorporated into informed consent documents. This proposal reflects the moral and legal constraints operative in the dominant culture, and there were a host of problems with it, as indigenist critics made clear.

a. The very concept of patenting genes clashes fundamentally with indigenous knowledge and value systems, as we have already seen in the case of the Maori. It is expressed as well in a number of the major statements of opposition to the Diversity Project issued by indigenous organizations: "We oppose the patenting of all natural

[78] Philip Bereano, "Patent Pending: The Race to Own DNA," *The Seattle Times*, 27 August 1995, B5.

[79] Henry Greely, "Mapping the Territory," *The Utne Reader*, 20 (1996): 87.

genetic materials. We hold that life cannot be bought, owned, sold, discovered or patented."[80]

b. The proposal still forces an intellectual property regime on indigenous peoples. Intellectual property rights are a western legal concept developed to facilitate private ownership of intangible resources and to protect individual, technological, and industrial inventions. The price of protecting indigenous knowledge with western intellectual property is, Chidi Oguamanam notes, the "forced epistemological assimilation"[81] of that knowledge. Indigenists argue that intellectual property rights are inappropriate instruments to impose on indigenous peoples' communitarian cultural and legal systems. As an Aboriginal activist notes:

> We assert that our identity and our rights are not reducible to the rights of individuals . . . With its cult of the individual and its emphasis on individual rights, non-indigenous people in the western world have failed to acknowledge the collective nature of indigenous societies, and have provided inadequate protection for the group rights of peoples.[82]

The Working Group on Traditional Resource Rights has proposed alternatives to intellectual property rights which attempt to determine the extent to which existing international customary law and practice can be used to defend indigenous knowledge and biogenetic resources. Indigenous peoples, indigenous legal systems, and concepts of property rights are guiding this debate.

c. No enforcement mechanisms were in place, or proposed, for ensuring that the materials transfer and database access agreements were honored. Brett Shelton, Native attorney and former policy analyst for the National Indian Health Board, asks "But who will enforce the contracts? Why should we trust the HGDP to enforce them for us?" He notes that, if someone misused the samples or violated the contract, it was unclear what, if anything, could be done about it:

80 "Declaration of Indigenous Peoples of the Western Hemisphere Regarding the Human Genome Diversity Project," available online at: www.ipcb.org.

81 Chidi Oguamanam, "Localizing Intellectual Property in the Globalization Epoch: The Integration of Indigenous Knowledge," *Indiana Journal of Global Legal Studies*, 11:2 (2004): 168.

82 Michael Dodson, "Social Justice for Indigenous Peoples" (October 1993). Available online at: http://catalogue.nla.gov.au/Record/1453330.

> The protocol is considered a model, yet it is not going to be helpful in protecting tribal rights. To have something like this be the definitive example on how our rights will be protected is not comforting at all – in fact, it's scary. We have some serious things to be concerned about, and this Protocol is not going to help at all.[83]

The proposal, then, would not prevent biopiracy. Genome scientists declared the patent system the "'mechanism of excellence' for commercializing the results of the Human Genome Project."[84] Given current biopatent trends, and the potential for corporate biotechnology funding, patenting would likely occur.[85] Researchers associated with the Diversity Project may agree not to patent indigenous genetic material, but others would not be similarly bound. Lest such an "end-run" seem far-fetched, note that it was actually proposed at one of the Diversity Project's workshops on "Ethical and Human Rights Implications":

> It would be useful to the Diversity Project to say, from the beginning, that no patents will be sought for genes taken from the Project's samples. A firm interested in patenting the gene could always go back independently to the country where the gene was found and make whatever financial arrangements were appropriate, but that would not implicate the Project.[86]

Even the President of the American Type Culture Collection, where the Diversity Project samples would be stored, expressed doubts that codes of ethical conduct, or even the law in this regard, could be successfully enforced. Raymond Ciphus believed that there would be a black market on this material, nationally and internationally:

[83] Brett Shelton, cited in Debra Harry "Tribes Meet to Discuss Genetic Colonization." Available online at: www.ipcb.org.

[84] Butler, "Genetic Diversity Proposal," 376.

[85] Recent empirical research, however, suggests that the pace of patenting and commercialization is not as fast as some have feared. Russel Barsh argues that, so far as intent or motivation goes, academic career promotion and intellectual curiosity rather than profit are driving human genetic diversity research. (See his "Pharmacogenomics and Indigenous Peoples: Real Issues and Actors," *Cardozo Journal of International and Comparative Law*, 11 (2003): 382.) He also notes that patents with indigenous origins were largely the result of data in publications of academic researchers placed in the public domain. (See Russel Barsh, "Intellectual Property and Indigenous Peoples," *American Society of International Law Proceedings*, 95 (2001).)

[86] United States Senate, "Human Genome Diversity Project: Hearing before the Committee on Governmental Affairs." 103rd Congress, 1st Session (1993). (Washington, DC: United States Government Printing Office, 1993). Available online at: http://www.archive.org/stream/humangenomediveroounit/humangenomediveroounit_djvu.txt.

> I think you are going to see materials being taken, tissues processed and cells produced and I don't see any way that patent laws and policing by the traditional methods are . . . going to be able to control this.[87]

Under these circumstances, as one lawyer has suggested, a truly fair disclosure on an informed consent form might well read as follows:

> We are gathering this data for the benefit of people other than you. It is likely that you will have negative consequences from this and no gain. We are asking you to give to us, with little or nothing given to you in return, and we expect you to absorb all losses that may accrue to you, and all of your people, from this project [both foreseen and unforeseen] without any liability on our part.[88]

d. There are serious problems with informed consent documents, especially in these contexts. One is a lesson from history and treaty making that suggests that prior informed consent documents would not serve to protect indigenous peoples: "This was exactly what did not happen in many First Nations/Wasichu treaty relationships[,] ultimately resulting in the theft of inherent rights . . . because it was beyond comprehension what might be important in the future."[89] The proposal also imposes a western model of individualized consent on indigenous peoples. How exactly does one secure the informed prior consent of entire indigenous populations or of the communities that make them up? Who will determine whether, and on what basis, a certain number of individuals must consent, or only a single "leader"? Who within a given community is authorized to give consent for research that implicates everyone? Is it a tribal governing committee – with no mandate for ethical decisions – or a spiritual leader? For native North American peoples, it was proposed that an officially recognized tribal government be the decision-making body. Anyone familiar with current controversies in Indian Country, and the

[87] "Sunday Morning: Biopiracy: The Gold Rush for Human Genes" (CBC Television Broadcast, May 1, 1994).

[88] Interview with Alan W. Clarke, J. D., in Chassell, Michigan (December 1, 1997).

[89] Jordan S. Dill, "Re: Papua New Guinea Patents," (October 29, 1995). Available online at: http://nativenet.uthscsa.edu/archive/nl/9511/0282.html.

struggle between progressives and traditionals over issues such as gambling casinos and nuclear waste repositories, will recognize in this a horribly divisive scenario. As Mead states: "the [Diversity Project] and other similar-type activities can serve to divide, and cause irreparable damage to the ability of indigenous communities to trust each other, let alone to trust others."[90]

The divisiveness would only be compounded if government officials of the nation-state in which the indigenous nation is located were given a role in deciding who has the authority to give "consent" to speak for the people. Given the historical relationships between many nation-states and indigenous peoples (e.g., Iraq and the Kurds, or Guatemala and the Mayans) this could be disastrous; this difficulty would only be exacerbated by the Diversity Project's regional organization.

e. Communication difficulties will undercut the basis for informed consent. There is a massive tangle of western institutions, beliefs, and values built into human genetic research, specific collection practices, libraries of cell collections, instruments such as materials transfer and database access agreements, intellectual property law, and royalties. How will the Diversity Project be explained? Anthropologists are touted as essential, but their own interests may figure in important ways. Will their research grants and careers be tied to success in sampling? How extensive and explicit will the information conveyed be? Finally, what of previous and current sampling? In some cases there has been no informed consent at all, much less that obtained in the manner outlined in the proposal. Will the Diversity Project allow access to this data?

Conclusion

The Diversity Project's violation of fundamental principles of social justice was manifest. The benefits of the Diversity Project to indigenous peoples were minimal to nonexistent, yet they were the ones who would bear whatever harms resulted, directly or indirectly, from Diversity Project activities

[90] Mead, "Letter from Aroha Mead."

and from the misuse of the data collected. Debra Harry drew on the 1964 Helsinki Declaration's injunction that "in research on man, the well-being of the subject takes precedence over science and society" to argue for a halt to the Diversity Project on the grounds that "indigenous people not only will not benefit from it, but may experience increased discrimination as a result."[91]

This is not an idle worry, given the history of western science when it comes to the study of human differences and the ease of accessing such a database. It will not do for Diversity Project scientists, from their comparative position of privilege and power, to invoke some dubious principle of double effect and accept only responsibility for the research consequences they intend and foresee, while eluding responsibility for the unintended consequences of their work which indigenous peoples predict. For one thing, the "experts" on the negative consequences of western intervention in indigenous societies are people from those societies, not western population geneticists. Predictions of indigenous societies must be given significant weight. For another, many of these unintended consequences are not only foreseeable but also probable, given the present surge in life-form patenting (and profiting), the biopiracy precedents already established in agriculture and botanicals, and the extensive human tissue trade.[92] As John Moore (a Seattle businessman who lost an infamous California Supreme Court case which declared that he had no ownership rights over cells his doctors removed from his body and patented) asked during a 1996 meeting of the National Academy of Sciences Committee on the Diversity Project: "Do you think a system that could not protect me will protect the rights of peoples or individuals that live in other countries?"[93]

Similar concerns were voiced by the UNESCO International Bioethics Committee in its refusal to endorse the HGDP. In their long list of criticisms of the Diversity Project, they protested that: "the enthusiasm of the project's supporters for scientific results has led to the neglect of

91 Butler, "Genetic Diversity Proposal," 373.

92 See generally the RAFI Communiqués "1996 Biopiracy Update" (December 1996) and "The Human Tissue Trade" (January/February 1997). Available online at: http://www.etcgroup.org/en/archives.htm.

93 RAFI Press Release, "US Funding of Human Biodiversity Collections Carries on Despite Contrary Scientific Advice." Available online at: http://www.etcgroup.org/en/materials/publications.html?pub_id=434.

wider issues, in particular human rights . . . although HGD has 'expressed urgency' in collecting samples from peoples in danger of cultural and physical extinction, it had not expressed concern about their extinction per se."[94]

The debate over the HGDP illustrates how its indigenist critiques not only demonstrated the conjoined operation of value-neutrality and value-bifurcation in the new imperial science, but also directly challenged it. Politics (the "social and collective"[95]) does not begin where ethics ("the behavior of individuals"[96]) ends. Ethics never finds its "limits." According to one Iroquois leader, Joagquisho (Oren Lyons): "Every question that is political is also moral. Every question. And you have to answer it morally."[97] Moreover, issues of power in ethics, especially in the ethics of science, are rarely, if ever, absent. They continue to be played out vividly and resolutely in ongoing struggles over biocolonialism.

In October 1997, the NRC finally released the results of its 30-month-long study of the HGDP proposal, rejecting it as ethically, legally, and scientifically inadequate: "Following an exhaustive examination, the committee found the proposal does not clearly explain the purpose of the project or provide the necessary safeguards for protecting participants."[98] Nevertheless, during this time, the NSF had continued to fund the HGDP; its Physical Anthropology Program almost doubled its support for this type of research, allocating $1 million, or 52% of its grant monies to support ten HGDP-related projects.[99] It was a mixed outcome. The determined, articulate opposition of the HGDP's critics and subjects had at least temporarily shaken the effectiveness of a rhetoric of research justification based on value-neutrality and value-bifurcation, yet, although the research would not proceed with all due haste, it would continue. The NRC committee recommended both that any future diversity study be under United Nations supervision (something the HGDP had steadfastly resisted) and

94 Butler, "Genetic Diversity," 373.
95 Elizabeth Grosz, *Sexual Subversions* (Sydney, Australia: Allen & Unwin, 1989): xvii.
96 Ibid.
97 Oren Lyons, "R.C.A.P. Public Hearings" (Akwesasne, May 1993). Available online at: http://sisis.nativeweb.org/mohawk/ovide.html.
98 RAFI, "Scientific Review Rejects the HGDP," (25 October 1997). Available online at: http://www.etcgroup.org/en/materials/publications.html?pub_id=436.
99 RAFI, "US Funding of Human Biodiversity Collections."

that limited funding be approved for (non-HGDP) diversity collection. As Hope Shand, Research Director of Rural Advancement Foundation International (RAFI[100]), noted:

> That would result in a piecemeal approach that is inconsistent with the NRC's call for a complete research protocol . . . to be in place before consent procedures, much less collection, can start.[101]

And so HGDP-related work proceeded apace, without normative safeguards in place.

Perhaps one of the most valuable counters to the justificatory rhetoric advanced by those promoting the HGDP was the persistent, emphatic, and thorough contextualization of this research initiative. Normative critiques of the HGDP invariably undermined the tendency of its advocates to abstract, isolate, and immunize the project from history and politics. The sidestepping of such issues was neither subtle nor oblique. The HGDP's official FAQ stated that if sampling is too long delayed, some human (i.e., indigenous) groups may disappear as discrete populations due to urbanization or loss of language or other characteristics that distinguished them as a separate group,[102] and the initial Call for a Survey observed that "isolated human populations are being rapidly merged with their neighbors":

> Population growth, famine, war and improvements in transportation and communication are encroaching on once stable populations . . . destroying irrevocably the information needed to reconstruct our evolutionary history.[103]

[100] RAFI was an advocacy organization that, at the time of the HGDP debates, was devoted primarily to issues of biodiversity and biotechnology. It, and the research it disseminated online via the RAFI Communiqué, played an influential role in these debates. It has since expanded its scope and undergone a name change. See "RAFI and RAFI-USA Announce Plans of Name Change for Globally-focused RAFI," 5 February 2001. Available online at: http://www.etcgroup.org/en/materials/publications.html?pub_id=282. The RAFI Communiqués crucial to the HGDP debates can now be found in the archives of the ETC Group, at http://www.etcgroup.org/en/archives.html.

[101] RAFI, "Scientific Review Rejects."

[102] Human Genome Diversity Project, "FAQ." For a more accurate and representative account, one might consider as an instance how the policies of the World Bank and of Brazil's National Institute for Colonization and Land Reform are destroying the Uru-eu-wau-wau people. See Chapter 1 and Paulo Celso de Oliveira, "Brazil: Uru-eu-wau-wau Need Help" (25 March 1996). Available online at: http://nativenet.uthscsa.edu/archive/nl/9603/0182.html.

[103] Luca Cavalli-Sforza, et al., "Call for A Worldwide Survey," 490.

Such priorities and callous dismissals of the many ways in which oppression historically has impacted, and continues to impact, the survival and well-being of indigenous peoples are in no small part the legacy of value-neutrality and value-bifurcation. So too is the failure to realize that – because contemporary biotechnoscience sustains that oppression by commodifying and patenting indigenous genetic resources – proposals like the HGDP cannot suppose that they are unanswerable to this political context. The response that "We are scientists, not politicians" is neither responsible nor convincing for bioscientists, whose work is commercialized – whether by themselves, by governments, or by the seed and drug industries – almost immediately upon completion.

Like most ideological commitments, value-neutrality, value-bifurcation, and the pure/applied science distinction are most powerful when most submerged. They are then most able to ensure that criticisms will not reach all the way to knowledge production, and will be managed and reformulated at the level of knowledge use. The resulting rhetoric of research justification can be difficult to detect, analyze, and assail. Yet indigenist critics of the HGDP did so consistently, and in ways that brought these ideological commitments to the surface where they could be faced and accounted for. Although the impact of these critiques forced some HGDP advocates to acknowledge, and look more closely at, the political face of science and of knowledge production, others have found the task too discomforting.[104] Too convinced, perhaps, of the primacy of their own good intentions and of the severability of bioscience initiatives like the HGDP from unequal relations of power, they enfolded themselves in a justificatory rhetoric which facilitated selective responsibility for the practice of science as it reinforced extant power relations.

[104] A case in point: Not a single representative of the thirteen-member North American Committee of the HGDP would attend a 1998 conference that brought together tribal leaders, elders, tribal legal advisors and educators, scientists, and health officials to discuss genetic research and native peoples. This, despite repeated invitations by its indigenous organizers, and despite the fact that the Diversity Project received foundation funding "for the specific purpose of communication with tribes" (Debra Harry, "Tribes Meet"). The reason? They objected to the conference's title and to the fact that they would be given no more time than other speakers to present their case. According to Greely, "anyone attending the conference on behalf of the HGDP would be cast, unfairly but irrevocably, in the role of arch villain and 'bio-pirate.'" (Ibid.) "The conference you organized was biased," the Chair of the North American HGDP Committee, John Moore, told the organizers, "so even if we had been free to attend, we probably would not have done so." (Ibid.)

PART III

LEGITIMATION: THE RULE AND ROLE OF LAW

The value-neutral/value-bifurcated ideology of the new imperial science is part of the rhetorical tool kit which masks the moral and political character of biocolonialism, deflecting indigenist critiques. There is a larger story to be told about power here, however, for biocolonialism is the product of an alliance forged by the biotechnology industry with the dominant legal system. In the remainder of this book, key aspects of this story, and their implications for indigenous peoples, are considered. The commodification of knowledge and the collusion of intellectual property law are central to my discussion.[1]

Indigenous resistance to biocolonialism, and notably the strong critiques that have been made of the Diversity Project, derive in part from a refusal to construe certain types of knowledge as a commodity. For many indigenous peoples, knowledge of the natural world (especially medicinal and agricultural knowledge) is only properly construed as a gift. Chapter 6 contrasts gift and commodity conceptions of knowledge, and links that contrast to biocolonialism. It concludes by examining the role of economic and political entrepreneurship in contemporary biotechnoscience.

Whether knowledge is regarded as a commercial exchange in the marketplace or as the reciprocal exchange of gifts, an understanding of power

[1] Wade Chambers and Richard Gillespie argue that it is essential for analyses of contemporary science to examine "those vectors of assemblage now devoted to the process of commodification in science, including such social mechanisms as copyright laws, the privatization of university research, as well as the appropriation of indigenous knowledge." "Locality in the History of Science: Colonial Science, Technoscience and Indigenous Knowledge," *Osiris*, 15 (2000). The present volume clearly endorses this view of science theory.

relations is integral to an understanding of knowledge systems. As we have seen in Chapter 3, several recent science theorists[2] have argued that questions of knowledge cannot be divorced from those of power. Plainly, biocolonialism, and indigenist critiques of it, cannot be adequately assessed without appreciating how power figures in the epistemological debate and, conversely, how divergent construals of knowledge enter into the political debate. Because law itself is a central factor in the knowledge/power equation, Chapter 7 addresses how western intellectual property law shapes research as it legitimates and extends biocolonialism and how, in so doing, it alters human relationships. It considers the ideological nature of the distinction between private property rights and the public domain, and illustrates how western legal concepts of "originality" and "innovation" embedded in intellectual property law are not only sharply at odds with their indigenous counterparts, but are primed to serve the interests of biocolonialism.

Although the rule of law aids and abets extractive biocolonialism, it is also being used to challenge and undermine it. In numerous national and international fora, indigenous peoples are pressing their case for the acknowledgement of their group right to self-determination, seeking to protect their lands, resources, and knowledge systems for present and future generations. This has involved both vigorous challenges to the dominant view of the sovereignty of nation-states (according to which nation-states may do whatever they wish within their borders), as well as efforts to articulate and assert their own conceptions of what it means to behave, and to be regarded, as a sovereign nation.

The final chapter takes up the issue of sovereignty, which is so central to resistance to biocolonialism. For a very long time, the story of sovereignty has been a story about borders and boundaries. Bright-line borders, as legal scholars say, that are supposedly clear and distinct, hard and fast. It has largely been a western story, the primary author of which is held to be Thomas Hobbes. In the literature, it is often dubbed absolute sovereignty.

This conception of sovereignty has come under sustained critique for some time, and various alternatives to it are being developed. Some of

[2] See, for example, Joseph Rouse, *Knowledge and Power: Toward a Political Philosophy of Science* (Ithaca, New York: Cornell University, 1987).

these originate in critiques of state sovereignty being made by a variety of academics from diverse fields. Others originate in the critiques of tribal sovereignty doctrine that indigenous scholars and activists have been formulating. Chapter 8 focuses on these latter accounts, examining the contribution that this work is making to the transformation of sovereignty and to the development of a very different story about what a sovereign nation is, and should be. It also demonstrates how this alternative account of sovereignty can be engaged in resisting the phenomenon of biocolonialism.

6

The Commodification of Knowledge

In the context of bioprospecting, scientific knowledge is not simply capitalized; it is politicized in the very particular sense of being inscribed with specific kinds of accountabilities, social relations and potential property claims, and interests. We might say it is neoliberalized. – Cori Hayden[1]

The ideology of the market, and the omnipresence of market forces, has left an indelible mark on the western conception of knowledge. Aided and abetted by the western legal system, and most strikingly by the rise of intellectual property law, knowledge has undergone a steady process of commodification. This is particularly true of knowledge produced in the microworld "factories" of western biotechnoscience, which have become crucial outposts in the establishment of an international intellectual property rights regime. Never content merely to maintain the status quo, as capitalism moves from an industrial to a global information economy, it continues to regenerate itself. Wealth, as Christopher Lind observes, is created

> not primarily from the manufacture of industrial goods, but from the generation of ideas and information. As existing pools of capital seek to capture the new sources of wealth, debates about intellectual property are moving to center stage.[2]

Although the market and market forces of late capitalism differ substantially from those envisaged by Adam Smith, they continue – notably under

[1] Cori Hayden, *When Nature Goes Public: The Making and Unmaking of Bioprospecting in Mexico* (Princeton, New Jersey: Princeton University Press, 2003): 9.
[2] Christopher Lind, "The Idea of Capitalism or the Capitalism of Ideas? A Moral Critique of the Copyright Act," *Intellectual Property Journal*, 7 (1991): 71.

the banner of intellectual property law – to transform the legal system in ways that impact directly the western conception of knowledge. Just as land and labor were metaphorically transformed to accommodate a market economy, so too is knowledge – human intellectual labor – being transformed by what Karl Polanyi calls a "commodity fiction" which hands over "the fate of man and nature to the play of an automaton running in its own grooves and governed by its own laws."[3]

The Market System and the Rise of Intellectual Property

Various commentators have noted how the market doctrine obtained political and philosophical hegemony over western society by pointedly ignoring the distinction between commodities and noncommodities. Commodities, for the economist, have a specific origin and purpose. They are manufactured goods which are produced for sale, sold, and eventually consumed. Because human labor – intellectual or manual – is not manufactured for sale and consumption, it is not a commodity strictly speaking. It is not a product, but a part of who we, as human beings, are; a

> personal, intimate and intrinsic part of ourselves. Human work cannot be separated from the whole person . . . it is a market fiction that there is a separation between the human and human work. We can no more sell our work than we can sell ourselves.[4]

Nor, of course, is land – a part of nature – a commodity that is produced by people for sale and consumption.

Yet to leave work and nature out of the market equation would challenge the market system. As Andrew Kimbrell observes:

> If market ideology was to be the central law of a society . . . it had to extend to all important aspects of life . . . Vital noncommodities had to be subsumed under the definition of commodity, treated like any other commodity, and subjected to the supply-and-demand laws of commodities.[5]

Thus, it was convenient to ignore the distinction between commodities and noncommodities. This metaphorical transformation of labor and land into

[3] Karl Polanyi, *Primitive, Archaic and Modern Economies: Essays of Karl Polanyi.* (New York, New York: Doubleday, 1968): 62.
[4] Andrew Kimbrell, *The Human Body Shop* (San Francisco, California: Harper, 1983): 269–70.
[5] Ibid., 270.

"fictitious commodities" also greatly enhanced the power of the market system, facilitating control of virtually all aspects of social behavior and natural resources. Karl Polanyi recounts this transformation and its full impact:

> The crucial step was this: labor and land were made into commodities, that is, they were treated *as if* produced for sale. Of course, they were not actually commodities, since they were either not produced at all (as land) or, if so, not for sale (as labor). Yet no more thoroughly effective fiction was ever devised . . . The true scope of such a step can be gauged if we remember that labor is only another name for man, and land for nature.[6]

The transformation and commodification of knowledge – of human intellectual labor – was part of this process. Knowledge is not produced by people for sale and consumption, and despite the tendency of recent work in science studies to speak of knowledge production and knowledge products, knowledge is not a product. Such talk merely reflects the effectiveness of the knowledge-as-commodity metaphor. Like manual labor, intellectual labor is a "personal, intimate and intrinsic part" of human beings. To paraphrase Kimbrell, human knowledge cannot be separated from the whole person; it is a market fiction that there is a separation. We can no more sell our knowledge than we can sell ourselves.

When market assumptions are extended to ideas and information, intellectual property results. Patents, copyrights, and trade secrets are protections that the state gives to innovations – to new ideas. These types of property rights are intended to provide for ownership of "noncorporeal, intellectual objects, such as writings, inventions and secret business information"[7] that can be bought and sold in the marketplace. Private intellectual property can restrict the use, the expression, and the methods of acquiring ideas.

The rise of intellectual property has also helped to transform the western conception of knowledge in another way. Scholarly, as well as popular,

[6] Polanyi, *Primitive, Archaic*, 61–2.

[7] Edwin C. Hettinger, "Justifying Intellectual Property," *Philosophy and Public Affairs*, 18 (1989): 31.

conceptions of knowledge have regarded it as nonexclusive[8] – as existing in many places at once and as not consumed by use: "the possession or use of (such) an intellectual object by one person does not preclude others from possessing or using it as well."[9] However, when it is commodified, and rendered as intellectual property, information becomes exclusive, and its value is seen to lie in part in that exclusiveness. The point of owning a song, or certain genetic information, is to ensure and secure exclusive profits.

Intellectual property laws serve as means of transforming indigenous knowledge and genetic resources into profitable commodities and of advancing the commodification of nature. For example, the chief of the Global Environment Division of the World Bank, discussing traditional plant knowledge in the Ethiopian Coptic Church, recently proposed: "Let's screen that knowledge stock . . . (and) explore how it might be commercialized."[10] Indigenous representatives to the Commission on Sustainable Development have challenged the practice of bioprospecting and the global imposition of western intellectual property laws. Victoria Tauli-Corpuz offers a compelling description of the cultural politics of science unfolding here, and of the contrasting metaphors of knowledge which help to sustain them:

> We have witnessed how indigenous seed varieties and medicinal plants which our women and healers have preserved and developed were appropriated by international and national research institutes and transnational corporations . . . Without our knowing, these seeds and medicinal plants were altered in laboratories and now we are told that the companies have intellectual property rights over these genetic plant materials because they have improved on them. This logic is beyond us . . . we, indigenous peoples . . . have developed and preserved these plants over thousands of years.[11]

Another particularly disturbing aspect of this debate is that the patenting of genetic information is simultaneously the patenting of life forms because

8 See R. J. Roberts, "Is Information Property?," *Intellectual Property Journal*, 3:2 (1987) and Steve Fuller, *Social Epistemology* (Bloomington, Indiana: Indiana University Press, 1991).

9 Hettinger, "Justifying Intellectual Property," 34.

10 Cited in Phil Bereano, Message posted to *Native-L* on 31 October 1995. Available online at: http://nativenet.uthscsa.edu/archive/nl/9511/0014.html.

11 Victoria Tauli-Corpuz, "We Are Part of Biodiversity, Respect Our Rights," *Third World Resurgence*, 36 (1993): 25.

the innovations in question are based upon and produce life forms. A 1995 report to the United Nations Educational, Scientific and Cultural Organization's (UNESCO's) International Bioethics Committee notes: "Genetic material is seen as part of what constitutes life; as such, patenting transforms this material into a commodity that can be owned and traded in."[12] Commenting on this phenomenon, José de Souza Silva observes that "genetic property rights subject nature to worldwide commodification, an important step in the ongoing biotechnological revolution."[13] This commodification is not limited to plants, of course; it involves nonhuman animals as well. In 1983, well before the Office of Technology Assessment (OTA) closed its doors, well over 190 genetically engineered animals (these include fish, cows, mice, and pigs) were "figuratively standing in line to be patented by a variety of researchers and corporations."[14] It also involves human animals, people, who are treated as sources of genetic information. As Okanagan activist Jeannette Armstrong states: "it is not only knowledge about plants and animals that is being made a commodity: The essential substance of the human life form – human gene lines – are now items for transnational trade and profit."[15]

Gifts and Commodities

Labor should not be sold like merchandise but offered as a gift to the community.
– Che Guevara

The nature, depth, and force of indigenous opposition to biocolonialism, and especially to the Diversity Project, tend to be poorly grasped by advocates of these extractive initiatives of western science – whether corporate or academic.[16] It is frequently assumed that after proper informed consent

[12] UNESCO, "Bioethics and Human Population Genetics Research" (November 15, 1995): section 2.3.2. Available online at: http://portal.unesco.org/shs/en/files/2303/10596456491-populationCIB3_en.pdf/populationCIB3_en.pdf.

[13] José de Souza Silva, "Plant Intellectual Property Rights: The Rise of Nature as a Commodity," in N. Patrick Peritore and Ana Karina Galve-Peritore (eds.), *Biotechnology in Latin America* (Wilmington, Delaware: Scholarly Resources, 1995): 57.

[14] Kimbrell, *The Human Body Shop*, 198. Congress withdrew funding for the OTA, and the Office closed on 29 September 1995.

[15] Jeannette Armstrong, "Global trade targets indigenous gene lines," *National Catholic Reporter* (January 27, 1995): 11.

[16] For examples, see the Summer 1996 special issue of *Cultural Survival Quarterly*, which was devoted to this topic.

documents, material transfer agreements, and database access agreements have been drafted, and the "hysteria" whetted by "professional alarmists" subsides, opposition to projects such as the Human Genome Diversity Project (HGDP) will and should dissipate.[17] At the least, it should be effectively disarmed. Such assumptions can be sustained only by wrenching certain indigenist critiques from their contexts. Some of the most substantive objections to the Diversity Project, and to biocolonialism more generally, contend that life forms, and indigenous knowledge of the natural world, are gifts; they must not be privatized, commercialized, and commodified.

This section contrasts a western commodity conception of knowledge with the construal of knowledge as a gift which is prevalent in many indigenous knowledge systems. I do not suggest that all knowledge within all western and indigenous knowledge systems conforms to these divergent metaphors of commodity and gift.[18] Certainly within the West, there has been resistance to life-form patents on analogous grounds. Similarly, some indigenous peoples have embraced such patents, to varying degrees and with varying degrees of consensus and reluctance. As Tom Greaves notes, "the arena of Western institutions are played in when the stakes are high and there is no other choice."[19] Knowledge systems, whether western or indigenous, are neither monolithic nor static; they are varied and changing, far more so than my discussion here will reflect.

Nevertheless, these diverging metaphors of knowledge do capture tendencies and features which are typical of, or prevail in, many indigenous and western knowledge systems. Moreover, they have not only intellectual but social and moral implications for what and how something can be known: Metaphors "shape our perceptions and in turn our actions, which tend to be in accordance with the metaphor."[20] These are politically significant insofar as they inform contemporary struggles within indigenous

[17] John Moore, "Native Americans, Scientists, and the HGDP," *Cultural Survival Quarterly*, 20:2 (Summer 1996): 62.

[18] Nor do I wish to assume the adequacy of the gift/commodity distinction as a way of contrasting entire economic systems. For further consideration of this, see Arjun Appadurai, *The Social Life of Things* (Cambridge, UK: Cambridge University, 1986).

[19] Tom Greaves (ed.), *Intellectual Property Rights for Indigenous Peoples* (Oklahoma City, Oklahoma: Society for Applied Anthropology, 1994): 6.

[20] Nancy Stepan, "Race and Gender: The Role of Analogy in Science," in Sandra Harding (ed.), *The "Racial" Economy of Science* (Bloomington, Indiana: Indiana University Press, 1993): 372.

and western knowledge systems over biocolonialist policies and practices. Indeed, part of what is at issue in resistance to the Diversity Project is whether a particular change should take place within indigenous knowledge and value systems – a significant change in how certain knowledge is understood and in how it is valued.

Consider Aroha Mead's statement of the basis of Maori opposition to the Project. Many of the Diversity Project's advocates, she notes, mistakenly supposed that indigenous critiques of the Project were based on a misunderstanding of its goals and on confusion regarding minor details.[21] Anyone who followed the long electronic debate on *Native-L* between opponents of the Project and its central apologist, Stanford law professor Henry Greely, discussed in the last chapter, will concur with Mead here. Greely and other Project proponents have repeatedly failed to address – or even to indicate they take seriously – what lay at the heart of indigenist resistance:

> It is difficult to articulate the degree to which the indigenous and western scientific philosophies differ on such a fundamental point, but . . . I wish to emphasize that it is the difference in understanding of the origin of humanity, the responsibility of individuals and the safety of future generations which sits so firmly at the core of indigenous opposition to the (Diversity Project) . . . the fundamental reason is that, according to an indigenous world view, this type of research proposes to interfere in a highly sacred domain of indigenous history, survival and commitment to future generations.[22]

As Mead explains, the Maori translate the word "gene" as *iratangata* ("life spirit of the mortals") or *whakapapa* ("geneology"), so a physical gene is understood to be "imbued with a life spirit handed down from the ancestors."[23] Each successive generation contributes to it, passing it on to future generations. Genes, thus, are part of the heritage of families, communities, tribes, and entire indigenous nations. They are not the property of individuals, nor is any part or derivative of them. The innovative manipulations leading to the isolation and storage of DNA segments, and the

21 Aroha Mead, "Letter from Aroha Mead, Director, International Association of the Mataatua Declaration, to Dr. Darrell Macer, Sub-Committee on Population Genetics," UNESCO International Bioethics Committee, UNESCO-Bioethics & Human Population Research, (29 July 1995). Available online at: http://nativenet.uthscsa.edu/archive/nl/9510/0350.html.

22 Ibid.

23 Ibid.

privatization and commercialization of cell lines, turn them into such and are therefore vigorously resisted.

Comparable concerns have been expressed by diverse indigenous peoples protesting the patenting of traditional medicines and crop varieties, and for whom knowledge of the natural world, particularly medicinal and agricultural knowledge, is regarded (like life itself) as given, not produced. There are normative implications to such an epistemological posture. When knowledge is construed as a gift, the *process* of knowing rather than the product of knowledge, and the nature and quality of the relationships with the nonhuman world which are constitutive of that process, become central. Moreover, given the inalienability of gifts, when a gift is offered the continuity of social relationships ensures that it always remains the giver's. Thus the giver remains in a position to influence and guide the disposition of a gift. Commodities, by contrast, are alienable. When they are exchanged, so is effective control over the disposition of the commodity. The "social distance and independence of the transactors" in the marketplace leave the seller of the commodity unable to influence its use.[24]

To properly engage in a process of reciprocal exchange, of giving and receiving, behavioral constraints must be accepted. The reciprocity of the exchange is to be respected and reflected in one's conduct. These normative constraints are simultaneously ecological and social. The process of knowing must be undertaken in a way that respects and reflects the fact that each individual, each community, each tribe, each nation, and each species has "a responsibility to the workings of the universe,"[25] to the generations to come and to those that have passed. As with knowledge of the natural world, for many indigenous peoples land itself is a

> gift . . . (so) they assume certain ceremonial duties which must be performed as long as they live on and use the land . . . Obligations demanded by the lands upon which people lived were part of their understanding of the world; indeed their view of life was grounded in the knowledge of these responsibilities.[26]

[24] Jeff Berg, "Moral Rights: A Legal, Historical and Anthropological Reappraisal," *Intellectual Property Journal*, 6 (1991): 363.
[25] Paula Gunn Allen, *The Sacred Hoop* (Boston: Beacon, 1986): 73.
[26] Vine Deloria, Jr. "Out of Chaos," in D. Dooling and P. Jordan-Smith (eds.), *I Become Part of It* (San Francisco, California: Harper, 1992): 262–3.

This construal of knowledge, and the normative constraints which attend it, can be readily illustrated by diverse indigenous knowledge practices. I emphasize here knowledge of healing, of hunting, and of crop cultivation.

Normative Dimensions of Knowledge

There are specific ceremonies and procedures which persons with knowledge of traditional medicines are generally careful to observe. Typically, a traditional healer will offer tobacco to the plants being collected. The plant will be addressed and thanked for being there, for allowing itself to be used in healing. Only certain plants will be culled, at certain stages of their life cycles, at certain times of the year and of the day. The comments of Diné healer Mae Tso richly demonstrate how conceiving knowledge as reciprocal exchange mediates behavior, what is done in the name of indigenous science, as well as how it is done:

> When you are collecting medicine healing herbs, you have to collect for the individual sick person. You make an offering to the plants in your prayers, you have to know the plant's name, the person's name and the reason. The medicine plants that you have gathered cannot be used for anyone else, nor can they be stored and kept for use at a later time. When you are collecting herbs, you cannot collect them in large quantities. There are specific sacred herbs for all kinds of sickness . . . All these medicine plants have a specific song and prayer to go along with them. When you collect these herbs, you have to make an offering to them to get the healing spirit of the herbs to work. You have to know the prayers and songs for the herbs to collect them. You only collect what is needed, nothing more or less.[27]

The ecological moral she conveys here is echoed in Jake Swamp's account of his training in the gathering of medicinal herbs:

> You don't just go out there and pluck it out by its roots and walk away. You have to prepare. You have to know the words that go with it. What I was taught was that when you see that plant, to first see that it's the one you offer thanksgiving to, that plant is still here with us, still performing its duty and that you wish it to continue. You walk past it

[27] Mae Tso, "Affidavit of Mae Tso, Jenny Manybeads, *et al. v.* United States of America, *et al.*," 730 F. Supp. 1515 (U.S. Dist. AZ 1989) (No. 88–410): 328.

> and you look for the other one, and that one you can pick. For, if you take that first one, who is to know, maybe that's the last one that exists in the world.[28]

The Cree goose hunter's practice of *pwaatikswaau*, or smoking to the game, expresses a similar attitude and acknowledgement of the gift relationship, or reciprocal exchange, which binds the human to the nonhuman world, and which "constitutes a root metaphor or paradigm for knowledge in general."[29] Smoke is an appropriate vehicle of exchange for creatures of the air, and tobacco is a traditional medicine, customarily offered to honor other beings – human and nonhuman – especially when something is being taken or requested. When the hunter is successful and a goose falls, "the gift is respectfully admired by the hunter and later received as a guest into the lodge by the women of the hunter's household."[30]

Something analogous is evident in the agricultural knowledge practices of Andean peoples, undertaking the cultivation of their *chacras*. According to Modesto Machaca, "to open a chacra I must ask permission of the Pachamama so that she will allow me to work this soil . . . I tell her that I will cultivate this soil with love, without mistreatment and the fruits she gives me we will all eat."[31] Cultivating a *chacra* is a reciprocal activity, necessarily involving both humans and the land. It is in this sense that Andean agricultural knowledge is to be seen as tied, or tethered, to the land:

> To raise a chacra is not merely to domesticate plants and animals; it is to nurture lovingly and respectfully, in other words, to nurture ritually, together with plants and animals, the soils, waters, microclimates and, in general, the whole land.[32]

All of the activities that go on in the *chacra* – sowing, weeding, hilling, harvesting, and even the storage, transformation, and consumption of harvested products – are ritual activities. These rituals express the Andeans'

[28] José Barreiro, "The Search For Lessons," *Akwe:kon*, Vol. IX, No. 2 (1982): 21.

[29] Colin Scott, "Science for the West, Myth for the Rest?: The Case of James Bay Cree Knowledge Construction," in Laura Nader (ed.), *Naked Science: Anthropological Inquiry into Boundaries, Power, and Knowledge* (New York, New York: Routledge, 1996): 74.

[30] Ibid., 82.

[31] Julio Valladolid Rivera, "Andean Peasant Agriculture: Nurturing a Diversity of Life in the *Chacra*" in Frédérique Apffel-Marglin and Julio Valladolid Rivera, *Regeneration in the Andes* (St. Urbain, Montréal, Québec: Intercultural Institute of Montréal, 1995): 25.

[32] Ibid., 24.

attitude of love, respect, and gratitude to the earth for its gifts, including the gifts of knowledge regarding how to cultivate a *chacra*.

The process of knowing exemplified by Diné healing, Cree hunting, and Andean farming practices is not exclusively or narrowly cognitive. It is also an evaluative activity, conditioned by respect and gratitude, in which certain normative constraints on knowledge – on what, how, and by whom things are known – are critical. These constraints spring from an acknowledgement that human beings play, and cannot help but play, a fundamental role in the natural world. Humans are, of course, not unique in this.

The knowledge that indigenous healers, hunters, and farmers are given binds them and the people they treat and feed to the land, just as the exchange of gifts between people binds them to one another. The giving of gifts establishes a relationship between those involved; their circulation within the human world, as well as between the human and nonhuman world, acknowledges and enhances community. Those involved in the exchange and sale of commodities, by contrast,

> do not look toward the person of each other, but only toward the commodity; there are no obligations of brotherliness or reverence, and none of those spontaneous human relations that grow out of intimate personal community. They all would just obstruct the free development of the bare market community . . . Such absolute depersonalization is contrary to all elementary forms of human relations.[33]

As one commentator observes:

> It seems no misnomer that we have called those nations known for their commodities "the free world." The phrase doesn't seem to refer to political freedoms; it indicates that the dominant form of exchange in these lands does not bind the individual in any way – to his family, to his community, or to the state.[34]

When something that is a gift is metaphorically transformed and treated as if it were a commodity, the social and moral ramifications are considerable. Aroha Mead's comments earlier in this chapter demonstrate that part of what indigenist critics of the Diversity Project were contesting is the

[33] Max Weber, *On Law in Economy and Society* (New York, New York: Simon & Schuster, 1954): 192.

[34] Lewis Hyde, *The Gift* (New York, New York: Random House, 1979): 67.

desirability and inevitability of just such a transformation. What was ultimately at issue were the transformation of certain kinds of knowledge and certain forms of life into commodities and the implications of this for indigenous knowledge and value systems. The Declaration of Indigenous Peoples of the Western Hemisphere Regarding the HGDP made this plain:

> We oppose the patenting of all natural genetic materials. We hold that life cannot be bought, owned, sold, discovered or patented, even in its smallest forms . . . We particularly oppose the Human Genome Diversity Project which intends to collect, and make available, our genetic materials which may be used for commercial, scientific, and military purposes . . . Our principles are based upon our profound belief in the sacredness of all Creation, both animate and inanimate. We live in a reciprocal relationship with all life . . . [35]

So too, in the Blue Mountain Declaration rejecting life-form patenting, we find the following:

> The humans, animals, microorganisms and plants comprising life on earth are part of the natural world into which we were all born. The conversion of these life forms, their molecules or parts into corporate property through patent monopolies is counter to the interests of the peoples of the world. No individual, institution, or corporation should be able to claim ownership over species or varieties of living organisms. Nor should they be able to hold patents on organs, cells, genes or proteins, whether naturally occurring, genetically altered or otherwise modified . . . [W]e call upon the world and the Congress of the United States to enact legislation to exclude living organisms and their component parts from the patent system. We encourage all peoples to oppose this attack on the value of life.[36]

A commodity conception of knowledge assumes certain values and facilitates certain behaviors that are inappropriate or inconceivable when knowledge is regarded as something given, rather than produced for sale. Increasingly, western technoscience – whether corporate, academic, or governmental – is committed to "producing" knowledge that is to be applied in industry. Although there is a growing failure to accept, appreciate,

[35] "Declaration of Indigenous Peoples of the Western Hemisphere Regarding the Human Genome Diversity Project" *Indigenous Woman*, Vol. II, No. II (1995): 32–3.

[36] "Blue Mountain Declaration," reprinted in *The Seattle Times*, 20 August 1995. Available online at: http://community.seattletimes.nwsource.com/archive/?date=19950820&slug=2137238.

and observe limits to such knowledge acquisition, the rise of intellectual property regimes does indicate a readiness to limit access to such knowledge in the interests of enhancing its value as a commodity. Biocolonialism arises when this conception of knowledge is conjoined to the scope and power of western legal institutions committed to extending intellectual property regimes globally.

Economic and Political Entrepreneurship in the New Imperial Science

By 2005, publicly traded biotech companies were worth $410 billion. One of the most research-intensive industries in the world, the U.S. biotechnology sector in 2005 alone spent $19.8 billion on research.[37] The interests of this U.S.-dominated industry are shaping the development, and the extension internationally, of an intellectual property regime that disadvantages less powerful groups – both nation-states of the Third World and indigenous nations of the Fourth World. Over the past two decades, U.S. patent law "has been tested, criticized, and expanded to fit the needs of biotech's seemingly unfettered development," while U.S. policy has promoted "globalization of stringent and broad patent protections similar to those found in the [United States]."[38] The rise of intellectual property in general, and that of biopatents in particular, is thus helping to mediate a confluence of science with the economy.

Recent research in science studies documents the newly emerging relationships between science and property in academia, government, and industry and how intellectual property rights have made the formerly independent concepts of science and property contingent upon one another.[39] Universities, focusing on the economic value of academic research, have joined industry and the government in using science to create and profit from new property. Science theorists Henry Etzkowitz

[37] "Biotechnology Industry Facts," available online at: http://bio.org/speeches/pubs/er/statistics.asp.

[38] Amy Carroll, "Not Always the Best Medicine: Biotechnology and the Global Impact of U.S. Patent Law," *American University Law Review*, 44 (1995): 2439.

[39] See Francis W. Rushing and Carole Ganz Brown (eds.), *Protection of Intellectual Property Rights in Science, Technology, and Economic Performance* (Boulder, Colorado: Westview Press, 1990).

and Andrew Webster suggest that science policy and industrial policy are merging into one: "capitalization of knowledge becomes the basis for economic growth ... The first step in the capitalization of science is to secure knowledge as intellectual property ... The second ... is to accrue value from knowledge that has been secured ... through marketing and licensing activities."[40] Others have noted that within biotechnology "a realignment drive by economic forces is taking place between free information and proprietary information" and that the implications of this for scientific practice are considerable.[41]

The growing intrusion of economic considerations in science plainly affects determinations of scientific promise. Both the identification of problem areas and the selection of a particular problem as worthy of pursuit frequently have a heavy economic component, turning on the availability of grants and the likelihood of attracting funding. In the United States, most of that funding comes from industry and the federal government. The $3 billion Human Genome Project (HGP), funded by the National Institutes of Health and the Department of Defense, is a case in point. After the $25 million Diversity Project was formally adopted by the Human Genome Organisation (HUGO), the organization responsible for the HGP, the National Science Foundation issued a call for pilot projects. We have already seen how the population geneticists who proposed the Diversity Project were frustrated by the difficulty of getting grants for their work. Were they to succeed in hitching their research wagons to a megascience project like the HGP, the availability of future funding would be virtually assured. Some anthropologists also mentioned the benefit to their field: "One of the strongest arguments in support of the [Diversity Project] is that it could represent a pot of 'free money' for anthropologists."[42] There was, moreover, an added payoff: Not only would they "be deluged" with data from the Diversity Project "if all goes well,"[43] but some contended

[40] Henry Etzkowitz and Andrew Webster, "Science as Intellectual Property," in Sheila Jasanoff *et al.* (eds.), *Handbook of Science and Technology Studies* (Thousand Oaks, California: Sage, 1995): 481, 482, 484.

[41] Ibid., 484.

[42] Jonathan Marks, "Commentary: The Human Genome Diversity Project," *Anthropological News* (April 1995): 72.

[43] John Moore, "Putting Anthropology Back Together Again," *American Anthropologist*, 96 (1994): 925.

that this had the potential to unify the badly divided discipline, "to bring the fields of anthropology back together again."[44]

Governments, universities, and industries attempt to recoup their economic investment in selected scientific projects by converting the results of research into private intellectual property. Thus, intellectual property considerations figure importantly. They do so not only at the outset of research by affecting pursuit decisions, but also by impacting both the process of scientific pursuit and its outcome.[45] The pace of scientific pursuit is affected as well. Etzkowitz and Webster comment that knowledge, by its nature, "is evanescent and temporary, because it is always in principle and practice replaceable by new knowledge. Thus property in knowledge with potential economic value must be captured quickly to secure value from it."[46] By compromising uninhibited exchange of information among scientists, intellectual property restricts the dissemination of reports on the progress and results of research efforts. Like other forms of property rights, intellectual property rights are concerned with establishing exclusions, restrictions, and control: Patents restrict the use of ideas, copyrights restrict the expression of ideas, and trade secrets restrict the methods of acquiring ideas. As with most other proprietary claims,

> those with the cultural, economic, and political resources will be most likely to secure their claim against competitors . . . Political and ethical matters, reflecting the global economic divide between haves and have nots, are therefore central to the debate over intellectual property rights.[47]

Existing patent laws are also being modified to better accommodate biotechnology. Descriptive requirements are being loosened and broadly interpreted so that genes, plants, and animals can be included in the scope of patent law, and new micro-organisms can be redefined as products of human inventiveness, rather than as unpatentable products of nature.[48] Such modifications enhance the scope and degree of patent holders' power.

44 Ibid., 941.
45 Etzkowitz and Webster, "Science as Intellectual Property," 482.
46 Ibid.
47 Ibid., 489–90.
48 See generally Cary Fowler, "Biotechnology, Patents, and the Third World," in Vandana Shiva and Ingunn Moser (eds.), *Biopolitics* (Atlantic Highlands, New Jersey: Zed Books, 1995).

The effect of this, Cary Fowler contends, is to maintain "the centralization of control over biodiversity which has existed since colonial times. The mode of control has simply shifted from physical to legal."[49] The only "originality," "novelty," and "inventiveness" recognized by the current intellectual property regime are those conforming to the highly individualized western conception. It fails utterly to recognize the generations of collective, indigenous, intellectual, and physical labor, the creative efforts of which have preserved and refined the pool of diverse genetic materials currently being mined as sources of new intellectual property. Yet, as Vandana Shiva has argued, there is no epistemological justification "for treating some germ plasm as valueless and part of the common heritage, and other germ plasm as a valuable commodity and private property. The distinction is not based on the nature of the germ plasm, but on the nature of political and economic power."[50] In this way law – like science – demonstrates its ability to exercise power, not only through its material effects or judgments, but also by disqualifying other knowledges and experiences.[51]

All of this amply undermines the presumptions and assertions of political and economic "disinterestedness" widely made by those engaged in pursuit of the new imperial science. Increasingly, scientists are acting like economic entrepreneurs,[52] as reputation and scientific credibility are linked to success in generating exploitable knowledge.[53] Yet some

49 Ibid., 218.

50 Ibid., 210.

51 In this I concur strongly with Carol Smart, who argues persuasively against Michel Foucault's position that juridical power is waning as disciplinary power waxes in contemporary western societies. See Carol Smart, *Feminism and the Power of Law* (New York, New York: Routledge, 1989). Alan Hunt argues for a conclusion similar to Smart's but along somewhat different lines. See Alan Hunt, "Foucault's Expulsion of Law: Toward a Retrieval, Law and Social Inquiry," *Law and Social Inquiry*, 1 (1992). Smart suggests that a focus on disciplinary mechanisms ought not displace law's significance as a site of power relations. She does not reject "the idea that non-juridical modes of regulation are increasingly important," but maintains that "juridical power remains a formidable obstacle to feminism and that whilst other mechanisms of discipline develop, law itself can deploy these mechanisms to enhance its own power." Smart, *Feminism*, 137. There is no question but that juridical power remains a formidable obstacle to indigenism. Biocolonialism, aided and abetted by intellectual property law, is ample demonstration of that.

52 Bruno Latour and Steve Woolgar describe at length how scientists invest their intellectual capital so as to enjoy the greatest return on their practice: "In this respect, scientists' behaviour is remarkably similar to that of an investor of capital. An accumulation of credibility is prerequisite to investment. The greater this stockpile, the more able the investor to reap substantial returns and thus add further to his growing capital." Bruno Latour and Steve Woolgar, *Laboratory Life* (Beverly Hills, California: Sage Publications, 1979): 197.

53 Etzkowitz and Webster, "Science as Intellectual Property," 487.

commentators have contended that political, not economic, entrepreneurship is the more appropriate analogy. Just as in politics the production of authoritative decisions "cannot proceed in a purely technical way, but depend[s] critically on justifications and their acceptance,"[54] so too in science – it is argued – success in mobilizing resources turns on scientists' justifications being accepted, not simply on a market taking up their products. Surely both sides of this debate are correct, and political entrepreneurship is conjoined to economic within the new imperial science. The Diversity Project underscores the fact that scientists pursuing it must justify their actions, procedures, and products if they are to succeed in mobilizing resources. So, too, must others. Even biotechnology corporations rely on intellectual property law to justify their appropriation of indigenous intellectual and genetic resources and to counter charges of biopiracy and theft.

Indigenous peoples are acutely aware that by commodifying both their knowledge and genetic resources, biocolonialism results in a substantial loss of power and control, and with that, the abandonment of crucial moral responsibilities to future generations. The Zuni, for example, have formulated a Cultural Resources Advisory Team to provide guidance concerning Zuni genetic resources. It has declared that Zuni seeds "should not be sold or given to outsiders for profit, resale, breeding, or trademarketing."[55] The reason is that, if Zuni seeds are transformed into a commodity and sold, the Zuni will no longer know how the seeds will be used. Because they will no longer be under Zuni control, their abuse cannot be prevented. To convert Zuni seeds into commodities would not only alter the nature of Zuni communal relationships, it would result in a significant and irreversible loss of power. The Zuni would no longer be able to monitor and control the use of their seeds and the generations of intellectual and physical labor that their cultivation represents. They would no longer be able to discharge their moral responsibility to ensure that the seeds be properly used.

Indigenous recognition that the process of commodification leads to a loss of power and an inability to control how something is used is widespread. It is not limited to the commodification of genetic materials,

[54] Ibid.

[55] Daniela Soleri *et al.*, "Gifts from the Creator," in Tom Greaves (ed.), *Intellectual Property Rights for Indigenous Peoples* (Oklahoma City, Oklahoma: Society for Applied Anthropology, 1994): 34.

but includes the commodification of knowledge as well. Consider the Maori account of this. The third of the three baskets of knowledge which form the basis of traditional Maori epistemology contains all knowledge of the natural world (agriculture, medicine, astronomy, fishing, crafts, etc.). Such knowledge is considered *tapu* – sacred and set apart, or removed from profane use. Thus, it is treated with special respect. It is also endowed with *mana* or power.[56] As a gift from the gods, it is not to be passed on lightly. Above all, knowledge that is *tapu* must never be transformed into a commodity:

> our elders never allow us to sell any knowledge of anything Maori that is really tapu. To them it is priceless. Money can never buy knowledge and when they teach they will tell people: "This knowledge I am passing over to you must never be sold."[57]

One is responsible for such knowledge and for how it will be used, or misused: "A *tapu* involves a restriction, and in the case of *tapu* knowledge, this requires making sure that the knowledge does not fall into the wrong hands."[58] Should this happen, the knowledge will lose its *tapu*, and thereby its power:

> There is . . . a fear that by giving things out they could be commercialized. If this happens they lose their sacredness, their fertility. They just become common. And knowledge that is profane has lost its life, lost its tapu.[59]

Resisting the Politics of Disappearance

There has recently been a surge of interest by the dominant culture in indigenous knowledge and indigenous knowledge systems. The reasons are multiple. They include the failure of development policies that have disregarded the social, political, and cultural contexts in which they were implemented and an as yet limited appreciation of the value and viability

[56] See Maori Marsden, "God, Man and the Universe: A Maori View," in Michael King (ed.), *Te Ao Hurihuri* (Auckland, New Zealand: Reed Publishing, 1992): 121.

[57] N. Pewhairangi, "Foreword: Learning and Tapu," in King, ibid., 11.

[58] John Patterson, *Exploring Maori Values* (Palmerston North, New Zealand: The Dunmore Press, 1992): 164.

[59] T. Manihera, "Foreword: Learning and Tapu," in King, *Te Ao*, 9.

of indigenous knowledge systems. The rhetoric of development, one commentator observes,

> has gone through several stages . . . Today indigenous knowledge is seen as pivotal, above all, in discussion on sustainable resource use and balanced development. This orientation is in stark contrast to the views of many earlier theorists, who saw traditional knowledge and institutions as obstacles to development.[60]

The study of indigenous knowledge has even been institutionalized, with the establishment of a Center for Indigenous Knowledge in Agriculture at Iowa State University, an Internet list on indigenous knowledge,[61] and a journal, the *Indigenous Knowledge and Development Monitor*. Such developments are consistent with the knowledge as commodity metaphor. The commodification of indigenous spiritual knowledge has become the specialty of the New Age Industry, the commodification of traditional medicinal knowledge has become the specialty of the pharmaceutical industry, and the commodification of plant genetic resources and indigenous agricultural knowledge has become the specialty of the commercial seed industry. In opposing the Diversity Project, what indigenous peoples were resisting was part of that continuum, the commodification of the genetic information in their cell lines.

After a period of dormancy, there has also been within academia a renewed interest in contrasting indigenous and non-indigenous knowledge, with attendant debate about terminology and the implications of adopting one terminological distinction rather than another. This debate has tended to proceed, as one might expect, on methodological and epistemological grounds. It often aims to secure some sort of dialogue between, if not integration of, indigenous and western knowledges of the natural world. A recent editorial in the *Indigenous Knowledge and Development Monitor*, for instance, calls for the development of "methodologies designed to build a bridge between various knowledge systems."[62] Hand in hand with this are calls for the gathering, documentation, archiving, and preservation of indigenous knowledge in national and international databases,

60 Arun Agrawal, "Indigenous and Scientific Knowledge: Some Critical Comments," *Indigenous Knowledge and Development Monitor*, 3:3 (1995): 2.

61 INDKNOW: Indigenous Knowledge systems List. The INDKNOW archives contain numerous sites reflecting the nature and scope of activity surrounding indigenous knowledge systems. Available online at: http://homepages.ihug.co.nz/~sai/indigen.html.

62 "Editorial," *Indigenous Knowledge and Development Monitor*, 4:1 (1996): 1.

presumably because no bridge can be built when there is nothing left to bridge.

For a long time, the existence of indigenous knowledge and knowledge systems was denied. When their existence was acknowledged, they were generally deprived of cognitive standing. They were dismissed as primitive, mystical, and unscientific – because they violated the fundamental methodological canons and commitment to value-neutrality of western science. And steadily, steadily throughout, political, economic, and cultural practices and policies of oppression have been eroding away at their very substance, at their conditions of existence.

The solution now is not the isolation, documentation, and storage of indigenous knowledge in international, national, and regional archives.[63] No more than is the preservation of indigenous cell lines in data banks the proper response to the "vanishing," "rapidly disappearing" "isolates (who are) of Historic Interest" to population geneticists. Nor is the answer a "bridge" to assimilation built in the context of unequal power relations, and with the bridging interests of the dominant culture setting the agenda; a proposal that promises to be simply another stage in the politics of disappearance.

The appropriate response from those interested in preserving genetic diversity has already been formulated by indigenist critics of the HGDP:

> Why don't they address the causes of our being endangered instead of spending $20 million for five years to collect and store us in cold laboratories? If this money will be used instead to provide us with the basic social services and promote our rights as indigenous peoples, then our biodiversity will be protected.[64]

And the appropriate response from those interested in preserving the diversity of knowledge systems has been proposed by Arun Agrawal. That response, he suggests, lies

> in attempting to reorient and reverse state policies to permit members of threatened populations to determine their own future, thus

63 As James Boyle has pointed out, the establishment of data banks for indigenous genetic resources raises concerns that there will no longer be any incentive to preserve those resources: "Precisely because of our increasing ability to record genetic information as information, its connection to its natural habitat will become less necessary." James Boyle, *Shamans, Software & Spleens: Law and the Construction of the Information Society* (Cambridge, Massachusetts: Harvard University Press, 1996): 129.

64 Tauli-Corpuz, "We Are Part of Biodiversity," 25–6.

> facilitating *in situ* preservation of indigenous knowledge. *In situ* preservation cannot succeed unless indigenous populations and local communities gain control over the use of the lands on which they dwell and the resources on which they rely. Those who are seen to possess knowledge must also possess the right to decide on how to conserve their knowledge, and how and by whom it will be used.[65]

It is, after all, the givers of gifts who must determine when, to whom, and how the gifts are to be given.

[65] Agrawal, "Indigenous and Scientific Knowledge," 5.

7

Intellectual Property Rights as Means and Mechanism of Imperialism

Indigenous peoples have linked their quest for self-determination to the protection of their knowledge.
– Chidi Oguamanam[1]

The means of justifying the new imperial science are inseparable from the means of its extension; the "rule of law,"– or as it is also known, the "supremacy of law," – accomplishes both. Law is, Alan Hunt maintains, a "primary agency of the advance of new modalities of power and constitutes distinctive features of their mode of operation."[2] The imposition of the "rule of law" by a dominant nation-state upon other peoples was a classic means of extending empire, part of the process of colonization. This was, and remains, especially true of property law. Indeed, the politics of property has long been the central historical dynamic mediating the relationships between indigenous peoples and imperial states. Whereas sovereignty over indigenous lands was typically justified by appeal to three international legal theories of territorial acquisition – occupation, conquest, and cession – acquisition of less tangible indigenous resources – cultural, intellectual, and genetic – is now widely legitimated by appeal to intellectual property laws.

Intellectual property policies are justified in the U.S. Constitution on utilitarian grounds as a means "to promote the progress of science and useful arts."[3] Yet the lack of evidential support for the claim that patents and copyrights indeed effectively promote these ends has been

1 Chidi Oguamanam, "Localizing Intellectual Property in the Globalization Epoch: The Integration of Indigenous Knowledge," *Indiana Journal of Global Legal Studies*, 11:2 (2004): 165.

2 Alan Hunt, "Foucault's Expulsion of Law: Toward a Retrieval," *Law and Social Inquiry*, 1 (1992): 21.

3 *U.S. Constitution*, Art. 1, Sec. 8, Cl. 8.

noted.[4] In its place, one is generally offered appeals to "faith" that they are doing so, for instance: "Faith in the private sector's ability to produce beneficial innovations is strong at the moment."[5] Intellectual property laws have been a particularly effective strategy for acquiring, commodifying, and rendering profitable intangible indigenous resources, such as artistic expressions and medicinal and spiritual knowledge. Current copyright laws, for example, support and facilitate the practice of cultural imperialism by consigning traditional music to the public domain, then providing for its facile "conversion" to private property. The appropriation by American artists and record companies of calypso music is a case in point. Millions of dollars have been made from a single song without any of this being returned to the communities of its origin.[6]

Patent law enables a similar practice in the case of genetic resources. The U.S. government is currently funding numerous major industry/university consortia which have planted their bioprospecting stakes throughout the world. The concrete repercussions of divergent construals of knowledge – as commodity and as gift – are painfully apparent in Exhibit Three (Chapter 1), in the case of the Guajajara. How the law has served to advance new modalities of power, and to regulate their mode of operation, might be better appreciated by considering the origins and development of intellectual property law. I will do so briefly, focusing on copyright law.

The Origins of Copyright Law

While guilds were instrumental in shaping patent and trademark law, mercantile interests played a major role in shaping the formation of copyright law in England. In particular, publishers sought to obtain monopoly control over the production of books. This control was challenged in the late seventeenth century by writers who needed to earn their livelihood from the sale of their writing.

Copyright is popularly viewed as a law for authors and artists. It originated, however, with publishers and has long benefited entrepreneurs far

4 See Gerald Dworkin, "Commentary: Legal and Ethical Issues," *Science, Technology, & Human Values*, 12:1 (1987).

5 Pamela Samuelson, "Innovation and Competition: Conflicts over Intellectual Property Rights in New Technologies," *Science, Technology & Human Values*, 12:1 (1987).

6 Roger Wallis and Krister Malm, *Big Sounds From Small Peoples* (New York: Pendragon Press, 1984): 193.

more than creators.[7] Martha Woodmansee has described how writers transformed themselves into "authors" in the modern sense by redefining the nature of writing. She recounts how, prior to the mid-eighteenth century, writing

> was considered a mere vehicle of received ideas which were already in the public domain, and, as such a vehicle, it too, by extension or analogy, was considered part of the public domain.[8]

At its best, writing was understood to be a process of inspired craftsmanship, and writers were understood to be a vehicle or instrument, neither distinctly nor personally responsible for their creations. Understood as craftspersons, writers had to prove themselves adept at following the body of rules that had been preserved and handed down to them for manipulating traditional materials to achieve goals dictated by their audience. Understood as inspired, they were

> equally the subject of independent forces, for the more inspired moments of (their) work – that which is novel and most excellent in it – are not any more the writer's doing than are its more routine aspects, but are instead attributable to a higher, external agency – if not to a muse, then to divine dictation.[9]

The production of poetical works, Goethe notes, was "regarded as something sacred, and it was considered close to simony to accept or bargain for an honorarium."[10]

As Woodmansee argues, this view of the writer changed, and the view of writer as author emerged, as the element of craftsmanship was eliminated or discarded, and that of inspiration was emphasized. Moreover, the source of inspiration was internalized, seen as emanating from within the writer. Literary inspiration came to be regarded as a matter of "original genius,"

[7] R. Patterson and S. Lindberg, *The Nature of Copyright* (Atlanta, Georgia: University of Georgia Press, 1991). James Boyle observes that actual authors are often disadvantaged by copyright, whereas large corporate entities succeed in acquiring sweeping intellectual property rights. See his *Shamans, Software & Spleens: Law and the Construction of the Information Society* (Cambridge, Massachusetts: Harvard University Press, 1996): xiii.

[8] Martha Woodmansee, "The Genius and the Copyright," *Eighteenth-Century Studies*, 17 (1984): 434.

[9] Ibid., 427.

[10] Cited in ibid., 435.

and the inspired work came to be regarded as the peculiar and distinctive product, and property, of the writer.[11]

The struggle between publishers and writers gradually intensified. Publishers attempted to reduce books to their physical foundations: "The book is not an ideal object . . . it is a fabrication made of paper . . . a commodity produced for hard cash."[12] Authors insisted their work transcended their material foundation, yet even so constituted property. It was Fichte who provided the distinction on which subsequent copyright law would largely depend, by describing three distinct shares of property in the book:

> When the book is sold ownership of the physical object passes to the buyer . . . the material aspect, the content of the book, the thoughts it presents also pass to the buyer. To the extent that (the buyer) is able, through intellectual effort, to appropriate them, these ideas cease to be the exclusive property of the author . . . the form in which these ideas are presented, however, remains the property of the author eternally.[13]

A book thus emerged as "the intellection of a unique individual."[14] The author, far from being a vehicle of ideas, transformed them, making them the expression of an individual's own unique mind. That original expression is private intellectual property. It, and the right to any profits from it, is what the copyright protects. In his influential study of law and the information society, *Shamans, Software and Spleens*, James Boyle critiques this romantic view of authorship and the influence it has had on the commodification of information. He argues that it "blinds us to the importance of the commons – to the importance of the raw material from which information products are constructed."[15]

In one influential legal definition, "writings" are defined as "any physical rendering of the fruits of creative, intellectual or aesthetic labor."[16] Copyright law, as we have seen, developed in response to the need for writers

[11] Ibid., 427.
[12] Ibid., 443.
[13] Ibid., 444–5.
[14] Ibid., 447.
[15] James Boyle, *Shamans*, xiv. However, in an interesting article, Madhavi Sunder cautions against reifying the public domain, as it may have the unintended effect of obscuring the inventiveness of indigenous knowledge, its dynamic and innovative aspects. See Madhavi Sunder, "The Invention of Traditional Knowledge," *Law and Contemporary Problems*, 70 (2007): 100.
[16] *Goldstein v. California*, 412 U.S. 546, 93 S.Ct. 2303, 37 L.Ed.2d 163 (1973), 304.

to sell their intellectual labor, to turn it into a commodity. As a result of eighteenth-century European writers' challenge to the existing power relations, publishers no longer retained the exclusive right to sell and profit from their writings. In the future, writers would have to surrender their copyright before this could take place.

This inclusion of intellectual laborers in the marketplace required a significant conceptual transformation. Not only did the nature of writing need to be reconceived, but so did the nature of knowledge. Knowledge, or more exactly ideas, became something that no longer needed to remain in the public domain. It was able to be transformed into private property, provided that it was "original" and was fixed in some physical form. It could then be exchanged in the marketplace, as a commodity to be bought or sold. Interestingly, the originality requirement, at least in U.S. law, has received a minimalist interpretation. A work is original if it is "one man's alone";[17] any "distinguishable variation" of a prior work is enough to constitute originality, and render it private intellectual property.[18]

Innovation and Individuality

The chasm between "inspired" writing and "original" authorship is deep. As we have seen, the writer, as a vehicle or instrument, was regarded as subject to independent forces that played a crucial role in the writing process. The inspired moments of a work, no less than its more routine moments, were not the writer's sole doing. With the shift to the notion of original authorship, inspiration was internalized and the writer was relieved of responsibility to traditions preserved and passed down. Such intellectual labor sprang from the "original genius" of an individual, and hence was that individual's personal product and property.

The criterion of originality in copyright law to which this led has its counterpart in the requirement of novelty in patent law. The result was the embedding within western intellectual property law of assumptions about individuality and innovativeness that are acutely at odds with the conceptual commitments of many indigenous cultures. This embedding

[17] *Bleistein v. Donaldson Lithographing Co.* 188 U.S. 239 (1903).

[18] M. Baker, "La(w) – A Note to Follow So: Have We Forgotten the Federal Rules of Evidence in Music Plagiarism Cases?," *Southern California Law Review*, 65:3 (1992): 1590.

has directly enabled the continued expropriation of indigenous cultural and genetic resources. As Aroha Mead comments,

> I query the concept of "innovation" as defined by western intellectual property laws – particularly when no recognition or value is accorded to the customary knowledge which links a species of plant to a particular usage, and details the most appropriate harvest, portion of the plant ... and method of preparation.[19]

Indigenous knowledge and generations of indigenous labor – mental and physical – are discredited. All that is credited is the "chop-shop" labor of individual corporate and academic scientists who interject "novelty" into what they have taken.

The justificatory rhetoric embedded in the expropriation of indigenous knowledge and genetic resources is essentially the same as that invoked by those, encountered at the outset of this book, actively engaged in the marketing of indigenous spirituality. In such cases, appeals to common property, private property, and usually both in succession constitute the legitimating rationale of cultural imperialism. It enables the dominant culture to secure political and social control as well as to profit economically from the cultural and genetic resources of indigenous cultures. Just as the concept of *terra nullius* once provided legal and moral cover for the imperial powers' treatment of indigenous peoples, the concept of public domain plays a comparable role within late capitalism.

As we have seen in Chapter 1, far from being mutually exclusive, these appeals function together to facilitate a conversion, or privatization, process. When intellectual property laws of the dominant culture are imposed on indigenous peoples, the first appeal to common property, or the public domain, lays the legal groundwork for the private ownership secured by the second. What "flows out ... as the 'common heritage of mankind' ... returns as a commodity."[20] This strategy is particularly effective for acquiring desired but intangible indigenous resources – medicinal and spiritual knowledge, ceremonies, artistic expressions. Ownership of

[19] Aroha Mead, "Letter from Aroha Mead, Director, International Association of the Mataatua Declaration, to Dr. Darrell Macer, Sub-Committee on Population Genetics," UNESCO International Bioethics Committee, UNESCO-Bioethics & Human Population Research (July 29, 1995). Available online at: http://nativenet.uthscsa.edu/archive/nl/9510/0350.html.

[20] Jack Kloppenburg and Daniel Kleinman, "Seed Wars: Common Heritage, Private Property, and Political Strategy," *Socialist Review*, 95 (September/October 1987), 25.

such intangibles may in turn (as in the case of genetic information) lead to control of, and denial of indigenous access to, tangible resources. This control is not only "legal theft" of indigenous resources, it is legally sanctioned and facilitated theft. As Vandana Shiva comments, "communities have invested . . . centuries of care, respect, and knowledge" in developing such resources, yet "today, this material and knowledge heritage is being stolen under the garb of IPRs (intellectual property rights)."[21]

The payoff of imperialistic cultural practice is substantial. There is considerable economic profit to be reaped from the commodification and marketing of indigenous cultural resources. It is also politically invaluable. As the established legal system extends and enforces the practice of cultural imperialism, it brings with it its own legitimating rationale. The latter is, simply put, a way of speaking about and a way of thinking about what is going on; a rhetoric and a reasoning that plays a politically diversionary role as, at the individual level, it nurtures self-deception.[22] Ultimately, it constitutes a logic of domination – a structure of fallacious reasoning that seeks to justify subordination. The dominant conceptual framework is held to have certain features that indigenous frameworks lack, and which render it superior. Such alleged superiority, it is assumed, justifies the assimilation of those frameworks and cultures to it.[23]

This logic of domination figures vitally in biocolonialism and in cultural imperialism more generally. If strategies of resistance to it are to be effective, they must be situated within the broader social context that informs it. The extension of the commodity form to new areas is one of the principal historical processes associated with the political economy of capitalism. It provides a way of reproducing the social relations needed if capital is to

[21] Cited in Beth Burrows, "How Do You Spell Patent? P-I-R-A-C-Y?," *The Boycott Quarterly*, 1:3 (1994), 6, 5.

[22] Intellectual property policies are justified in the Constitution on utilitarian grounds as a means "to promote the progress of science and useful arts." *U.S.*, *Constitution*, Art. 1, Sec. 8, Cl. 8. However, the lack of evidence for the claim that patents and copyrights have indeed effectively promoted these ends has been noted by Dworkin, among others. (See Gerald Dworkin, "Commentary: Legal and Ethical Issues," *Science, Technology, & Human Values*, 12:1 (1987).) Appeals to "faith" that they are doing so are common. (See Pamela Samuelson, "Innovation and Competition: Conflicts over Intellectual Property Rights in New Technologies," *Science, Technology & Human Values*, 12:1 1987.)

[23] For a characterization of oppressive conceptual frameworks, and discussion of the logic of domination, see Karen Warren, "A Philosophical Perspective on the Ethics and Resolution of Cultural Properties Issues," in Phyllis Messenger (ed.), *The Ethics of Collecting Cultural Property* (Albuquerque, New Mexico: The University of New Mexico Press, 1989).

survive and grow in a particular sector.[24] The development of the notion of intellectual property, and the articulation of intellectual property laws, is a significant moment in the self-expansion of capital, another instance of "the relentless extension of market assumptions into areas where the market has not ruled."[25] We are, as Christopher Lind protests, "forced to genuflect before the great god market in yet one more area of . . . life."[26] It is also a significant move in the dynamics of power that structures dominant/indigenous relations, in the growth of cultural imperialism. It wrests away from indigenous peoples the power to control their cultural, spiritual, and genetic resources. As Jack Kloppenburg notes, "business interests in the developed nations have worked very hard over the past ten years to put in place a legal framework that ensures that genetically engineered materials . . . can be owned."[27]

Forged by and in the interests of the dominant powers, particularly the United States, intellectual property laws and western concepts of "originality" and "novelty" are thus imposed on the world through coercive instruments such as the General Agreement on Tariffs and Trade (GATT) and its provisions on Trade-Related Aspects of Intellectual Property Rights (TRIPS). The latter offers an interesting twist on an earlier expropriative colonial rationale based on coercive trade policies. English acquisition of indigenous lands was once held to be justified if the "infidels" refused to engage in trade, according to Peckham's version of the Laws of Nations.[28] According to the U.S. initiative in the GATT, if other nation-states want to engage in trade with the United States, they must adopt U.S. stipulations regarding intellectual property which are contrary to their customary practice and which enable acquisition of their genetic and cultural resources. As one critic notes, TRIPS fail to acknowledge "the more

[24] Jack Kloppenburg, *First The Seed: The Political Economy of Plant Biotechnology, 1492–2000* (Cambridge: Cambridge University Press, 1988): 11. See also Kloppenburg and Kleinman, "Seed Wars."

[25] Christopher Lind, "The Idea of Capitalism or the Capitalism of Ideas? A Moral Critique of the Copyright Act," *Intellectual Property Journal*, 7 (1991): 70.

[26] Ibid.

[27] Jack Kloppenburg, Jr., "No Hunting! Scientific Poaching and Global Biodiversity," *Z Magazine* (September 1990): 106.

[28] See Glenn Morris, "International Law and Politics," in M. Annette Jaimes (ed.), *The State of Native America: Genocide, Colonization, and Resistance* (Boston, Massachusetts: South End Press, 1992): 63.

informal, communal system of innovation through which Third World farmers produce, select, improve and breed a plethora of diverse crop varieties."[29] The U.S. government, for some time, pressured Ecuador to ratify a bilateral agreement on intellectual property rights, part of the "strategy to unilaterally push developing countries to broaden the scope of industrial patent law, even beyond the scope that was agreed in GATT."[30] It opened the door to life-form patenting, despite the fact that the Andean Pact Law on Patents forbids any patents on human genes or organs. Ecuador's refusal, in 1996, to ratify this agreement was influenced by the indignation of the Ecuadorian public when it learned that the United States held a ten-year-old patent on ayahuasca, a plant sacred to indigenous Amazonians.[31]

As for indigenous nations – which are not recognized as such by the United Nations – there is usually no pretense of "trading" involved. Intellectual property rights are "a sophisticated name for modern piracy."[32] Across the planet, at an accelerating pace, collectively owned traditional medicines and seeds are being privatized and commodified. Altered sufficiently to render them patentable, they are transformed into the "inventions" of individual scientists and corporations, and placed on sale in the genetic marketplace. The knowledge systems that produced the impressive medicinal, pharmaceutical, botanical, and agricultural achievements of indigenous peoples are dismissed as hostile to creativity and change, even as indigenous knowledge and genetic resources – carefully nurtured, developed, and preserved for centuries – are expropriated, mined as "raw materials," processed in labs and through the intellectual property system, to emerge as valuable commodities. This conjunction of western law and technoscience provides the history and context which informs indigenist critiques of the Diversity Project and other biocolonialist initiatives.

[29] See Darrell A. Posey and Graham Dutfield, *Beyond Intellectual Property: Toward Traditional Resource Rights for Indigenous Peoples and Local Communities* (Ottawa, Ontario: International Development Research Centre, 1996): 103.

[30] Susanne van de Wateringen, "USA Pushes Ecuador to Sign IPR Agreement," *Biotechnology and Development Monitor*, 33 (December 1997). Available online at: http://www.biotech-monitor.nl/3309.htm. The struggle between the United States and Ecuador continues. See "Ecuador, Columbia to have talks on FTA with US" (31 December 2005). Available online at: http://www.bilaterals.org/article.php3?id_article=3392.

[31] Ibid.

[32] Beth Burrows, "How Do You Spell Patent? P-I-R-A-C-Y?," *Boycott Quarterly*, 1 (1994): 4, 5.

The Assimilative Potential of Intellectual Property Rights

Indigenous resistance to biocolonialism faces a difficult dilemma: how to challenge a form of power – in this case, western intellectual property law – "without accepting its own terms of reference and hence losing the battle before it has begun."[33] On the one hand, unless indigenous peoples have "control over their intellectual products, their knowledge stands to be expropriated without any material benefits reaching them."[34] Arguably, one way to maintain such control is to play the legal game upon which the dominant culture insists and adopt intellectual property protection in order to thwart biopiracy. The "Isolates of Historic Interest" to Diversity Project scientists could, for example, embrace the elaborate materials transfer and database access agreements designed for them by Diversity Project proponents.

On the other hand, however, there is good reason to question both the adequacy and appropriateness of intellectual property rights as a means of protecting indigenous rights and resources. As Darrell Posey and Graham Dutfield have argued, intellectual property right protection is purely economic, whereas the interests of indigenous peoples are not just economic but political, linked to self-determination[35] and the profoundly entrenched inequalities of power and wealth that divide indigenous communities, corporations, and the governments of nation-states. To acquire and defend IPR protection is also a time- and capital-consuming process, requiring costly legal advice and information unavailable to and beyond the means of many indigenous peoples,[36] although not of the corporations or governments who would be their opposition in any legal battle. Moreover, Posey and Dutfield note, intellectual property rights have the potential to engender conflict and protracted legal battles between different indigenous communities laying claim to the same technical knowledge regarding a specific resource and its use.[37]

We have already seen that western intellectual property law is at odds with vital features of many indigenous knowledge systems – by imposing

[33] Carol Smart, *Feminism and the Power of Law* (New York, New York: Routledge, 1989): 5.
[34] Arun Agrawal, "Neither Having One's Cake, Nor Eating It: Intellectual Property Rights and 'Indigenous' Knowledges," *Common Property Resource Digest*, 30 (1995): 5.
[35] Posey and Dutfield, *Beyond Intellectual Property*, 92.
[36] Ibid., 76.
[37] Ibid., 92.

individualized concepts of originality, inventiveness, rights, and informed consent; by eroding the shared nature of much indigenous knowledge; and by converting both knowledge and life forms into commodities to be harvested, altered, packaged, and sold for personal profit. Biocolonialism's critics regard it as an assimilative process that threatens to transform indigenous knowledge and value systems, as well as the natural world itself, in unwelcome and lasting ways. The adoption of western intellectual property rights to resist biocolonialism is ultimately to be transformed by the same unwanted western values, concepts, and practices: "Protecting traditional knowledge with Western IP is possible at the price of forced epistemological assimilation of the former."[38]

Biocolonialism endangers the knowledge, resources, and labor of generations of indigenous peoples. The price of preventing this, by playing along with the dominant society and adopting the protection of intellectual property law, is ultimately assimilation – transformation by the values and practices of that society: "We cannot buy the arguments that we have to play within the field of existing patent and copyright laws to be able to protect our resources and knowledge."[39] Yet the other horn of this dilemma is that "without control over their intellectual products, their knowledge stands to be expropriated without any material benefits reaching them."[40]

Meanwhile, indigenous knowledge systems are condemned (when their existence is acknowledged) as closed, changeless, stultifying, and stifling of originality. Such characterizations not only ignore the massive contributions of indigenous peoples – especially medicinal, pharmaceutical, botanical, and agricultural – they also egregiously distort indigenous knowledge systems themselves. If indigenous knowledge systems did not foster agricultural innovation or plant-breeding "originality" (to cite but one instance), the rich diversity of the geneplasm currently held in seed banks and field gene banks would be wholly inexplicable.

Within most indigenous knowledge systems, the source of originality is not internalized as the genius of one individual. Rather, the natural world, the community, and the individual are all integrally involved. Individuals are subject to independent forces and constrained by the need to act with respect for the natural world and for future generations. The community

[38] Chidi Oguamanam, "Localizing Intellectual Property," 168–9.
[39] Tauli-Corpuz, "We Are Part of Biodiversity," 26.
[40] Agrawal, "Neither Having One's Cake," 4.

grounds and informs the individual. However, because the process of knowing is experientially based, and what one learns depends on individual development, abilities, and preparation, individuals play an essential role in contributing new knowledge to the community. As one young Keres man explains: "You don't ask questions when you grow up. You watch and listen and wait, and the answer will come to you. It's *yours* then, not like learning in school."[41]

Such an approach to innovation requires receptivity, reciprocity, and responsibility to the natural and human worlds in which one is situated. It is the result of conducting oneself in, and of relating to, the natural and human worlds in accordance with that normative constraint. This relationship is evident in the Andean practice of conversing with the natural world which is central to their agricultural science. Such dialogue leads one "to emphasize and attune oneself with (the other's) mode of being, and in company with that other, to generate and regenerate life."[42] It is manifested in their effort to increase the diversity of their cultivated plants by "testing" new varieties. The cultivator does this

> without obligating the new seed "to get accustomed by force." It is accepted for a seed that does not "accustom" itself to move away . . . the (cultivator) says simply: "this seed does not get used to me . . . " . . . and continues "testing" others "to see if they follow him or her."[43]

The new knowledge that results from such conversing is a gift. To paraphrase an earlier comment: When gifts are given, the continuity of social relationships (and, we should add, of relationships with the natural world) has the effect that the gift given always remains the givers'. It is inalienable.

[41] Larry Bird, cited in Terry Tafoya, "Coyote's Eyes: Native Cognition Styles," *Journal of American Indian Education* (February 1982): 24. The other side of this is nicely captured by Thomas Buckley: "To explain too much is to steal that person's opportunity to learn." Cited in D. Dooling and P. Jordan-Smith (eds.), *I Become Part of It* (San Francisco, California: Harper, 1989): 39.

[42] Grimaldo Rengifo Vasquez, cited in Frédérique Apffel-Marglin, "Development or Decolonization in the Andes?," in Frédérique Apffel-Marglin and Julio Valladolid Rivera, *Regeneration in the Andes* (St. Urbain, Montréal, Québec: Intercultural Institute of Montréal, 1995): 13. Rengifo Vasquez is the coordinator of PRATEC, a nongovernmental organization formed in 1987 which researches Andean science, technology, and philosophy. This remarkable group has developed an accredited university course which critiques the contemporary western knowledge system from an Andean perspective. For more on this see ibid.

[43] Ibid., 33.

Altering Communal Relationships

The decision to treat life forms, and knowledge or information, as if they were "transactions and products" has far-reaching consequences.[44] The manner in which the introduction of an intellectual property system alters communal relationships provides additional grounds for opposing bio-colonialism. Legal theorists have begun to examine the potential political, economic, and social effects of the expansion of the proprietary control over information. Shelley Wright contends that designating something as private property and a valuable commodity involves a decision about how human relationships are recognized and regulated by law. How the law characterizes information has implications for how people are perceived to, and do, interact. When relationships are characterized in terms of property, and information is regarded as a product, "Human interaction becomes closed, exclusionary, coerced and hierarchical . . . Other human actors are seen as either potential trespassers or potentially useful partners to relationships that are largely seen as forms of transaction or exchange."[45]

> To treat human relationships as constituting property is to regard individuals as atomized entities, whose communicative and relational connection is determined by power, i.e., competition over control, or . . . rights . . . Property is about control . . . control over other human beings through categorization and exclusion . . . and control over the World.[46]

The exclusionary nature of property rights was emphasized by Blackstone himself, in the Commentaries, where he grounds English law on the right to property: "that sole and despotic dominion which one man claims and exercises . . . in total exclusion of the right of any other individual in the universe."[47] It is because property rights are exclusionary that they can be characterized as "private"; the public domain is whatever remains after private rights are exhausted. Wright observes that, although patents require that the protected information be made public in the sense of

[44] Shelley Wright, "Property, Information and the Ethics of Communication," *Intellectual Property Journal*, 9 (1994): 49.
[45] Ibid., 51, 59.
[46] Ibid., 51, 64.
[47] Sir William Blackstone, 1 *Commentaries on the Laws of England: Of the Rights of Things* (1st edition, Oxford, 1765).

being accessible, use of that information remains the private right of the patent holder or licensee. As a commodity, information is treated "as if it were an object that can be separated and dealt with quite apart from the relationships within which it is created."[48] The public/private distinction becomes "a polarized division in which relationships are juxtaposed and granted legal attributes that fix them within regimes of power, rights and obligations . . . It is always an ideological structure, even where it has real effects."[49]

The way the ideological distinction between private rights and the public domain is invoked in biocolonialism illustrates its effectiveness as a process of imperialism. We saw earlier how, just as the concept of *terra nullius* at one time provided legal and moral cover for the imperial powers' treatment of indigenous peoples, the concept of public domain plays a comparable role in late capitalism. Declaring that the land belonged to no one prepared the way for its conversion into private property. Similarly, maintaining that the intellectual, cultural, and genetic resources are in the public domain, that they belong to everyone as part of the common heritage, now prepares the way equally effectively for their conversion into private property. The notions of property that belongs to no one and of property that belongs to everyone are functionally similar, as we argued earlier, enabling a conversion process which leads to the privatization of property.

Wright's discussion is particularly valuable for what it suggests about the aftermath of this process. Because exploitation rights are temporally limited for both copyrights and patents, at some point the protected property ceases to be private and falls into the public domain. When this happens, the information contained, for example, in a patent specification, may be used by anyone. However, Wright contends, this does not guarantee subsequent free and equal competition in the marketplace as the ideological justification for intellectual property would have it. The original patent holder will still benefit from the "private rights of property within which the information was in fact created and used."[50]

> [These] will still govern its continuing existence even after the rights themselves come to an end. The effect of the continuing influence

[48] Wright, "Property, Information," 50.
[49] Ibid., 52, 64.
[50] Ibid., 57.

> of property rights is to exclude those who cannot replicate or create an adequate context of relationships in which the information can be used and exploited.[51]

Thus, Wright explains, although the patent holder's exclusive use monopoly may end with the expiration of the patent, the benefits secured by it are not immediately severed. They continue to accrue to the patent holder or to anyone else able to reproduce a relational setting conducive to use of the information. Information cannot readily be divorced from the context of the relationships in which it was created. If information is the product of private rights, as western intellectual property law maintains, it will carry its history with it when rights to its use pass from the individual patent holder to everyone as it enters the public domain. What Wright emphasizes is how this alters the nature of the public domain. When information is construed in terms of private proprietary rights, it limits our understanding of the public domain

> to a diminishing zone of undefined space, in which information can never be free because it has been created as a product of private rights. What remains of the public domain cannot be visualized as a single unitary entity: rather it is seen as fragmented into overlapping concepts of expression, accessibility, and exploitation. The public realm . . . is riven and distorted by the shadows of pre-existing private rights of property.[52]

These types of consideration reinforce the need for indigenous communities to continue their efforts to develop alternatives to the intellectual property rights which have been formulated to advance the interests of high-tech corporations and the initiatives of western science.[53] With such a great deal at stake, arguably with everything at stake, a growing number of alternatives are currently being investigated.[54] First, community intellectual property rights are being proposed to replace individualized western intellectual property rights. Criteria for such communal rights have been

[51] Ibid., 57–8.

[52] Ibid., 58–9.

[53] Graham Dutfield provides a useful summary of additional reasons why patents are poor choice as a means of protecting indigenous knowledge. See his *Intellectual Property, Biogenetic Resources and Traditional Knowledge* (Sterling, Virginia: Earthscan, 2004): 104–5.

[54] A more extended consideration of these can be found in Posey and Dutfield, *Beyond Intellectual Property*. It offers a comprehensive overview of the varied, complex issues raised for indigenous communities by western intellectual property rights, to which my discussion is indebted.

developed. Because future generations are unable "to consent to transactions that threaten their existence as a group,"[55] some of these require recognition of the inalienability of cultural property.

Second, a Model Community Intellectual Rights Act ("MCIRA") has been drafted. The concept of community intellectual rights moves away from the concept of property which is problematic for many indigenous peoples and focuses on preventing the "privatization and usurpation of community rights and knowledge through existing definitions of innovations."[56] The act recognizes indigenous peoples as innovators because their knowledge is unknown to the outside world. One possibility is a community register, which allows people to document all known plant and animal species with details of their uses and to determine the conditions of access, if any, to this information. Such a register may also be of value in supporting land claims because it provides evidence of intimate knowledge of the local environment. Third, model provisions have also been proposed by the United Nations Educational, Scientific and Cultural Organization (UNESCO) and the World Intellectual Property Organization for extending conventional copyright so that intangible expressions, as well as fixed works, are protected. Arguably, these could include traditional genetic resources.

An additional development, which recognizes the importance of political as well as economic considerations, is the emerging concept of traditional resource rights. This is an integrated rights concept which articulates the many "bundles of rights" that can be used for protection, compensation, and conservation and that may form the basis for a *sui generis* system. These include intellectual property rights, but also included are major legally binding international agreements (the Convention on Biological Diversity; the International Covenant on Economic, Social and Cultural Rights; the International Covenant on Civil and Political Rights; etc.) as well as various soft law instruments and mechanisms (such as the Universal Declaration of Human Rights, the United Nations Economic and Social Council, and the Working Group on Indigenous Populations, Agenda 21, and the Rio Declaration). The concept of traditional resource rights emphasizes that control over knowledge and biogenetic resources is

[55] James Odek, "Bio-Piracy: Creating Proprietary Rights in Plant Genetic Resources," *Journal of Intellectual Property Law*, 2 (1994): 177.

[56] Posey and Dutfield, *Beyond Intellectual Property*, 98.

central in indigenous struggles for self-determination and covers a very broad range of rights.[57]

However, there are at least two problems with such an approach. The Four Directions Council, a Canadian-based indigenous peoples organization, contends that no single international *sui generis* model can be imposed on all, given the wide variation in indigenous jurisprudential systems:

> Indigenous peoples possess their own locally-specific systems of jurisprudence with respect to the classification of different types of knowledge, proper procedures for acquiring and sharing knowledge, and the rights and responsibilities which attach to possessing knowledge, all of which are embedded uniquely in each culture and its language . . . Any attempt to devise uniform guidelines for the recognition and protection of indigenous peoples' knowledge runs the risk of collapsing this rich jurisprudential diversity into a single "model" that will not fit the values, conceptions or laws of any indigenous society.[58]

Also, traditional resource rights clearly embrace and reflect a western conception of rights, a fact which may render them problematic for various indigenous nations. Addressing the protection of indigenous cultural property, United Nations Special Rapporteur Erica-Irene Daes comments that "possessing a song, story or medicinal knowledge carries with it certain responsibilities to show respect to and maintain a reciprocal relationship with the human beings, animals, plants and places with which the song, story or medicine is connected."[59] Consequently, it may be more appropriate to speak in terms of "a bundle of relationships, rather than a bundle of economic rights."[60] Despite this, there are strong convictions, if not a consensus, about the value and efficacy of human rights discourse as an essential tool in the struggles of historically oppressed peoples.[61] Central

57 Ibid., 99–100.

58 Cited in Dutfield, *Intellectual Property*, 123–4.

59 U.N. Commission on Human Rights (UNCHR), Sub-Commission on Prevention of Discrimination and Protection of Minorities, *Study on the Protection of the Cultural and Intellectual Property of Indigenous Peoples*, P 26, U.N. Doc. E/CN.4/Sub.2/1993/28 (July 28, 1993) (prepared by Erica-Irene Daes).

60 Ibid. Similarly, David Alexis asserts that "Indian people do not think in terms of rights but in terms of responsibility." See his "Obscurity as a Lifestyle," *Borderlines*, 23 (1991–1992): 15.

61 See Robert A. Williams, "Encounters on the Frontiers of International Human Rights Law: Redefining the Terms of Indigenous Peoples' Survival in the World," *Duke Law Journal* (1990).

among these are calls for the recognition of group rights in intangible property.[62]

Finally, we should note the development, by the Indigenous Peoples Council on Biocolonialism, of a model ordinance to assist in the protection against unauthorized research – particularly as regards genetic resources and indigenous knowledge. The Indigenous Research Protection Act recognizes the tribe's "inherent sovereign right to be the exclusive owner of its own cultural property"[63] and to maintain control over its resources. A comprehensive document, it nevertheless is a flexible one, leaving many of the difficult decisions open to be settled by individual tribes, including the matter of intellectual property rights and benefit-sharing arrangements. Debra Harry and Le'a Malia Kanehe offer this warning about unanticipated impacts from the latter, which bears on the issues raised in Chapter 2 regarding indigenous peoples' responsibilities for how their knowledge is used:

> once IPR protection expires, the protected subject matter goes into the public domain. Once released into the public domain, the Indigenous knowledge is no longer considered tribal property, and consequently, the tribe loses the ability to control its use because it is considered public knowledge. The net result is a permanent alienation of tribally held knowledge and/or resources.[64]

A similar caveat has been extended by Cori Hayden, who observes that benefit-sharing provisions "only make more explicit the historically entrenched gaps in power of the actors involved," exacerbating existing inequalities.[65]

Conclusion

What intellectual property law offers biocolonialism is validation, the legitimating rationale that is needed to make plausible, palatable, and respectable the acquisition by a dominant power of indigenous genetic

[62] See, for example, Angela R. Riley, "Recovering Collectivity: Group Rights to Collectivity in Indigenous Communities," *Cardozo Arts & Entertainment Law Journal*, 18 (2000).

[63] Debra Harry and Le'a Malia Kanehe "Indigenous Land and Property Rights: Asserting Sovereignty over Cultural Property: Moving Towards Protection of Genetic Material and Indigenous Knowledge," *Seattle Journal of Social Justice*, 5 (2006): 48.

[64] Ibid., 52.

[65] Cori Hayden, *When Nature Goes Public: The Making and Unmaking of Bioprospecting in Mexico* (Princeton, New Jersey: Princeton University Press, 2003): 4.

resources. Law has a long history of meeting such ideological needs, providing a veneer of justification for existing power relations and legitimating practices that conform to, support, and preserve the status quo.[66] A conservative bias is built into law "by rule of law doctrines such as the observance of precedent and faithfulness to the intentions and practices of the past."[67] It is reflected as well in legal education, where

> Law is studied to strengthen, not challenge, it . . . and questions of coercion and control are seldom considered . . . The terms of legal discourse are taken for granted.[68]

Law, legal discourse, and legal institutions are part of the process of legitimization and social conflict management invoked by a dominant elite. As radical theorists have argued, the modern capitalist nation-state "needs to validate itself ethically, not just to the ruling elites but to society as a whole."[69] To successfully maintain power, the interests of the elites must be "conceived of and presented, as being the motor force of a universal expression, of a development of all 'national energies.' "[70] Although legitimating domination is one vital function of law within dominant nation-states, law also functions as a political–economic institution the mandate of which is the management of political and economic struggles:

> Law interprets and resolves social conflicts and relationships, mediates the potentially disruptive tensions in economic substructures and issues authoritative proclamations which purport to be the product of an objective, neutral process.[71]

66 Raymond Belliotti describes the processes of purification and internalization that are involved:

> The dominant ideology is filtered through a series of legal surrogates, purified of direct contamination by the ruling class, sanctified as the outcome of eminently fair procedures, and solidified as part of society's core commonsense normative beliefs . . . citizens further internalize the decrees of law, and come to accept these judgments as their own . . . and are thereby less likely to vent the rage necessary for meaningful social transformation.

Raymond Belliotti, "The Legacy of Marxist Jurisprudence," in David Caudill and Steven Jay Gold (eds.), *Radical Philosophy of Law: Contemporary Challenges to Mainstream Legal Theory and Practice* (Amherst, New York: Humanity Books, 1995): 14.

67 Ibid.

68 Carl Swidorski, "Constituting the Modern State," in Caudill and Gold, *Radical Philosophy*, 164.

69 Ibid., 163.

70 Antonio Gramsci, in Quintin Hoare and Geoffrey Nowell Smith (eds. and trans.), *Selections from the Prison Notebooks of Antonio Gramsci* (London, England: Lawrence & Wishart, 1971): 182.

71 Belliotti, "The Legacy of Marxist Jurisprudence," 14.

Its suitability to fulfill this mandate turns on its alleged ability to transcend such struggles, to act upon them from the outside: "Law sets itself outside the social order, as if through the application of legal method and rigour, it becomes a thing apart which can in turn reflect upon the world from which it is divorced."[72]

The legal method relies, no less than does scientific method, on value-neutrality and value-bifurcation to deflect moral and political critique. Just as the latter engages in boundary-work to establish its authority and exclude values from its domain, so – as Mary Jane Mossman argues – does the former engage in boundary definition, designating certain matters as political or moral, and hence outside the realm of law.[73] The delineation of boundaries confers neutrality on the law. It is the purview of judges and lawyers to interpret the law, not to make judgments about moral or political issues which lie outside the law. In this way they are able to "assert a terrain within which legal method is entirely appropriate" while appearing to avoid "subjective areas like moral evaluations, or political bias."[74] This rhetorical stipulation enables law, like science, to present itself as "a force of linear progress, a beacon to lead us out of darkness."[75] Meanwhile, it conceals what Carol Smart calls law's juridogenic potential – its capacity for generating harm and creating wrongs as the consequence of its operation. The result is that political and economic struggles such as those being waged in resistance to biocolonialism are "subsumed in a discourse about legality instead of morality," and politics is "reduced to the maneuverings of lawyers and judges."[76] The latter is well demonstrated by the development of elaborate materials transfer and database access agreements in response to critiques of the Diversity Project that called for a political reordering of priorities, including recognition of indigenous rights to self-determination and a more socially just allocation of scarce resources.

Let us be clear about what is being critiqued. It is not the concepts of public domain or common heritage, nor even that of private property, per se. It is a particular set of social and power relations – specifically, the dynamic of oppression and domination mediating western and indigenous

[72] Smart, *Feminism and the Power of Law*, 11.
[73] Cited in Smart, *Feminism and the Power of Law*, 22.
[74] Ibid.
[75] Ibid., 12.
[76] Swidorski, "Constituting the Modern State," 164.

cultures that sustains the practice of cultural imperialism. As outlined here, that practice is one wherein elements of the dominant culture's conceptual framework – notably, its concepts of ownership and property – are thrust upon indigenous cultures and enforced by the power of the state. These concepts tend to dictate the terms of the struggle, to reinforce current relations of power, and to sustain existing inequities between dominant and indigenous cultures. Resistance to this practice is pronounced, adamant, and growing. Although indigenous representatives to the Commission on Sustainable Development acknowledged that many of the cultural and genetic resources of indigenous cultures can be shared with the rest of the world, they were resolute that

> we will be the ones who will determine how these will be shared based on our own conditions and our own terms... Is there a way of preserving and promoting biodiversity and indigenous peoples' knowledge and technology without necessarily being pushed into the field of intellectual property rights? We are still seeking for the answers to this.[77]

The task is as daunting as it is vital. Law professor Morton Horwitz has documented how, during the post–Revolutionary War period, merchant and entrepreneurial groups rose to political and economic power, forging an alliance with the legal profession to advance their own interests through a transformation of the legal system. By the mid-nineteenth century, they had succeeded in reshaping the legal system to their own advantage, and at the expense of other less powerful groups in society.[78] A comparable phenomenon appears to be currently in process at the international level. Through coercive instruments such as the GATT, the United States and leading industrial nations have succeeded in furthering their interests at the expense of indigenous peoples and developing nations by strengthening western intellectual property systems worldwide. All of this demonstrates the degree to which law, as various critical legal theorists have insisted,[79] is a form of politics. The politics of property and ownership that we have seen played out in various examples in previous chapters, is ample testimony

77 Tauli-Corpuz, "We Are Part of Biodiversity," 26.

78 Morton Horwitz, *The Transformation of American Law, 1780–1860* (Cambridge, Massachusetts: Harvard University Press, 1977).

79 See Joseph William Singer, "Legal Realism," *California Law Review*, 76 (1988).

to the fact that, when it comes to dominant/indigenous relations, law has never been separate from politics. Whether as appeals to *terra nullius* or to the public domain, legal theories of acquisition have, since contact, provided the legitimating rationale for territorial and cultural imperialism, and for the privatization of indigenous land and resources. A first step in undermining this process (although it is no more than that) may be to set to rest the fractured fairytale of a neutral, apolitical legal system.

8

Transforming Sovereignties

Sovereignty carries the horrible stench of colonialism. It is incomplete, inaccurate and troubled. But it has also been rearticulated to mean altogether different things by indigenous peoples. In its link to concepts of self-determination and self-government, it insists on the recognition of inherent rights to the respect for political affiliations that are historical and located and for the unique cultural identities that continue to find meaning in those histories and relations.

– Joanne Barker[1]

Law, as we have seen, can provide a means of resistance to oppression as well as serve as an instrument of oppression. Indigenists are drawing upon a variety of legal systems and instruments to block the continuation of extractive biocolonialism. They are also working to create legal concepts more reflective of diversity and more responsible in the face of it. The biocolonialism which indigenous peoples are currently experiencing cannot continue without the assistance and support, and often the active collusion, of both surrounding and distant states, the coercive power of which buttresses and overlaps that of transnational corporations. A significant part of the legitimating rhetoric of biocolonialism appeals to a particular understanding of sovereignty, one currently being challenged by a wide array of contemporary critics, including indigenists, who are also shaping alternatives to it. Because the hope of ending biocolonialist practices rests in part upon our ability to move past these oppressive but

[1] Joanne Barker, "For Whom Sovereignty Matters," in Joanne Barker (ed.), *Sovereignty Matters: Locations of Contestation and Possibility in Indigenous Struggles for Self-Determination* (Lincoln, Nebraska: University of Nebraska Press, 2005): 26.

well-entrenched understandings of sovereign power, such efforts to transform the concept and practice of sovereignty has considerable import for our topic.

As we have already seen at various points throughout this book, indigenous peoples have regarded the preservation of indigenous knowledge systems and genetic resources as vitally linked to self-determination and self-governance. This view is reflected in international documents. According to the United Nations Economic and Social Council Commission on human rights, "the protection of cultural and intellectual property is connected fundamentally with the realization of the territorial rights and self-determination of indigenous peoples."[2] It is also demonstrated by the way indigenous peoples involved in drafting the Declaration on the Rights of Indigenous Peoples chose to represent those rights

> as indivisible and interdependent aspects of their identities as sovereigns. Human rights for indigenous peoples, in other words, became translated to mean rights to a self-determination that was indelibly linked to sovereignty. So strong is this conceptualization that it is now virtually impossible to talk about what sovereignty means for indigenous peoples without invoking self-determination.[3]

Biocolonialism is a political act, and so is indigenous resistance to it. It was this recognition and acknowledgement of their political status that indigenous peoples kept insisting upon in the debate over the Human Genome Diversity Project, and that Luca Cavalli-Sforza, Henry Greely, and other Project proponents kept missing. The latter could see only populations to be sampled and preserved rather than peoples who needed first of all to be consulted, negotiated with, and respected as legitimate self-determining political entities who would (or would not) authorize whatever scientific research was to be done.[4] As Rosemary Coombe has noted, "Assertions of indigenous intellectual and cultural property have indeed been made, but they have been made secondary to and inherent

[2] United Nations Educational, Scientific and Cultural Organization (UNESCO), Report of the Sub-Commission on Prevention of Discrimination and Protection of Minorities, 45th Sess., U.N. Doc. E/CN.4/Sub.2/1993/28 (1993).

[3] Joanne Barker, "For Whom Sovereignty Matters," in Barker, *Sovereignty Matters*, 19–20.

[4] For an illuminating discussion of the populations/peoples divide in the HGDP see Joanne Barker, "The Human Genome Diversity Project," *Cultural Studies*. 18:4 (2004).

components of aboriginal title and self-determination which recognizes the primacy of indigenous territoriality."[5]

Two Strands of Sovereignty Research

When political and legal theorists grope wildly for metaphors, something strange is afoot. And metaphors for sovereignty have been flying thick, and frantically, of late; metaphors that clash and conflict with one another. Sovereignty, it is said, is crumbling, pooling, maturing, diffusing, leaking, evaporating, eroding, shifting, and diminishing.[6] It is fuzzy, misty, and obsolete. It is "a mistake built upon mistakes, which has barnacled an unfortunate mythology."[7] It is a shibboleth and a dead duck. Some will not let the word pass their lips, referring to it as "That 'S' word," whose "birth is illegitimate and [which] has not aged well."[8] Others reach for the literary, calling it "the Banquo's ghost of the academic feast – rattling the soothsayers by reappearing at inconvenient intervals just when many assumed its final departure was at hand."[9] Others have simply sat in frustration and asked whether it is "the word we wish to throw out, or the concept, or the implications of the concept or the word?"[10] To say that the concept of sovereignty is currently contested and in flux is to understate the obvious.

Our foray into this conceptual turmoil begins with a brief sketch of the concept of absolute, or Westphalian, state sovereignty that has dominated the international system for well over three centuries, together with some of the developments that are prompting its current transformation. Two different strands of research that are contributing to this transformation from very different perspectives will then be examined. For all their distinctiveness, they converge at several points in interesting and surprising

[5] Rosemary J. Coombe, "Works in Progress: Traditional Knowledge, Biological Diversity and Intellectual Property in a Neoliberal Era," in Richard W. Perry and Bill Maurer (eds.), *Globalization under Construction: Governmentality, Law and Identity* (Minneapolis, Minnesota: University of Minnesota Press, 2003): 302.

[6] See, for example, Michael R. Fowler and Julie M. Bunck, *Law, Power and the Sovereign State* (University Park: Pennsylvania State University Press, 1995): 1–3.

[7] Louis Henkin, "Human Rights and State 'Sovereignty,'" *Georgia Journal of International and Comparative Law*, 25 (1995): 31.

[8] Louis Henkin, "That 'S' Word: Sovereignty, Globalization and Human Rights, et cetera," *Fordham Law Review*, 68:1 (1999): 1.

[9] Fowler and Bunck, *Law, Power and the Sovereign State*, 3.

[10] Charles Merriam, cited in Fowler and Bunck, *Law, Power and the Sovereign State*, 3.

ways. A variety of theorists from diverse disciplines have contributed to the first strand of research that focuses on state sovereignty and seeks either to displace absolute sovereignty with some alternative, such as relational sovereignty or thin state sovereignty, or to do away with a state system and with sovereignty entirely.

The second strand of research, on indigenous sovereignty, will be of particular interest in light of the issues raised in previous chapters. Indigenous scholars and activists on both sides of the Canadian/U.S. border have been preoccupied for some time with the critique of the tribal sovereignty doctrine embedded within U.S. Federal Indian law, as well as, more recently, with the prospects of an emergent sovereignty that have been opened up by the Canadian Constitution Act. Frustration has nearly always attended such efforts, and increasingly, there have been calls for a reappraisal of them. As Wallace Coffey and Rebecca Tsosie observe, instead of turning to external definitions of what sovereignty means,

> it is important to construct this tool from *within* our Native societies... Too often, we as Indian people are forced to litigate our rights within the dominant society's appraisal of tribal sovereignty. We cite the Marshall Trilogy as if the concept of "domestic dependent nation" really means something in terms of our legal rights. In fact, we see cases like *Oliphant*, *Montana*, and *Strate* as wrong because they ignore the tribal sovereignty doctrine set forth in the Marshall Trilogy!... To the extent that we litigate our right to sovereignty within this legal framework, we have lost the true essence of our sovereignty.[11]

Part of the reason for this last is that the history of sovereignty is deeply implicated in the colonial project. Not only did it become identified "with a specific [European] set of cultural practices to the exclusion of others"[12] but, as various scholars have argued, in order to acquire sovereignty, the non-European world had to be absorbed into, assimilated by, Europe. No other viable conceptions of sovereignty were recognized by the positivist jurisprudence of the time, and so the denial of indigenous sovereignty

[11] Wallace Coffey and Rebecca Tsosie, "Rethinking the Tribal Sovereignty Doctrine: Cultural Sovereignty and the Collective Future of Indian Nations," *Stanford Law and Policy Review*, 12 (2001): 191, 196.

[12] Anthony Anghie, "Finding the Peripheries: Sovereignty and Colonialism in Nineteenth Century International Law," *Harvard International Law Journal*, 40 (1999): 5.

became an integral part of the process of imperialism. By reaching within the rich traditions of indigenous governance beliefs and practices, this second strand of research contributes to the development of a very different story about sovereignty, one that no longer "implies a set of values and objectives that put it in direct opposition to the values and objectives found in most traditional indigenous philosophies,"[13] one that suggests (if we are not to abandon the word, or concept entirely) the need to speak less of state sovereignty and more in terms of multiple sovereignties enjoyed by numerous nonstate as well as state actors where relationality and responsibility have displaced delusions of absolute immunity. These accounts of indigenous sovereignty hold great promise for facilitating indigenous participation in international governance and thereby enabling the struggles of indigenous peoples globally to protect their lands and resources from the powerful and varied forces that continue to encroach upon them.

The Crises of State-Sovereignty

State sovereignty is a concept the historical contingency of which it seems particularly easy to forget. However, the world in which it came to be was one characterized by "diffuse power relations . . . not rulers with exclusive powers . . . rulers encapsulated by well-defined territorial boundaries, capabilities and functions as we now know them."[14] Those concerned to make the case for leaving a purely state-centered view of sovereignty behind, and for embracing more complex constitutional arrangements, often point out that the historical image of the nation-state "has been transformed, from an *empirical fact* that shaped life in Europe from the Thirty Years War onward, into a *metaphysical entity* with its own soul and volition which is taken for granted as the prime actor in political discourse."[15] They point to a European Union characterized by coexisting, overlapping power centers, the members of which have agreed to act together instead of alone in certain areas, as evidence of and hope for actually transcending the sovereign state rather than reproducing it at a new level as some kind of superstate.[16] So we

[13] Taiake Alfred, *Peace, Power, Righteousness: An Indigenous Manifesto* (Don Mills, Ontario: Oxford University Press, 1999): 57.

[14] Konrad Schiemann, "Europe and the Loss of Sovereignty," *International and Comparative Law Quarterly*, 56 (2007): 477.

[15] Ibid.

[16] Ibid., 487.

might begin by underscoring sovereignty's contingency; it emerged within a particular historical context and, metaphysical aura notwithstanding, is capable of disappearing into another.

For most of its history, the story of sovereignty has emphasized borders, idealized as hard and fast bright-lines, given to clarity and distinctness. This has been, for the most part, a western story, rooted in two complementary mid-seventeenth-century texts: the 1648 *Treaty of Westphalia* and the 1651 *Leviathan* of Thomas Hobbes. It ascribed to nation-states what is most often described as absolute sovereignty, sometimes as territorial or Westphalian sovereignty, sometimes as thick sovereignty or statism. Diverse accounts of such sovereignty generally agree that internally, or domestically, the power and authority of the sovereign is absolute, final, and incontestable. Sovereign states are held to enjoy exclusive control over those inside their borders and to be wholly self-determining entities with unqualified rights of nonintervention and noninterference: "No state or group of states has the right to interfere directly or indirectly, for any reason whatever, in the internal or external affairs of any other state."[17] The notion of sovereign immunity – from law, from scrutiny, from justice – is central to this account. Indeed, according to the Hobbesian conception of sovereignty, no moral law binds the sovereign, so it is impossible for the sovereign to treat subjects unjustly. The sovereign has the right to lay down any laws that can be enforced, and such laws cannot be unjust: "The law is made by the sovereign power, and all that is done by such power is warranted."[18] Such sovereignty is also monolithic. It cannot be shared or divided: "Sovereignty is one and indivisible, inalienable and imprescriptible."[19]

As various state systems developed, the concept of sovereignty began to encompass not just the nature of power and authority within a state, but its political independence from other states. Externally, or internationally, sovereignty is constituted by separation, by bounding one entity off from another. Sovereignty in the relations among states signified independence,

[17] The only exception is for humanitarian intervention in the case of a severe violation of human rights. UN General Assembly, "Declaration on Principles of International Law," (October 24, 1970), Available online at: http://www.un.org/documents/ga/res/25/ares25.htm.

[18] Thomas Hobbes, *Leviathan*, 2nd ed., (original publication: London: Printed for Andrew Crooke at the Green Dragon in St. Paul's Church-yard, 1651), (New York: Washington Square Press, 1969): 250.

[19] 1791 *French Constitution* (Paris), adopted by the French National Constituent Assembly (September 1791), Article 3.

that is, the right of a state to exercise within its borders, "to the exclusion of any other state, the functions of a state."[20] A state that is sovereign in this sense is not accountable to any outside authority and has no inherent responsibilities to any entity beyond its territory save for those it may voluntarily assume. Absolute sovereignty, as one commentator observes, "renders international relations anarchical, for it makes states wholly autonomous; they are not required to yield or genuflect to any outside authority."[21] The difficulties that this view of sovereignty generated for international legal theory would be exacerbated by the rise of positivism in the late eighteenth and nineteenth centuries, a period which saw "the steady rise of the national state and its increasingly absolute claims to legal and political supremacy."[22] The central problem preoccupying international legal theorists quickly became the problem of order: How, in the absence of a global sovereign, can order among states whose sovereignty is thus conceived be established, justified, and maintained?

The narrative of absolute state sovereignty became widespread and well entrenched over the next 300 years, from the rise of the modern nation-state in 1648 through World War II. This meant, in Louis Henkin's words, that "until 1945 . . . how a state treated its own inhabitants was not a subject of international concern . . . (it) was nobody else's business. That was Hitler" he continues: "The world stood by, and had nothing to say about it. International law said nothing about it. What went on behind territorial frontiers was cloaked by an iron curtain of sovereignty."[23]

Unfortunately, such a view of state sovereignty remains very much in play today. The cloaking effect of absolute sovereignty makes it a powerful rhetorical tool. Far from being a dry expression of legal status, appeals to sovereignty are typically crucial diplomatic moves, taken by politicians intent on expressing and justifying foreign as well as domestic policies. The United States is especially, if selectively, attached to it. Former Attorney General John Ashcroft's frequent invocation of American sovereignty is a case in point. When asked about likely international protest to a pending

20 See the opinion of Arbitrator Max Huber, Island of Palmas Case (*U.S. v Netherlands*), 2 R.I.A.A. 829, 838 (Judge Anzilotti), 1928.

21 Daniel Philpott, "Sovereignty: An Introduction and Brief History," *Journal of International Affairs*, 48:2 (1995): 358.

22 Louis Henkin *et al.*, *International Law: Cases and Materials* (St. Paul, Minnesota: West Publishing Company, 3rd edition, 1993): xxv.

23 Henkin, "That 'S' Word," 4.

decision by the Justice Department to seek the death penalty against Zacarias Moussaoui, he responded, "We are a sovereign nation. We make judgments about crimes and the penalties that exist here."[24] Sovereignty, thus, is not merely an empirical claim about the way political power is in fact exercised, but a normative claim about how it should be exercised; it not only describes certain political arrangements, but attempts to justify them, shaping social and political policy.[25]

Perhaps nowhere, though, is the selectivity of America's attachment to this version of sovereignty more pronounced than when it comes to the presence, within its borders, of other nations. At the founding of the country, when the need to establish international legitimacy was acute, things were otherwise. The United States, in treating with Indian nations, regarded their sovereignty and independence as on a par with its own. "Like all other independent nations," an early U.S. attorney general affirmed, "their territories are inviolable by any other sovereignty... They are entirely self-governed, self-directed."[26] This assessment of tribal sovereignty changed as the comparative power and territorial ambitions of the United States grew and as its domestic jurisprudence began formulating rationalizations for state actions. From John Marshall's *Cherokee* cases to the plenary power doctrine, and via the mechanism of official Federal Indian Policy, the United States proceeded to assert its power over those nations within its physical borders, to compromise, qualify, and abrogate

[24] "Ashcroft to announce a decision on Moussaoui in coming week," *Agence France Presse*, (March 24, 2002) (Available online on LexisNexis Academic, News Wire Services). This parallels China's response to international criticism:

> Such arguments as "human rights taking precedence over sovereignty" and "humanitarian intervention" seem to be in vogue these days. Some countries even put such arguments into practice... Sovereign equality, mutual respect for state sovereignty and noninterference in each other's internal affairs are the basic principles governing international relations today... Any deviation from or violation of these principles would destroy the universally-recognized norms governing international relations.

Tang Jiaxuan, "Statement by Foreign Minister Tang Jiaxuan at the 54th Session of the U.N. General Assembly," *United Nations General Assembly*, 54th Session, (November 15, 2000). Available online at: http://www.fmprc.gov.cn/eng/gjwt/gjzzhy/2594/2602/t15218.htm.

[25] See: Michael Jacobsen and Stephanie Lawson, "Between Globalization and Localization: A Case Study of Human Rights Versus State Sovereignty," *Global Governance*, 5 (1999): 216.

[26] William Wirt, cited in Glenn W. Morris, "International Law and Politics: Toward a Right to Self-Determination for Indigenous Peoples," in M. Annette Jaimes (ed.), *The State of Native America: Genocide, Colonization, and Resistance* (Boston, Massachusetts: South End Press, 1992): 65.

the sovereignty of Indian nations. The Marshall decisions "invalidated, for purposes of American law, any conception of the Indigenous nations as sovereigns on a co-equal basis with the United States."[27]

Indigenous nations, whose governance structures had thrived for thousands of years, and whose willingness to treat with a rebellious young nation lent it the international legitimacy it required, were thus paternalistically reduced to "wards" of the enveloping state, "domestic, dependent nations . . . in a state of pupilage"[28] whose sovereignty "is of a unique and limited character" which "exists only at the sufferance of Congress and is subject to complete defeasance."[29] Today, the United States draws on the mantle of absolute sovereignty to argue vigorously in international fora that it is not accountable outside its borders for its treatment of these nations because "relations between states and indigenous peoples are purely matters of internal, domestic jurisdiction."[30]

This concept of state sovereignty is plainly undergoing transformation, however, and has been for some time. Two of the most often cited reasons for it are the phenomenon of globalization and the growth of international concern for human rights. Because both these developments are transsovereign events that address, and raise, transsovereign problems – problems that, by transcending borders, escape the control of individual nation-states – it is not surprising that they have contributed significantly to the conceptual ferment that surrounds state sovereignty. Globalization, "the terrible nearness of distant places,"[31] is a multidimensional phenomenon that is bringing disparate parts of the world into contact and changing the nature and distribution of power in the world in substantive and often unforeseen ways. With the rise of transnational corporate entities, of nonstate actors such as nongovernmental organizations, of critical social movements acting across borders,[32] and with the proliferation

[27] Robert Porter, "The Meaning of Indigenous Nation Sovereignty," *Arizona State Law Journal*, 34:75 (2002): 82.

[28] *Cherokee Nation v. Georgia*, 30 U.S. 1; 8 L. Ed. 25, (5 Pet.), (Decided: March 18, 1831): 17–18.

[29] *United States v. Wheeler*, 435 U.S. 313; 98 S. Ct. 1079; 55 L. Ed. 2d 303, (Argued: January 11, 1978; As amended: March 22, 1978).

[30] Morris (1992): 66.

[31] Okwui Enwezor, cited in Gayatri Sinha, "Diatribe or Art?, *The Hindu* (1 September 2002). Available online at: http://www.hindu.com/thehindu/mag/2002/09/01/stories/2002090100340200.htm.

[32] R.B.J. Walker and Saul H. Mendlovitz, *Contending Sovereignties: Redefining Political Community* (Boulder, Colorado: Lynne Rienner Publishers, 1990): 181–2.

of new information communication technologies, the power of sovereign nation-states is being either bypassed or undermined.

Globalization is, however, a phenomenon that may best be described as Janus-faced when it comes to human rights. It has the potential both to significantly enhance and to significantly undermine them. On the one hand, the international community's effort to protect human rights "can itself be seen as an aspect of globalization . . . reduc[ing] the sphere of sovereignty," while on the other hand, globalization is attended by powerful nonstate actors fully capable of violating human rights "in ways that were not contemplated during the international human rights movement."[33] As Louis Henkin notes:

> [I]f state sovereignty has resisted the human rights movement, and if globalization has begun to threaten state sovereignty, that may sound promising for the human rights movement. But I do not find comfort for human rights in the various forms of globalization. The fact is that human rights, and the human rights movement depend on governments and on the state system . . . I do not see the withering away of the state as a result of globalization . . . In any event, if the state is going to wither away, the time has not come, and will not come soon.[34]

Whereas some theorists, such as Michael Hardt and Antonio Negri, have maintained that the nation-state is withering, and hence we must begin to make sense of a notion of "global sovereignty,"[35] others see in globalization the promise of a third revolution in, or transformation of, sovereignty. The previous two, according to law professor Helen Stacy, were efforts to win national freedom from oppressive empires and gave primacy to the demarcation of borders. During the first, the Peace of Westphalia, the Vatican's territorial vassals were transformed into the nation-states of Europe. The second revolution was the partial decolonization period of the twentieth century, when the aspirations of many former colonies for self-determination were realized. Both revolutions, Stacy observes, "had embedded within them the idea of sovereignty as a strong claim of a new

33 Dinah Shelton, "Globalization & the Erosion of Sovereignty," *Boston College International and Comparative Law Review*, 25 (2002): 273, 279.

34 Henkin, "That 'S' Word," 7.

35 See: Michael Hardt and Antonio Negri, *Empire* (Boston, Massachusetts: Harvard University Press, 2001).

dotted line on the map."[36] Globalization, she contends, now presents us with an opportunity to choose between an account of sovereignty where border demarcation is even more pronounced, or one where it is defined in crucially different ways.

If globalization frustrates the process and point of drawing borders, the development of human rights law has undermined the ability of states to pull sovereignty around them as though it were an immunity cloak, shielding them from charges of human rights violations. According to the 1992 Helsinki Declaration, human rights "are matters of direct and legitimate concern to all participating states and do not belong exclusively to the internal affairs of the state concerned."[37] The degree to which this commitment to human rights permeates international affairs is vividly illustrated by Turkey's bid for membership in the European Union. Its admission was made conditional upon conformance with the Copenhagen criteria.[38] This required abolition of the death penalty and the provision of greater cultural rights for the Kurds, an indigenous people within Turkey's borders. In 2002, Turkey complied, ending state executions and lifting a ban on Kurdish language education and broadcasts. Furthermore, a series of international humanitarian interventions has recently been heralded as demonstrating that sovereignty no longer functions as "an absolute shield against the world . . . a force field repelling other nation states at the border."[39]

Critiques of State Sovereignty

The impact of globalization, the expansion of international human rights law, and the rise of the European Union and of institutions like the International Criminal Court all argue for, if they do not necessitate, an alternative to absolute state sovereignty, a different account of the way those with power may rule – one in which the legitimacy of criticism of state

[36] Helen Stacy, "Relational Sovereignty," *Stanford Law Review*, 55 (2003): 2038.

[37] Helsinki Summit Declaration 1992. Available online at: http://www1.umn.edu/humanrts/peace/docs/helsnk92.htm.

[38] The Copenhagen European Council, in 1993, recognized the right of central and eastern European countries to join the European Union provided they met various criteria. These included having stable political institutions guaranteeing human rights and respect for minorities. Available online at: http://ue.eu.int/ueDocs/cms_Data/docs/pressdata/en/ec/72921.pdf.

[39] Stacy, "Relational Sovereignty," 2034.

conduct is not circumscribed by geography, by where territorial borders begin or end, and one which provides no moral, or legal, cover for a state insisting that how it treats those individuals and peoples that lie within it is its own business and its own business alone. There are, in fact, a number of such accounts being developed. Indeed, as one commentator observes, there seems to be a shared sense, across disciplinary boundaries, that the dominant model of state sovereignty needs to be renegotiated, although the reasons for this, and the changes needed, differ:

> Sovereignty has become the new obsession in international law, in international relations, in political science, and in sociology scholarship. All of these scholars point, in one way or another, to the profoundly structured nature of sovereignty.[40]

We turn next to several proposals that attempt such a renegotiation.

According to Helen Stacy, sovereignty is being transformed by a different understanding of the social contract. The social contract must now accommodate "the increasingly complex range of transnational interactions under the conditions of globalization, and also the enlarging role of international human rights norms."[41] The Westphalian view of sovereignty that the United States appeals to in refusing to sign and ratify international human rights treaties "is unsuited to contemporary geopolitical, economic, and cultural conditions."[42] The days of a clear-cut distinction between a government's domestic activities and its international activities are behind us; the idea of sovereignty as a rigid border around national lands and national interests is insufficient. Contemporary sovereignty requires responsibility and accountability. Stacy proposes a relational account in which sovereignty is "the measure of care by government for its citizens"[43] and is "conditional upon the ruler discharging responsibilities of care towards the citizen."[44] These responsibilities extend to the interactions of citizens with the international community, and the international community has a role in assessing them. Contemporary human rights, she contends, cannot be adequately addressed by

[40] Ibid., 2040.
[41] Ibid., 2044.
[42] Ibid., 2054.
[43] Ibid., 2028.
[44] Ibid., 2036.

Hobbesian distinctions between the citizen and the noncitizen, between the "inside" and "outside" of territorial borders, because such distinctions "do not go far enough … they remain fixed, with the idea of sovereignty stopping at the border."[45]

Adeno Addis similarly rejects the idea of a thick, or strongly autonomous state, arguing that it is neither sustainable nor desirable. He defends a version of thin state sovereignty in which sovereignty is developed relationally and contingently, and is grounded on participation rather than isolation and noninterference. His account stresses the importance of groups in the lives and identities of individuals, rejecting views of sovereignty whose unit of analysis is the abstract individual "unaffected by, and prior to, the community within which it (is) located."[46] The communication revolution has seriously destabilized the traditional view of territorial sovereignty, he maintains, curtailing the power of the state and its claim to final authority within its physical borders. Yet the demise of the state system would be dangerous because an unregulated international information market would threaten diverse ways of life: "The state may be the only institution … capable of minimizing the international tendency to uniformize cultures and individuals."[47] He distances himself from those who regard the state's loss of authority and of border control with alarm, as well as from those who celebrate it. These opposing views, he claims, "misunderstand the ambiguous and even paradoxical nature of territorial boundaries."[48]

Political theorist Iris Marion Young argues for a postsovereign global polity which she terms decentered, diverse, democratic federalism. Involving "a global system of regulatory regimes to which locales, regions and states relate in a nested federated system,"[49] it provides for local self-determination but not for sovereignty *per se*. It embraces a thin level of global governance that will enable "more local control as compared with the current states system,"[50] one in which "locales can relate directly

[45] Ibid., 2058.
[46] Adeno Addis, "The Thin State in Thick Globalism: Sovereignty in the Information Age," *Vanderbilt Journal of Transnational Law*, 37 (2004): 1, 66.
[47] Ibid., 71.
[48] Ibid., 106.
[49] Iris Marion Young, "Hybrid Democracy: Iroquois Federalism and the Postcolonial Project," in Duncan Ivison, Paul Patton, and Will Sanders (eds.), *Political Theory and the Rights of Peoples* (Cambridge, UK: Cambridge University Press, 2000): 255.
[50] Ibid., 255.

to global authorities in order to challenge and limit the ability of nation-states to control them."[51] This model of governance is inspired in part by accounts of the democracy and federalism practiced by the Iroquois confederacy and by indigenous accounts of relational self-determination. It offers a situated, relational view of governance in which self-determining units acknowledge the need for, and reality of, interconnectedness and of mutually informative influences. These units, moreover, do not enjoy rights to noninterference and nonintervention at all, much less unqualified ones, because such rights fail to acknowledge interdependency and the possibilities for domination that threaten interdependent relationships. They do, however, enjoy a right not to be dominated. Whereas nondomination, or the absence of arbitrary interference,[52] involves a presumption of (rather than a right to) noninterference, interference to reduce relations of domination is acceptable.

What these three critiques share is a conviction that Westphalian, absolute sovereignty fails to acknowledge that sovereign entities are interdependent; they are embedded in and constituted by their relationships and are accountable to one another. Stacy and Addis propose alternative accounts of sovereignty that allow for an international system that is not restricted to states, one in which sovereignty implies standing to participate in international regulatory regimes.[53] Young offers a more radical critique of the dominant narrative which, although similar to theirs in many respects, abandons the state system entirely and replaces sovereignty with relational self-determination. Entities that enjoy relational sovereignty or self-determination see themselves as embedded in and constituted by their relationships, some voluntary or chosen, some (such as geographical proximity) not. They acknowledge and assume responsibility for governing and promoting the well-being of a human community and for respecting the legitimate claims and interests of all those affected by actions taken in the course of meeting this responsibility.[54] Such entities are indeed

51 Ibid., 255.

52 See: Iris Marion Young, "Two Concepts of Self-Determination" in Austin Sarat and Thomas R. Kearns (eds.), *Human Rights: Concepts, Contests, Contingencies* (Ann Arbor, Michigan: University of Michigan Press, 2001): 39.

53 Understanding sovereignty in terms of such compliance has been supported by Abram Chayes and Antonia Handler Chayes, *The New Sovereignty: Compliance with International Regulatory Treaties* (Cambridge, Massachusetts: Harvard University Press, 1995).

54 Young, "Two Concepts," 35. My discussion here is indebted to Young's work in this article, as well as in Iris Marion Young's "Responsibility and Global Labor Justice," *Political Philosophy*,

accountable to those outside their borders, and must consider the interests and claims of all those (individuals, groups, peoples or states) they impact – whether or not an explicit agreement, contract, or treaty binds them. Within all three accounts, the notion of responsibility replaces that of immunity. Self-determining or sovereign entities have certain responsibilities because they exist in certain relationships, occupy certain roles, and have certain powers. Their control and authority is not unqualified, and can be overridden to protect the rights of others (individuals, groups, peoples, or states).

This strand of research is responsive to the deepening crisis in which the dominant, Westphalian narrative of sovereignty has been submerged as a result of the expanding human rights regime and the growing awareness that many of the problems impacting the state system (such as pollution and environmental degradation, crime, infectious diseases, and refugee flows, among others) give the lie to the notion of impermeable state borders. They are, rather, transsovereign matters escaping the territorial boundaries of individual sovereign states. Indeed for Young, the morally and conceptually problematic nature of absolute or Westphalian sovereignty, with its denial of interdependency and its commitment to principles of noninterference and nonintervention, is so acute as to lead her to reject the state system and to envision a postsovereign world: "[b]ecause the existing international system of nation-states cannot meet [the] demands [of indigenous peoples for self-determination], commitment to justice for indigenous peoples entails calling those state-systems into question."[55] We should take this discussion a step further, however, by introducing another critique of state sovereignty, one based on a very different reading of the history and theory of international law, by a scholar focused on the colonial world and on how international law facilitated the cultural and political subordination of non-European peoples.

Colonialism and the Sovereignty Doctrine

Anthony Anghie has recently argued that colonialism has a constitutive effect on the sovereignty doctrine and that issues of culture are intimately

12 (2004) and "Hybrid Democracy: Iroquois Federalism and the Postcolonial Project," in Duncan Ivison *et al.* (eds.), *Political Theory and the Rights of Indigenous Peoples* (Cambridge, UK: Cambridge University Press, 2000).

[55] Ibid., 237.

tied to issues of sovereignty. As his reading of the history of international law in the nineteenth century demonstrates, "imperial, European international law decreed that only certain civilized cultures and societies were capable of being sovereign."[56] The positivist jurisprudence which flourished at the time obscured this, however, with "a legal discourse about coequal sovereigns that masked a series of diverse theoretical and doctrinal techniques" which proved effective in creating "a hierarchy of different sovereignties . . . justified in terms of the cultural differences between European and non-European peoples."[57] What such jurisprudence offered instead was a European vision of an international legal order which was state-centered and where states were constrained only by what they voluntarily consented to. This positivist narrative "continues to operate as the basic premise of the international legal system,"[58] despite diverse efforts to reformulate the basis of international law.

How were cultural differences translated into differences in legal status during the nineteenth century? The key move, Anghie claims, was the introduction of the concept of society into international law, and its use in articulating the sovereignty doctrine.[59] International legal theorists and jurists of the time were profoundly influenced by John Austin's legal positivism but, given his critique of international law, his legacy was an acutely problematic one. Although they shared Austin's belief that legal authority must derive from a determinate source (namely, the sovereign), they emphatically rejected his belief that, because there is no global sovereign, "the law obtaining between nations is not positive law."[60] In response, they argued that there were two sources of international law: treaties which were expressions of sovereign will and the developing body of customary law which, as the practice of states, similarly manifested the will and consent of the sovereign. Custom, however, presupposed the existence of a society of sovereign states, and it was through a circular interplay between

[56] Anthony Anghie, "Sovereignty: Nationalism, Development and the Postcolonial State: The Legacies of the League of Nations," *Texas International Law Journal*, 41 (2006): 447.

[57] Dan Danielsen, "Book Review: Imperialism, Sovereignty and the Making of International Law by Anthony Anghie," *American Journal of International Law*, 100 (2006): 757, 758.

[58] Anthony Anghie, "Finding the Peripheries: Sovereignty and Colonialism in Nineteenth-Century International Law," *Harvard International Law Journal*, 40 (1999): 1, 2.

[59] Ibid., 28.

[60] John Austin, in David Campbell and Philip Thomas (eds.), *The Province of Jurisprudence Determined* (Aldershot, UK: Ashgate Publishing, 1998 (1832)): 101.

law and society that, according to these accounts, international law was created and order among sovereign states achieved.[61] As John Westlake, Whewell Professor of International Law at Cambridge, asserted: "Without society no law, without law no society. When we assert that there is such a thing as international law, we assert that there is a society of states: when we recognise that there is a society of states, we recognise that there is international law."[62]

The concept of society would prove crucial in the development of a sovereignty doctrine which imposed a hierarchy of legal statuses, and pseudo- or quasi-sovereignties, on the non-European world, for it brought with it the idea of membership: "only those states that are accepted into society and agree upon principles regulating their behavior can be regarded as belonging to society."[63] It also facilitated "the various cultural distinctions that were crucial to the constitution of sovereignty doctrine."[64] Central among these was the distinction between civilized and uncivilized states. The practices and customs that counted as international law were those that derived from the civilized institutions of the civilized states. Only such states were qualified to be full members of international society, of the "family" or "community" of nations. The political implications of this distinction were openly embraced by nineteenth-century jurists. Westlake, for example, used it to justify his claim that "the occupation by uncivilized tribes of a tract, of which according to our habits a small part ought to have sufficed for them, was not felt to interpose a serious obstacle to the right of the first civilised occupant."[65]

A serious problem remained, however, for positivist jurisprudence and its sovereignty doctrine. Many of those excluded from full membership in, and so from the rights and powers enjoyed by, the family of nations on grounds of being "uncivilized" appeared internally to meet the Austinian criteria of sovereignty. So "[h]ow could it be claimed within this jurisprudence that the barbarian nations, 'a wandering tribe with no fixed territory to call its own,' a 'race of savages,' and a 'band of pirates' were not sovereign?"[66] For in

[61] Anghie, "Finding the Peripheries," 17.
[62] John Westlake, *Chapters on the Principles of International Law* (Cambridge, UK: Cambridge University Press, 1894): 3.
[63] Anghie, "Finding the Peripheries," 17.
[64] Ibid., 17.
[65] Westlake, *Chapters on the Principles of International Law*, 137.
[66] Anghie, "Finding the Peripheries," 26.

them, it was acknowledged, commands were given by a leader and obeyed. If they possessed these crucial positivist attributes of sovereignty, how is it that they were not sovereign? The answer given was that they lacked territorial control within fixed and stable borders. As legal theorist Thomas Lawrence declared, in his 1895 volume on *The Principles of International Law*:

> International Law regards states as political units possessed of proprietary rights over definite portions of the earth's surface. So entirely is its conception of a state bound up with the notion of territorial possession that it would be impossible for a nomadic tribe, even if highly organised and civilized, to come under its provisions.[67]

Such nomadic roaming peoples, these tribes wandering so aimlessly about, failed, in other words, to meet a necessary condition for being sovereign. Even if they were to be regarded (counterfactually) as "highly organized and civilized," they were not in exclusive occupation, much less in territorial possession, of a determinate, well-defined bit of land the borders of which were bright and fixed. Thus they were not sovereign. Yet Lawrence, and the jurisprudence of the time, is careful to add that, even if one were to regard them (counterfactually) as sovereign, they still would be excluded from the family of nations, and so from the realm of international law and society, because they lacked certain unspecified but required "characteristics." Addressing himself to the legal status of a "wandering" tribe, Lawrence articulates this no-win situation: "Yet none of these communities would be subject to International Law, because they would want various characteristics, which, though not essential to sovereignty, are essential to the membership of the family of nations."[68]

Thus, what we might think of as the "wandering tribes" dilemma can be stated as follows: If they were regarded as civilized, they could not be regarded as sovereign, and if they were regarded as sovereign, they still could not be regarded as civilized. The status for the non-European states of Asia and Africa was only slightly less skewed. Because they met both the Austinian criterion of sovereignty and the requirement of exclusive territorial control, they might seem to be formally sovereign, but the decisive issue, when it came to legal status, was whether they were appropriately civilized, and so entitled to "the comprehensive range of powers enjoyed by

[67] Thomas Lawrence, *The Principles of International Law* (London: Macmillan, 1895), 136.
[68] Ibid., 58.

the European sovereigns who constituted international society."[69] Because they were deemed not to be appropriately civilized, they were, in the words of Lassa Oppenheim, "not-full Sovereign States."[70] Different classifications of the differing legal status of different peoples ensued. Westlake, for example, distinguished the Asian states – which he characterized as civilized in some respects but still "different" – from the uncivilized tribes who were "more severely denounced as completely backward."[71] As Anghie notes, however,

> these classifications were irrelevant in terms of the broad issue of the central distinction between the civilized and uncivilized. All non-European societies, regardless of whether they were regarded as completely primitive or relatively advanced, were outside the sphere of law, and European society provided the model that all societies had to follow if they were to progress.[72]

Nineteenth-century sovereignty doctrine, he concludes, is "a history of the processes by which European states, by developing a complex vocabulary of cultural and racial discriminations, set about establishing and presiding over a system of authority by which they could determine who was and was not sovereign."[73]

It is interesting to note how much of all of this remains with us. Consider the following, contemporary, account of sovereignty from the *Stanford Encyclopedia of Philosophy*, which has many of the same ingredients – territoriality, membership, even "wandering tribes," and cultural assumptions about what kind of governance structures "count":

> A final ingredient of sovereignty is territoriality, also a feature of political authority in modernity. Territoriality is a principle by which members of a community are to be defined. It specifies that their membership derives from residence within borders . . . Most vividly contrasting with territoriality is a wandering tribe, whose authority structure is completely disassociated with a particular piece of land.[74]

[69] Anghie, "Finding the Peripheries," 28.
[70] Lassa Oppenheim, *International Law: A Treatise* (2nd edition, 1912), 110.
[71] Anghie, "Finding the Peripheries," 30.
[72] Ibid., 31.
[73] Ibid., 66.
[74] "Sovereignty," *Stanford Encyclopedia of Philosophy*, available online at: http://plato.stanford.edi/entries/sovereignty.

There are at least two things worth commenting on here. First, this eight-page discussion never mentions any form of sovereignty other than state sovereignty, the sovereignty granted to those sufficiently civilized to qualify as members of the family of nations. Second, few North American indigenous peoples would recognize anything close to themselves in this account. Some tribes, such as the Pueblo, have always resided on the same land and settled into organized villages, although this fact, notably, did not enhance their claims for sovereignty under Federal Indian Law. The Supreme Court, in *United States v. Sandoval*, appealed to their "cultural inferiority" to assert federal power over their lands, claiming that despite their settled lifestyle, they were

> nevertheless Indians in race, customs, and domestic government. Always living in separate and isolated communities, adhering to primitive modes of life, largely influenced by superstition and [fetishism], and chiefly governed according to the crude customs inherited from their ancestors, they are essentially a simple, uninformed and inferior people . . . They have been regarded and treated by the United States as requiring special consideration and protection, like other Indian communities.[75]

No tribes, in any event, were given to wandering adrift, to roaming aimlessly about. Many moved twice annually from relatively stable winter to summer homelands and back. Far from being "completely disassociated with a particular piece of land," the political, cultural, and spiritual ties of most tribes to particular lands virtually defined their collective identities, as we have seen in Chapter 2. That bond with the land is, in fact, a central feature of indigenous sovereignty.

Reclaiming Indigenous Sovereignty

Indigenous legal scholars in the United States continue to comb through both treaties and Supreme Court decisions to make the strongest readings possible for tribal sovereignty under Federal Indian Law. Yet another strategy has also begun to take shape – one not limited to legal and political research but pursued by scholars in other areas as well. It begins, for some,

[75] *U.S. v. Sandoval*, 231 U.S. 28, 39 (1913).

with the recognition that Americans embrace a certain mythology about the founding of their nation, one that depicts the harsh realities of conquest as a benevolent civilizing campaign. It then shifts to the troubling concern that perhaps that myth is being "supported by us – the scholars who are charged with teaching, thinking, and writing about these things," when the dominant society's narratives of sovereignty, or of property rights, are simply accepted and "we force ourselves to think of creative arguments for why Native peoples' rights are as deserving as non-Native peoples' rights. Maybe we have it all turned around and should adopt a different lens. . . . "[76] For others, it springs, above all, from the fact that concepts of tribal sovereignty modeled upon state sovereignty are "incompatible with traditional indigenous notions of power . . . sovereignty is an exclusionary concept rooted in an adversarial and coercive Western notion of power."[77] Not only have such terms been "used to negate indigenous jurisdictional and territorial rights by excluding indigenous people from their definition, but they have worked against indigenous epistemologies of governance and law to negate the values of egalitarianism and reciprocity on which those systems are based."[78]

In North America and elsewhere, indigenous scholars are increasingly turning to traditional governance beliefs and practices[79] that have survived the imposition of western legal and political structures and the relentless process of cultural imperialism. In places these systems of belief and practice remain vital; in places they remain elusive but extant; in places they are disappearing; in places they have been "disappeared." But they are actively being recovered and reclaimed, and where necessary "reappeared." Although many communities and individuals are involved in such efforts, the contributions of only a handful, primarily legal scholars, will be alluded to below. This work – by Rebecca Tsosie, Wallace Coffey, Gordon Christie, and Robert Williams – constitutes the second strand of sovereignty research considered here, although it repeatedly acknowledges and embraces predecessors and contemporaries, including

[76] Rebecca Tsosie, "Land, Culture, and Community: Reflections on Native Sovereignty and Property in America," *Indiana Law Review*, 34 (2001): 1312.
[77] Alfred, *Peace, Power and Righteousness*, 55, 59.
[78] Barker, "The Human Genome Diversity Project," 572.
[79] These are many and diverse. My discussion here acknowledges that fact, even though it takes place at a level of generality where these differences among indigenous peoples are not articulated.

Vine Deloria Jr., Robert Warrior, Oren Lyons, John Borrows, Robert Porter, and Taiake Alfred among many others.

Although the United States, unlike Canada, formally recognized indigenous sovereignty in domestic law, that sovereignty was rapidly qualified as not being equivalent to that of foreign states, but of a "unique and limited character"[80] appropriate to "domestic, dependent nations."[81] In "Rethinking the Tribal Sovereignty Doctrine: Cultural Sovereignty and the Collective Future of Indian Nations," Wallace Coffey and Rebecca Tsosie review some of the key Supreme Court cases that have steadily restricted the scope and nature of tribal sovereignty. They observe that, in each of these, the federal government is perceived "to have affirmatively 'granted' Native sovereignty through statutes and treaties and to have the authority to decide when that sovereignty should end."[82] Accordingly, they conclude that it is time for a "reappraisal of the tribal sovereignty doctrine – one that is based in the conceptions of sovereignty held by Indian nations and . . . responds to the challenges that confront Indian nations today."[83]

Coffey and Tsosie set aside externally imposed accounts of limited or diminished tribal political sovereignty to work on an account of inherent sovereignty which locates political sovereignty within cultural sovereignty. The practices and processes of indigenous governance must, in other words, be informed by, and cohere with, the cultural values and traditions that are distinctive of their particular communities. The historical imposition of corporate forms of governance within indigenous communities, such as the tribal councils of American Indian nations and the band councils of First Nations, failed to be culturally coherent in just this respect.[84] They were not, and are not, integrated with, or reflective of, indigenous cultural norms and values. This, as we will see momentarily, is a source of particular concern for Gordon Christie in his account of emergent indigenous sovereignty within the Canadian context.

80 *United States v. Wheeler*, 435 U.S. 313, 323 (1978).

81 *Cherokee Nation v. Georgia*, 30 U.S. (5 Per.) 1, 17 (1831).

82 Coffey and Tsosie, "Rethinking the Tribal Sovereignty Doctrine," 195.

83 Ibid., 195.

84 For an account that reveals the extent of colonial domination in the area of governance, see Donald Grinde's discussion of the Canadian government's "abolishment" of the traditional Haudenosaunee government at the Six Nations Reserve. Donald A. Grinde Jr., "Iroquois Border Crossings: Place, Politics and the Jay Treaty," in Claudia Sadowski-Smith (ed.), *Globalization on the Line: Culture, Capital and Citizenship at U.S. Borders* (New York, New York: Palgrave, St. Martin's Press, 2002).

One of the points which Coffey and Tsosie stress, and which is reflected in the accounts of Christie and Williams, is that within a cultural understanding of indigenous sovereignty, the concept of relationship is fundamental. Not only is it "used to forge connection between Indian nations and other sovereigns, whether Indian or non-Indian,"[85] it also is vital to the process of building community which is "an essential part of the exercise of sovereignty."[86] This process, according to Vine Deloria, involves supporting social structures through which "communities exercise political, economic, and spiritual power along with responsibility."[87] Such sovereign communities (as noted in Chapter 2) are seen primarily as bearers of responsibilities rather than of rights, and as constrained by the relationships in which they find themselves. Euro-American notions of sovereignty and self-determination are regarded as failing to capture the perspective shared by many indigenous peoples "that human power and agency are limited in very fundamental ways by their relationship to other parts of the natural world."[88]

The latter includes relationships with other peoples. Narratives of indigenous sovereignty begin with an acknowledgement of interdependency, and unfold in terms of respect and responsibility, both of which are essential if human beings, both as individuals and as communities, are to thrive in relationships capable of sustaining present and future generations. This is succinctly captured in the observations of one delegate to the United Nations Working Group on Indigenous Populations, law professor Craig Scott:

> If one listens, one can often hear the message that the right of a people to self-determination is not a right for peoples to determine their status without consideration of the rights of other peoples with whom they are presently connected and with whom they will continue to be connected in the future. For we must realize that peoples, no less than individuals, exist and thrive only in dialogue with each other. Self-determination necessarily involves engagement with and responsibility to others (which includes responsibility for the implications of one's preferred choices for others) . . . We need to begin to think

[85] Coffey and Tsosie, "Rethinking the Tribal Sovereignty Doctrine," 198.

[86] Ibid., 199.

[87] Vine Deloria, Jr., cited in Robert Allen Warrior, *Tribal Secrets* (Minneapolis, Minnesota: University of Minnesota Press, 1995): 92.

[88] Coffey and Tsosie, "Rethinking the Tribal Sovereignty Doctrine," 197.

> of self-determination in terms of peoples existing in relationship with each other. It is the process of negotiating the nature of such relationships which is part of, indeed at the very core of, what it means to be a self-determining people.[89]

Indigenous sovereignty assumes an interdependency with the land, and in this it contrasts markedly with the territoriality of state sovereignty. The latter involves an understanding of power as "control over" land and people, which is absent from the former. It also serves to define the members of a community by their residence within borders, "in a way that may not correspond with identity."[90] For many indigenous peoples, however, land is constitutive of culture and identity. Far from being "disassociated" with the land, traditional indigenous forms of governance hold themselves accountable above all for protecting the land and resources which constitute them as distinct peoples and toward which they have crucial role responsibilities. This is one of the reasons that the replacement of traditional forms of governance by tribal councils modeled on corporate governance structures was a priority for the colonizing powers. It facilitated the alienation of land and resources and the demise of collective land ownership. Conversely, the calculated demise of the latter (via instruments such as the General Allotment Act of 1887[91]) further weakened indigenous governance. As Coffey and Tsosie state, "the most compelling

[89] Craig Scott, "Indigenous Self-Determination and Decolonization of the International Imagination: A Plea," *Human Rights Quarterly*, 18 (1996): 814, 819.

[90] "Sovereignty," *Stanford Encyclopedia of Philosophy*, available online at: http://plato.stanford.edu/.

[91] The function of the Dawes, or General Allotment, Act of 1887, "was to expedite the process of Indian 'civilization' by unilaterally dissolving their collectively (i.e. nationally) held reservation land holdings" and reallocating them "in accordance with the 'superior' (i.e. Euroamerican) concept of property: individually deeded land parcels . . . " M. Annette Jaimes, "Federal Indian Identification Policy," in Jaimes, *The State of Native America*, 126. It also thereby facilitated the acquisition of Indian lands: "White settlers had been clamoring for Indian land. The Indian tribes controlled nearly 135 million acres. If, the argument went, that land were divided on a per capita basis . . . the *surplus* would be available to the white settlement . . . By 1934 Indians had lost nearly 90 million acres through land sales, many of them fraudulent." (Vine Deloria Jr., *Custer Died For Your Sins* (Norman, Oklahoma: University of Oklahoma Press, 1988): 46–7). This occurred despite the fact that "a minority opinion in the report on the Dawes Allotment Act stated that perhaps the Choctaw method of holding land in common was superior to that of the white man because there was so little poverty among the members of the Five Civilized Tribes" and notwithstanding the fact that in the Treaty of 20 January 1825 "the United States provided that the Congress of the United States shall not exercise the power of apportioning the lands." Ibid., 42.

examples of cultural sovereignty . . . are the cases in which Native people actually fought for and achieved repatriation of sacred lands,"[92] such as the return of Blue Lake to the Taos Pueblo. It also includes "the tangible repatriation of Native culture,"[93] such as the return of ancestral remains and cultural objects and restoration of language, spirituality, and educational systems.

What more effective, and devastating, way was there to "diminish" indigenous sovereignty than by the displacement of traditional governance systems? And what more effective and powerful way to enhance it than to enable their continuance? These questions lie at the heart of Gordon Christie's discussion of the emergent sovereignty of indigenous peoples in Canada. In contrast to the United States, the Canadian government never expressly recognized indigenous sovereignty in the nineteenth century.[94] Indeed, it enacted the singularly oppressive 1876 Indian Act, which "sought to impose . . . a form of municipal government under which Tribal Band Councils elected according to Canadian standards, were delegated authority over a few minor matters."[95] Specifically, it stated:

[92] Coffey and Tsosie, "Rethinking the Tribal Sovereignty Doctrine," 205.

[93] Ibid., 207.

[94] By contrast, Canada attributed an absolute magical power to its own powers of sovereignty. Anishinabe law professor, John Borrows, offers the following comment on the Supreme Court of Canada's contention, in *Delgamuukw v. British Columbia*, that "*Because it does not make sense* to speak of a burden on the underlying title before that title existed, aboriginal title crystallized at the time sovereignty was asserted."

> Sovereignty is pretty powerful stuff. Its mere assertion by one nation is said to bring another's land rights to a "definite and permanent form"; simply conjuring sovereignty is enough to change an ancient peoples' relationship with their land. A society under sovereignty's spell is ostensibly transformed, for use and occupation are found to be extinguished, infringed, or made subject to another's designs. How can lands possessed by Aboriginal peoples for centuries be undermined by another nation's assertion of sovereignty? What alchemy transmutes the basis of Aboriginal possession into the golden bedrock of Crown title? . . . Aboriginal peoples wonder how it "makes sense" that *Crown title* "crystallized at the time sovereignty was asserted." The Court might as well speak of magic crystals being sprinkled on the land as a justification for the diminution of Aboriginal occupation and possession. Crown title simply does not make sense to Aboriginal people (and one suspects to many non-Aboriginal people). The contemporary reliance on assertions of sovereignty seems to "perpetuate the historical injustice suffered by aboriginal peoples at the hands of colonizers who failed to respect the distinctive cultures of pre-existing aboriginal societies." (John Borrows, "Sovereignty's Alchemy: An Analysis of *Delgamuukw v. British Columbia*," *Osgoode Hall Law Journal*, 37 (Fall 1999): 558, 563. (Citations omitted.)

[95] Kevin Worthen, "The Grand Experiment: Evaluating Indian Law in the 'New World,'" *Tulsa Journal of Comparative and International Law*, 5 (1998): 299, 308.

> The Governor may order that the Chiefs of any tribe, band or body of Indians shall be elected by the male members of each Indian settlement of the full age of twenty-one years at such time and place, and such manner, as the Superintendent General of Indian Affairs may direct, and they shall in such case be elected for a period of three years, unless deposed by the Governor for dishonesty, intemperance, or immorality, and they shall be in the proportion of one Chief and two Second Chiefs for every two hundred people . . .[96]

However, also unlike the United States, Canada began to negotiate modern treaties with indigenous nations in the 1970s. When the Canadian Constitution was repatriated from the United Kingdom, a section of the 1982 Constitution Act (Section 35) was included, providing that "existing aboriginal and treaty rights of the aboriginal peoples of Canada are hereby recognized and affirmed."[97] Considerable ferment and discussion has ensued, with a number of scholars arguing that section 35 provides what is needed to enable recognition of indigenous sovereignty.

Christie's concern is that, for all the promise of these developments, they may lead to a situation in which the resulting sovereignty and forms of governance are indigenous in name only. The federal and provincial governments are emphasizing the transference of power and authority to indigenous governments "with no concomitant suggestion that there would be any substantive change to the forms of governance put in place in Indigenous communities by colonial authorities"[98] over the last 150 years. Elected band councils centralize power "in the mould of European political institutions"[99] and were, in many cases, "deliberately created so as to displace the Indigenous mechanisms of political authority, the councils of wise men and women that deliberated on communal issues."[100] In what sense then, Christie asks, "are we talking about the re-emergence

[96] *1869 Act for the Gradual Enfranchisement of Indians and the Better Management of Indian Affairs Act* c. VI section 10. Available online at: http://www.ainc-inac.gc.ca/ai/arp/ls/pubs/a69c6/a69c6-eng.pdf. This was part of the legislation consolidated in the 1876 Indian Act. For a discussion of some of the differences in Canadian and American policies toward indigenous peoples, see Ralph W. Johnson, "Fragile Gains: Two Centuries of Canadian and United States Policy Toward Indians," *Washington Law Review*, 66 (1991): 643.

[97] *Canadian Constitution* (Constitution Act, 1982) pt. II, section 35(1).

[98] Gordon Christie, "Emergent Sovereignty in the Canadian Context," presented at the Western Division meeting of the American Philosophical Association (March 2006), 6.

[99] Ibid., 4.

[100] Ibid.

of Indigenous sovereignty when we are contemplating a transfer of more power and authority to these colonial creations?"[101]

How to respond to this situation is a subject intensely debated among indigenous communities in Canada, which have remained connected to traditional governance beliefs and practices to varying degrees. The process of reinvigorating traditional governance structures within these communities should begin, Christie suggests, with the practice of sovereignty, that is, "by engaging in a long and searching process of internal deliberation [and] . . . by reclaiming the ability to construct their own senses of collective identity."[102] What must be initially reclaimed, he contends, "is what was fundamentally lost – the power to collectively decide how to think about the future of the community, and about how to move toward that vision of the future."[103] The resonance of this with Coffey and Tsosie's process-oriented account of cultural sovereignty is strong.

Christie's discussion also addresses the nature of power within indigenous sovereignty. Within traditional governance structures, power is not exercised through hierarchies of domination. Traditional leaders did not command, exert their authority upon, or exercise control over, others who obeyed them.

> [T]hey did not – and could not – order anyone to do anything. They lacked this power, and to try to act this way would have been met with astonishment, followed soon by derision, and likely capped with the abandonment of this person.[104]

Acting in such ways, in fact, was invariably the model of how not to act, frequently instantiated by trickster figures. Someone who had to adopt coercive means was not a leader, for such behavior would only undermine, not sustain, communal ties. An effective leader was someone who, among other things, was able to persuade others to follow a certain course of action, to convince them that it was appropriate, and to fashion a consensus that all could live with. This reflects the respect that was traditionally accorded to each individual within indigenous communities. As Willie Ermine comments,

[101] Ibid., 5.
[102] Ibid., 7.
[103] Ibid., 7.
[104] Ibid., 3.

> within the Aboriginal community a paradox seemingly exists. In no other place did the individual have more integrity or receive more honour than in the Aboriginal community. The individual's ability as a unique entity in the group to become what she or he is ultimately meant to be was explicitly recognized. There was explicit recognition of the individual's right in the collective to experience his or her own life. No one could dictate the path that must be followed.[105]

Christie adds that indigenous societies functioned reasonably well not because responsible adults could not be ordered about by others, but

> because this sort of person was the end product of a long process of careful moral education . . . powerful modes of character building were employed to foster and strengthen the natural social tendencies of the individual. A process of instruction in how to live in a good way, as a member of a community of interdependent individuals, was in constant motion, so that the young would emerge into adulthood with powerful internalized societal drives.[106]

Another way of capturing this last point might be to say that within indigenous sovereignty value is placed not on the assertion of sovereign rights (to self-determination, noninterference, etc.), but on the acknowledgement of sovereign responsibilities (to sustaining and respecting the affiliational ties which bind individuals and communities together).

Similar themes are apparent in the understanding of indigenous sovereignty that emerges from the work of Robert A. Williams, Jr. In *Linking Arms Together*, Williams focuses closely on treaty making during the Encounter era. From the early seventeenth century through most of the eighteenth century, North America – especially in the woodlands of the East – was a multicultural frontier in which a number of competing, intersecting, and more or less equal cultural groups struggled together to establish and maintain a workable social order. Williams displaces the colonizing legal narrative of the West with a counter-mythology in which Indians are cast as accommodators of, rather than obstacles to, European survival on a Native American continent. His is a richly detailed account of how indigenous peoples responded to the numerous multicultural encounters

[105] Willie Ermine, "Aboriginal Epistemology," in Marie Battiste and Jean Barman (eds.), *First Nations Education in Canada* (Vancouver, British Columbia: University of British Columbia Press, 1995): 108.

[106] Christie, "Emergent Sovereignty," 8.

in which they found themselves immersed, drawing on their own unique traditions of diplomacy and governance to help resolve the problems of achieving law and peace among different peoples on the multicultural frontier. Although he rarely mentions sovereignty, what Williams offers is a close and nuanced narrative of indigenous sovereignty in practice. Indeed, it too is a process-oriented understanding of sovereignty; a sovereign nation is not one that has achieved a certain state (of, say, supreme political authority within and control over a territory) but one that acts in certain ways, in particular, one that actively treats with other nations.[107]

The purpose, conduct, and implications of treaty making for indigenous nations during the North American Encounter era were distinctive. Treaty making was also extensive. One thing that Europeans were acutely and uneasily aware of when they landed on the continent was that they were surrounded "by a large number of highly organized confederacies."[108] Treaties, whether among indigenous peoples or between indigenous peoples and various groups of Europeans, were primarily a means of establishing relationships among different peoples. Quite literally, the process of treaty making was a "rite of making relatives,"[109] as the kinship rhetoric which pervaded treaty-making ceremonies, and inflected the practice of indigenous sovereignty, suggests. Establishing affiliational ties with differing peoples was a way of resolving disputes and making peace; treaty making enabled peoples who were different from, and often strangers to, one another to unite and form ties of solidarity. Creating and maintaining connections was also a prerequisite for survival on the multicultural frontier: "[t]reaties, as constitutionalized connection, gave rise to customary bonds that treaty partners could rely on in times of need or crisis."[110] However, as Williams notes,

> Indian diplomats recognized that making connections with others was a most difficult process. Successful treaty-making required the use of great acts of imagination so that the two sides could come

[107] An especially effective demonstration of this was the issuance, by the Iroquois Confederacy at Onondaga, of their own international passports, which are now accepted worldwide for Iroquois travelers. See Grinde, "Iroquois Border Crossings," 176.

[108] Robert A. Williams, Jr., *Linking Arms Together: American Indian Treaty Visions of Law & Peace, 1600–1800* (New York: Oxford University Press, 1997), 33. This is a compelling and powerful scholarly work.

[109] Ibid., 50.

[110] Ibid., 99.

> to see themselves as related in their needs and sufferings as fellow human beings. This is why, in Indian diplomacy, a treaty was told as a special kind of story, a way of imaging a world of human solidarity, where we regard others as our relatives.[111]

A treaty was, in fact, regarded as a sacred text, "a narrative that committed two different peoples to live according to a shared legal tradition,"[112] sanctified by the smoking of the peace-pipe. This helps explain the moral gravity with which treaty making was conducted, as well as the depth of the indigenous commitment to honor treaties, to respect their terms. The pursuit of treaty-relations – the exercise of indigenous sovereignty – was "a divinely mandated responsibility in and of itself."[113] It fulfilled what indigenous nations regarded as "a sacred obligation to extend their relationships of connection to all of the different peoples of the world"[114] and embraced a vision of a society "in which different peoples were connected to each other as relatives"[115] and "could rely on the customary bonds of multicultural unity created by their treaty relationship in times of crisis or need."[116] According to American Indian multicultural constitutionalism, "different peoples in a relationship of close connection were expected to embrace the sacredly revealed truth of their shared humanity as a basis of normative action toward each other."[117]

By exercising their sovereignty and forming these alliances, different peoples agreed not only to form relationships of trust and reliance that would help ensure mutual survival, but to accept the responsibilities that those relationships entailed. Kinship, Williams observes, "is a form of social insurance."[118] Using kinship terms of address during treaty making "could be a highly effective way of impressing upon a colonial official a unique sense of the responsibilities he had taken on by making treaties with indigenous nations."[119] Treaty partners were responsible for behaving like proper relatives, maintaining connections, providing for one another's

[111] Ibid., 113.
[112] Ibid., 47–8.
[113] Ibid., 50.
[114] Ibid.
[115] Ibid.
[116] Ibid., 123.
[117] Ibid., 123.
[118] Ibid., 63.
[119] Ibid., 74.

needs, protecting one another's interests, and resolving disputes in ways that drew upon and strengthened the existing ties between them.

This approach is reflected in peace-making, or dispute-resolution, processes that continue today, such as those of the Comanche, mentioned in Chapter 2, for whom efforts to resolve disagreement among the members of a group begin with an exercise to strengthen bonding. Each person in the group is called upon to track his or her kinship ties to the rest of the group, reminding them that and how they are bound to one another, as well as what their reciprocal responsibilities are.[120] The responsibilities entailed by treating, by making relatives of one another, were regarded by indigenous nations as binding not only present but future generations in powerful and lasting ways. The treaty involved partners in relationships of trust and reliance, as is evident in the words of an Iroquois diplomat following the signing of a treaty granting a large parcel of land to the English:

> What We are now going to say is a matter of great Moment, which we desire you to remember as long as the Sun and Moon lasts. We are willing to sell you this large tract of land for your people to live upon, but We desire this may be considered as Part of our Agreement, that when we are all dead and gone, your Grandchildren may not say to our Children, that your Forefathers sold the land to our Forefathers, and therefore be gone off them. This is wrong. Let us all be Brethren as well after as before of giving you deeds for the land. After we have sold our land, we in a little time have nothing to shew from it, but it is not so with you, your Grandchildren will get something from it as long as the world stands, our Grandchildren will have no advantage from it. They will say we were fools for selling so much land for so small matter, and curse us; therefore let it be part of the present agreement that we shall treat one another as Brethren to the latest generation, even after we shall not have left a foot of land.[121]

Weaving the Strands Together: Prospects, Problems, and Promises

Each of these two strands of research present sovereignty narratives that contrast markedly with the dominant narrative of Westphalian state

[120] Ladonna Harris *et al.*, "Returning to Harmony: A Comanche Effort to Reactivate the Wisdom of the People," *Native Americas* (Fall/Winter 1996).

[121] Williams, *Linking Arms Together*, 130.

sovereignty. Although they are situated within different traditions – the concerns of which differ regarding issues of governance in a globalizing era, and the fundamental intellectual commitments and cultural allegiances of which are not the same – there are some surprising commonalities. Themes of relationality, of interdependency, and of responsibility have emerged repeatedly, themes sharply at odds with Westphalian sovereignty. Although they do not all do so to the same degree, much less in the same ways, these researchers are collectively working to transform thinking about state sovereignty into thinking about sovereignties, and to envision a very different global society in which the dominant, state-centered, Westphalian narrative of governance is displaced by multiple sovereignties – state and nonstate – in which power is construed very differently. The remainder of this chapter reflects on the prospects of weaving these strands together – however loosely, tentatively, and provisionally. There are very good reasons – some rather general, some quite specific – for doing so, although there are also reasons to be cautious and circumspect, if not wary.

Indeed, the theorist with which each strand in the account offered here ends – Iris Marion Young in the first instance and Robert Williams in the second – seems to invite such an interweaving. Young actually attempts it, by drawing directly both on Iroquois forms of democracy and federalism and on contemporary indigenous accounts of relational self-determination as well as on mainstream political theorists, in fashioning her account of decentered, diverse, democratic federalism. She is clearly concerned to secure, with this account, a type of polity that will be responsive to, and proactive regarding, the claims to justice being advanced by the world's indigenous peoples. These claims would certainly encompass the struggles to protect the indigenous knowledge and genetic resources considered earlier in this book. Such claims to justice are incompatible with the concept of state sovereignty that predominates in international relations. If they are to be properly recognized, she believes, the dominance of sovereign states in the international arena must be challenged and eventually replaced by something like decentered, diverse, democratic federalism. It is worth noting that other considerations of global justice support her vision, including the need to address human rights intervention, environmental protection, migration, and economic regulation. Certainly there are evolving regimes of international law in diverse areas – including human rights – which suggest the need for, if not the emergence of, a "thin" global regulatory regime such as the one she envisions.

Williams considers at one point, from the nonindigenous perspective, the usefulness of the counter-mythology he constructs. What might be gained by revisiting these Encounter era attempts to achieve an indigenous vision of law and peace among different peoples along the North American multicultural frontier? What can be learned from examining these rich and compelling expressions of indigenous sovereignty? The efforts made during the Encounter era "to achieve and sustain relationships of interdependence and solidarity," he contends, "can spur the development of critical perspectives on visions of law and peace for our own multicultural world."[122] We may learn a great deal from them "about the process of how different peoples from radically divergent cultural backgrounds try to achieve peace and accommodation with each other ... and perhaps how different peoples can agree to link arms together today."[123] From the indigenous perspective, such a re-envisioning of the Encounter era may help in the process of recovering an understanding of sovereignty that is congenial to and reflective of indigenous forms of governance. Doing so, he adds, may also "suggest new metaphors and new languages for better understanding and resolving this fundamental problem of indigenous peoples' survival in a multicultural world,"[124] including presumably the contemporary and pressing need to respond to biocolonialism.

Of course, as Williams points out, one of the things that was distinctive about the Encounter era is the rough equality which existed between certain European and indigenous peoples. The former "had no choice but to listen seriously to American Indians"[125] and indeed in many recorded documents from the time Europeans adapted to, compromised with, and occasionally expressed admiration for "Indian approaches and solutions to problems of human diversity and conflict on the North American colonial frontier."[126] So the current, profoundly unequal, relations of power were not an issue during this period; the Encounter era was the pause before the onslaught of imperialism. Nor do power, and the current inequities of power, play much of a role in Young's discussion, despite the fact that her goal is to offer an account of a global democratic polity where

[122] Robert A. Williams, "Linking Arms Together: Multicultural Constitutionalism in a North American Indigenous Vision of Law and Peace," *California Law Review*, 82 (1994): 981, 995.
[123] Ibid., 994.
[124] Ibid., 995.
[125] Ibid., 986.
[126] Ibid., 987.

oppressive relations of power can be destabilized and better addressed, if not overcome.

Today, still powerful nation-states, deeply invested in maintaining the contemporary unequal relations of power, dominate the international system. They will bring, and are bringing, their histories of power with them as the world moves into a post-Westphalian governance regime; the discussion of the Convention on Biological Diversity (CBD) to which we will turn momentarily is illustrative of that. There is every reason to be concerned that the existing realities of power not be overlooked in these efforts to envision alternative futures for global governance, where Westphalian presumptions are left behind. This problem may be more pressing for proposals like Addis's and arguably Stacy's, which call for the continuation of some form of state system, but it cannot be ignored even by proposals like Young's, which have us leaving the state system entirely behind. Such proposals call out for a consideration of transitional issues and the kinds of challenges that their realization poses, as well as for some reflection on how the demise of the state system may evolve, or be encouraged to evolve, from the current players and the current power imbalances.

The extant relations of power have, in any event, privileged a certain narrative of sovereignty over others. If other narratives of indigenous sovereignty, such as those addressed here, are to be better listened to, learned from, and accommodated, those relations of power will need to be altered. More importantly, such narratives must first be allowed the intellectual and political space to survive. The diverse processes of recovery of traditional governance systems in which various indigenous peoples are currently engaged must be allowed to unfold from within, taking whatever time is needed, and free from coercive forces from without. Almost certainly, the result will be as diverse as the peoples themselves, and it is perhaps here that the lessons of Encounter era indigenous diplomacy that Williams relates will prove most valuable. There is, after all, a great deal that links these two strands of sovereignty narratives together. They are both concerned with remedying the continuing injustices of early and contemporary imperialism, including the Westphalian reservation of sovereign status to the few, the civilized, the European, as well as its characterization as absolute. They both would displace Westphalian sovereign immunity and unaccountability with sovereign responsibility and interdependency. They are also both profoundly worried, at this point, about simple survival.

What is very clear, however, is that all peoples need to be involved in the revision and implementation of global governance if transglobal problems are to be effectively resolved, if transglobal inequities are to be fairly addressed, and if the indigenous peoples of the world are to survive. A global governance system or regulatory regime that can accommodate diverse, interdependent sovereignties, as well as embrace and be informed by a robust legal pluralism will be far better positioned to secure justice and ensure survival for all peoples. It would stand committed to what Young might have described as a global politics of difference, one which lays down institutions and ideological means for recognizing and affirming differently identifying peoples, giving political representation to their interests and celebrating their distinctive cultures and characteristics.[127]

How might a global governance system, transformed by the recognition of multiple sovereignties, respond differently to biocolonialism, and do so in ways that further both survival and justice? To see how, consider the issue of biodiversity, which is among many values threatened by biocolonialism, and the proposals for its protection advanced by the CBD. Alarm over the loss and degradation of ecosystems, together with species and genetic diversity, led to the negotiation of the CBD in 1992. Although alarm over the concomitant loss of cultural diversity – and the disappearance of a growing number of indigenous peoples globally – was not part of what brought the CBD into being, the latter was recognized as linked in some way to the former. Article 8(j) of the CBD requires Parties to

> [r]espect, preserve and maintain knowledge, innovations and practices of indigenous and local communities embodying traditional lifestyles relevant for the conservation and sustainable use of biological diversity and promote their wider application with the approval and involvement of the holders of such knowledge, innovations and practices and encourage the equitable sharing of the benefits arising from the utilization of such knowledge, innovations and practices.[128]

This provision acknowledges the relevance of indigenous peoples to in situ conservation, and is the first time that "the special function of indigenous and local communities in the innovation and preservation of

[127] See Iris Marion Young, *Justice and the Politics of Difference* (Princeton, New Jersey: Princeton University Press, 1990).

[128] CBD, June 5, 1992, art. 8(j), 1760 United Nations Treaty Series. Available online at: http://www.un.org/Depts/dhl/resguide/spectreat.htm#unts.

biological knowledge"[129] has been recognized in a global treaty. Yet to achieve one of its main objectives, namely, "the fair and equitable sharing of the benefits arising out of the utilization of genetic resources, including by appropriate access to genetic resources and by appropriate transfer of relevant technologies,"[130] the CBD vests ownership of, and sovereign rights to, biological and genetic resources firmly in the surrounding, or "host" state.[131] The dominant role which the CBD grants to recognized states in biodiversity protection was further enhanced by the 1996 Leipzig Declaration on Conservation and Sustainable Utilization of Plant Genetic Resources, which entrenched the idea that "states have sovereignty over the resources of biological diversity."[132] Indigenous peoples regard this as a "sovereignty grab"

> by nation states over all biological and ecological resources . . . [they] are both frustrated and angry that while Amazonian countries do little to protect their interests or guarantee even their most basic rights, they are nonetheless anxious to claim sovereignty over even local knowledge systems.[133]

[129] Naomi Roht-Arriaza, "Of Seeds and Shamans: The Appropriation of the Scientific and Technical Knowledge of Indigenous Local Communities," *Michigan Journal of International Law*, 17 (1996): 919, 949.

[130] CBD, (1992) at art. 1.

[131] This displays what some commentators on these issues have referred to as a "tug of war between two alternative property visions: state ownership of biological resources, as articulated in Article 8j of the Convention on Biological Diversity, and private ownership of these resources under the WTO's Trade Related Aspects of Intellectual Property (TRIPS) agreement." Yet, they note, there is another aspect to "this struggle over traditional knowledge and biological resources. Most of the world's remaining biodiversity exists within indigenous lands and territories. Rather than as an aspect of state sovereignty over territory, or the fruits of private invention, indigenous leaders conceive of these resources as an aspect of self-determination – as a recognition of their fundamental rights to property and culture. Indigenous groups are thus trying to expand the discourse over biological resources so that it includes their interests and their hopes for wresting back control over their territories, resources and heritage." (Rebecca M. Bratspies, "Symposium: Lands, Liberties and Legacies: Indigenous Peoples and International Law: Theoretical Approaches to International Indigenous Rights: The New Discovery Doctrine: Some Thoughts on Property Rights and Traditional Knowledge," *American Indian Law Review*, 31 (2006/2007): 316–17.)

[132] Erik B. Bluemel, "Separating Instrumental from Intrinsic Rights: Toward an Understanding of Indigenous Participation in International Rule-Making," *American Indian Law Review*, 30 (2005/2006): 108.

[133] Darrell Addison Posey, "Biodiversity, Genetic Resources, and Indigenous Peoples in Amazonia," Prepared for: *Amazonia 2000: Development, Environment, and Geopolitics*. Institute of Latin American Studies, University of London (24–26 June 1998). Available online at: http://www.ubcic.bc.ca/files/PDF/Posey_Biodiversity.pdf.

This vesting of sovereignty over genetic resources on indigenous lands with the surrounding state illustrates Anghie's contention that modern international law, and most notably the sovereignty doctrine, is informed by the dynamic and legacy of nineteenth-century colonialism. Certainly, if the interests of indigenous peoples had been a genuine concern of the CBD it would not have granted sovereignty over indigenous resources and knowledge to the nation-states in which they and their lands are situated. States, as Ronald Niezin notes, "are not the proper guardians of the politics, culture and economies of indigenous peoples for the same reason that states are not always the purveyors of unbiased justice toward them: they are too much interested in the outcomes of contests."[134] It also jeopardizes a number of things, at least some of which the CBD was intended to enhance, such as: (a) the protection of traditional indigenous agricultural and medicinal knowledge, because states have historically not only failed to protect but have facilitated the destruction of indigenous cultures and interests; (b) the effectiveness and equity of benefit sharing, because such sharing is subject to national legislation, and is unlikely to be passed on to the indigenous peoples – a good number of whom are not in any event interested in commercialization of their resources; (c) resource conservation itself, because the indigenous peoples who sustainably cultivated, protected, and used the resources in question for centuries need not be involved in the process; (d) the sovereign responsibilities of indigenous peoples, because the only sovereignty recognized is that of existing states; and (e) the cultural and often physical survival of the indigenous peoples whose genetic resources are being exploited in multiple and varied instances of biocolonialism.

The case of the Guajajara people, discussed in Exhibit Three, demonstrates this point. The likelihood of scenarios such as this one would be less were sovereignty to be exercised along the lines endorsed by both strands of sovereignty research examined here. If sovereignty were not restricted to nation-states, if it involved acknowledging interdependency and respecting the legitimate claims and interests of those impacted by sovereign acts, and if it required the assumption of responsibility for governing and promoting the well-being of human communities, the ability of the host of agents

[134] Ronald Niezin, *The Origins of Indigenism: Human Rights and the Politics of Identity* (Berkeley, California: University of California Press, 2003): 196.

involved in the Guajajara case to successfully conduct such projects would be significantly checked. And international legal instruments such as the CBD would have to be significantly revamped.

This is not the end of the story of the CBD, however. It is at least as significant for what was achieved in the penumbra of the document as for what occurred in the process of implementing it. We noted in the introduction to this chapter that the protection of indigenous knowledge and genetic resources has been cast from the outset, by indigenous peoples, in terms of their right to self-determination and self-governance. What the CBD did was to serve as an effective vehicle for raising and contesting this issue in an international arena. It enjoined states to do several things, without specifying how they should proceed in doing so, and this gave indigenous peoples an effective wedge to enter as participants in the process of dialogue and debate surrounding the document. If the latter did not give them a place at the table alongside nation-states, it could be said to have left the door open so that indigenous peoples could pull up their own chair. And so they did, energized perhaps by the negotiations over the Draft Declaration of Indigenous Peoples Rights, which were taking place at roughly the same time.

Article 8 of the CBD, In Situ Conservation, argues for the inclusion of indigenous peoples in the drafting of comprehensive conservation plans, while 8(j), as we have seen earlier in this chapter, specifically enjoins states: (a) to respect and preserve indigenous knowledge and practices regarding sustainable biological diversity; (b) to promote wider application of the latter but only with the approval and involvement of indigenous peoples; and (c) to encourage equitable benefit sharing arising from this. One legal scholar, who attended numerous meetings where implementation of Article 8(j) was under consideration, has this to say about the depth and nature of indigenous involvement in those debates:

> Many indigenous peoples . . . are resident in or enclosed and contained by the jurisdictions of states with whom they have long historical relationships of distrust, betrayal and violence. Rather than trust state delegates to the CBD to represent their interests, they have used the CBD agenda, forums, funding and publicity opportunities to further press global indigenous human-rights struggles for self-determination.[135]

[135] Coombe, "Works in Progress," 286.

In her assessment of the broader significance of this intervention, Coombe adds that the discourses of international human rights and of environmental preservation "are perhaps the only legitimate rhetorics of sufficient scope to counter languages of neoliberalism and the imperatives of capital's insistence upon the magical benefits of free trade."[136]

Other scholars are drawing attention to these and related developments. The authors of a recent article document a fundamental change that is occurring in international environmental law. Previously ignored or overlooked, indigenous peoples' rights, knowledge, and aspirations are being addressed. They have become increasingly involved in the formulation of policies that may impact them, and are doing so in the context of human rights and environmental justice. There is a noticeable shift underway, away from the state-centered nature of earlier international law "where dominant cultures impose their cultural norms and values on non-dominant cultures – to a model based on a shared understanding and treatment of indigenous peoples as separate. As such, indigenous peoples may be at the vanguard of an era of post-state sovereignty."[137] Howard Vogel argues that a new dynamic view of self-determination as an ongoing process is now in place in the United Nations, largely as the result of indigenous participation. This new understanding "may be restated as a right to self-determination that serves the well-being of groups who define themselves as a people by addressing the conditions under which they live and are governed through an on-going process of negotiation of the terms on which they live with their neighbors."[138] He believes it enables, in turn, a new relational theory of international human rights the conceptual basis of which is communal interdependency.

There may actually be some hope that alternative sovereignty narratives, alternative legal and political visions of global governance, can have some impact on current discussions focused on reforming the United Nations, the urgency of which has grown following the December 2004 report on

136 Ibid., 296.

137 Jeremy Firestone, Jonathan Lilley, and Isabel Torres de Noronha, "Cultural Diversity, Human Rights, and the Emergence of Indigenous Peoples in International and Comparative Environmental Law," *American University International Law Review*, 20 (2005): 291.

138 Howard J. Vogel, "Reframing Rights From the Ground Up: The Contribution of the New U.N. Law of Self-Determination to Recovering the Principle of Sociability on the Way To a Relational Theory of International Human Rights," *Temple International and Comparative Law Journal*, 20 (2006): 446.

UN reform.[139] As one commentator has noted, "It now appears that for the first time since the U.N. Charter was adopted in 1945, the idea of constructive and tangible change for the U.N. system is receiving serious attention from a wide array of national and international actors."[140] Most of the proposed reforms, however, emphasize structural and procedural changes intended to enhance efficiency and accountability. They do not envision the radical restructuring which will be required if we are to fashion a global regulatory regime which is responsive to the kinds of critiques of Westphalian sovereignty, and the efforts to develop or recover alternatives to it, that we have explored elsewhere in this chapter. Yet these critiques and efforts may be invaluable in moving us toward such radical restructuring insofar as they remind us, as David Kennedy has put it, that "it is possible to reinvent global political life,"[141] that "new modes of global political life come undone across some number of years and new ones are invented."[142] The strength of the two strands of sovereignty narratives traced in this chapter lies in their joint commitment to an understanding of sovereignty "in which the capacity to articulate and defend heterogeneity"[143] is high, and in their potential for coming together to reshape global political life so as to leave legacies of colonialism and of domination behind.

[139] "Report of the High Level Panel on Threats, Challenges and Change," *A More Secure World: Our Shared Responsibility*, U.N. Doc. A/59/565 (2 December 2004). Available online at: http://www.un.org/secureworld.

[140] Darren C. Zook, "Decolonizing Law: Identity Politics, Human Rights, and the United Nations," *Harvard Human Rights Journal*, 19 (2006): 95.

[141] David Kennedy, "Sovereignty: Responding to Anghie and Aravadum," *Texas International Law Journal*, 41 (2006): 468.

[142] Ibid., 466.

[143] Ibid.

Conclusion – The Politics of Knowledge

Resistance and Recovery

If we do not resist, we will not survive. Our resistance will guarantee our children a future.
– Winona LaDuke[1]

Knowledge has not become politicized; it always has been so. Indigenous knowledge systems explicitly recognize this by their responsiveness to the normative aspects of knowledge, to how human power and agency must be constrained if relations of affiliation with other entities are to be acknowledged and maintained – relations which enable our mutual, and multigenerational, survival. Yet the ideology of western science, wedded as it is to the thesis of value-neutrality, insists that issues of power do not enter into knowledge making or shape the dynamics of knowledge systems. The relations of domination and assimilation which characterize imperialism (whether in its historical or contemporary variants), and which facilitate biocolonialism, are thus neither acknowledged nor acknowledgeable.

And so the endangered status of indigenous knowledge systems is recognized, but responsibility for it, complicity in it, is denied:

> [C]ritical analysis of *why* Indigenous Knowledge is threatened . . . rarely moves beyond the rather simplistic assertion that the "Elders are dying" or the assumption that IK systems are more vulnerable . . . because they are oral . . . The answers to how and why our knowledge has become threatened lie embedded in the crux of the colonial infrastructure.[2]

1 Winona LaDuke, "Voices from White Earth: Gaa-waabaabiganikaag,"in Hildegarde Hannum (ed.), *Peace, Land and Community* (New Haven, Connecticut: Yale University Press, 1997): 35.

2 Leanne R. Simpson, "Anticolonial Strategies for the Recovery and Maintenance of Indigenous Knowledge," *American Indian Quarterly*, 28:3 and 4 (Summer & Fall 2004): 374–5.

With the aid of such depoliticization, corporate, academic, legal, and governmental institutions pool their interests and immense resources to extract from these knowledge systems what they find valuable in them. Indigenous agricultural and medicinal knowledge, along with traditional medicines, plant genetic resources, and the cell lines of the peoples themselves, are "discovered," processed in laboratories, legally transformed into private intellectual property, rendered as commodities, and placed for sale. A pattern that began with indigenous land and tangible resources continues now with indigenous knowledge and genetic resources. With the aid of such depoliticization, and often under the guise of humanitarian concern, these same powerful western institutions have joined together to "save" indigenous knowledges by documenting them before they disappear. What is held to be of value is removed and processed, made over in the image of knowledge as formulated within the dominant knowledge system, by methods which "seek to remove knowledge from the person, its proper place (location), and the process from which it is embedded . . . its context."[3] Thus are the rich contexts which constitute living indigenous knowledges reduced to texts: "Documenting or digitizing Indigenous Knowledge is a seemingly benign way of appearing to recover Traditional Indigenous Knowledge while at the same time increasing access to the knowledge and vastly increasing the potential for its exploitation."[4] The disappearance of indigenous peoples, their languages, and resources is, by contrast, assumed to be inevitable.

The response to these developments from indigenous communities, elders, activists, and scholars has been twofold: a fierce resistance to and critique of such ongoing imperialism coupled with a wide-ranging effort to recover and preserve indigenous knowledge systems and all that they inhere in – language, land, and culture.

The resistance begins with an insistence that this contemporary phase of colonization be recognized for what it is. Because the way in which knowledge is conceived has ethical and political implications, knowledge systems must be assessed in those terms. The tendency to abstract, isolate, and immunize the various "extractive" projects of the dominant knowledge system has been subjected to vigorous critique. Indigenists have insisted

[3] Debbie McGregor, "Coming Full Circle: Indigenous Knowledge, Environment, and Our Future," *American Indian Quarterly*, 28:3 and 4 (Summer & Fall 2004): 402.

[4] Simpson, "Anticolonial Strategies," 380.

on contextualizing biocolonialist research initiatives such as the Human Genome Diversity Project, both historically in terms of the impact of earlier comparable research as well as currently in terms of how such research is situated within powerful social alignments which perpetuate inequities. They have mounted strong advocacy internationally for the inclusion of broader human rights standards in scientific research. Individual tribes and tribal members have initiated lawsuits to protect genetic materials and resources. And first, last, and always, they have insisted in international legal and political fora on the recognition of their right as self-determining peoples to engage in decision making that impacts them, their resources, and future generations. As Sa'ke'j Youngblood Henderson notes of the successful effort to get the United Nations General Assembly to approve the Declaration on the Rights of Indigenous Peoples: "Thousands of Indigenous peoples participated over thirty years in the development of Indigenous diplomacy. They refused to accept the colonial narrative, refused to stand by and watch the destruction of Indigenous legal traditions and knowledge in the structuring of the global order."[5] Throughout these struggles, extraordinarily effective use has been made of modern communication technologies to exchange information, to generate solidarity, and to ensure publicity and exposure. Organizations such as the Indigenous Peoples Council on Biocolonialism is representative of these efforts by indigenous peoples across the globe. It provides educational and technical support "to assist indigenous peoples in the protection of their genetic resources, indigenous knowledge, cultural and human rights from the negative effects of biotechnology."[6]

Resistance in turn has spawned numerous projects of recovery. In article after article, indigenous scholars and activists speak of "an Indigenous renaissance," of how native peoples are "taking control of their destiny," and of the "revitalization of aboriginal societies." Evidence for this is plentiful and promising in efforts to recover traditional understandings of sovereignty, such as those examined in Chapter 8, where sovereignty is understood to be conditioned by responsibility and respect. Relations of domination and assimilation have no place within such a view of

[5] James (Sa'ke'j) Youngblood Henderson, *Indigenous Diplomacy and the Rights of Peoples: Achieving UN Recognition* (Saskatoon, Saskatchewan: Purich Publishing, 2008): 10. In this book, Henderson shares his insights as a participant in this process.

[6] The Indigenous Peoples Council on Biocolonialism can be accessed at: www.ipcb.org.

sovereignty; self-determination is held to be compatible with, and constrained by, mutual interdependence. Differing peoples retain their full distinctiveness and ability to live according to their own laws, customs, and ways, yet may be allied and interdependent: "We shall each travel the river together, side by side, but in our own boat. Neither of us will steer the other's vessel."[7] Indeed, connection or affiliation with them makes survival possible, and because we are so connected our survival can only be mutual. We are allied, responsible for one another.

Other moves toward recovery involve a range of related initiatives to take control of education through curricular development and the creation of tribally controlled programs and schools. These initiatives include various measures to restore indigenous languages, such as language immersion programs and internet classes. The connection between language preservation and knowledge preservation is often underscored:

> Our native language embodies a value system about how we ought to live and relate to each other . . . It gives a name to relations among kin, to roles and responsibilities among family members, to ties with the broader clan group . . . There are no English words for these relationships . . . if you destroy our languages you not only break down these relationships, but you also destroy other aspects of our Indian way of life and culture, especially those that describe man's connection with nature, the Great Spirit and the order of things.[8]

Efforts are also underway to revive spiritual ceremonies and protect the land and ecosystems which sustain indigenous peoples themselves: "The ecologies in which we live are more to us than settings or places; they . . . do not surround Indigenous peoples; we are an integral part of them and we

[7] Keith Penner, "Indian Self-Government in Canada: Report of the Special Committee" (Ottawa, Ontario: Government of Canada, 1983). This is visually captured in the *Gus-Wen-Tah*, the Two Row Wampum Treaty Belt that the Iroquois presented to the United Nations.

[8] Eli Taylor, *Towards Rebirth of First Nations Languages* (Assembly of First Nations, Ottawa, Ontario: Assembly of First Nations Education Secretariat, 1992): 14. Moreover, for those whose first concerns are conservation of biological diversity: "Those ecosystems that are most at risk are those that harbor the greatest biological diversity, and those peoples who know the most about these habitats and the relationships between and distinctions within their species hold this knowledge in linguistically specific ways." Rosemary J. Coombe, "Works in Progress: Traditional Knowledge, Biological Diversity and Intellectual Property in a Neoliberal Era," in Richard W. Perry and Bill Maurer (eds.), *Globalization under Construction: Governmentality, Law and Identity* (Minneapolis, Minnesota: University of Minnesota Press, 2003): 279.

inherently belong to them."[9] What is at stake in all of this is more than continued physical existence:

> Survival for Indigenous peoples . . . is an issue of preserving Indigenous knowledge systems in the face of cognitive imperialism. It is a global issue of maintaining Indigenous worldviews, languages and environments . . . a matter of sustaining spiritual links with the land.[10]

These and other strategies of resistance and recovery are being pursued by indigenous people and communities worldwide, determined to thwart biocolonialism, to reassert their sovereign responsibilities, and to replace "the politics of disappearance [with] the politics of debate and dialogue."[11] "Disappeared" knowledge systems, languages, resources, and peoples are acts of omission as much as commission, and assumptions that such disappearances are somehow inevitable often lie behind both. The indigenous response has been that nothing in this is foreordained. It is in our power to prevent further loss:

> It was not inevitable that Western knowledge would conquer Indigenous knowledge, or that our ways of life had to end. At any point in history we could have worked jointly toward conditions that would facilitate the return of Indigenous ways of being while appreciating the knowledge that supported those ways. Even now this is not an impossible task.[12]

[9] Marie Battiste and Sa'ke'j Youngblood Henderson, *Protecting Indigenous Knowledge and Heritage* (Saskatoon, Saskatchewan: Purich Publications, 2000): 9.

[10] Ibid., 12.

[11] Vandana Shiva, *Monocultures of the Mind* (Atlantic Highlands, New Jersey: Zed Books, 1993): 9.

[12] Angela Waziyatawin Wilson, "Indigenous Knowledge Recovery is Indigenous Empowerment," *American Indian Quarterly*, 28:3 and 4 (Summer & Fall 2004): 361.

Bibliography

Addis, Adeno, "The Thin State in Thick Globalism: Sovereignty in the Information Age," *Vanderbilt Journal of Transnational Law*, 37 (2004).

Agence France Presse, "Ashcroft to announce a decision on Moussaoui in coming week," (March 24, 2002). Available on LexisNexis Academic, News Wire Services.

Agrawal, Arun, "Indigenous and scientific knowledge: some critical comments," *Indigenous Knowledge and Development Monitor*, 3:3 (1995).

Agrawal, Arun, "Neither Having One's Cake, Nor Eating It: Intellectual Property Rights and 'Indigenous' Knowledges," *Common Property Resource Digest*, 30 (1995).

Agrawal, Arun, "On Power and Indigenous Knowledge," in Darrell A. Posey (ed.), *Cultural and Spiritual Values of Biodiversity* (London: United Nations Environmental Programme Intermediate Technology Publication, 1999).

Aldred, Lisa, "Plastic Shamans and Astroturf Sun Dance," *American Indian Quarterly*, 24:3 (2000).

Alexis, David, "Obscurity as a lifestyle," *Borderlines*, 23 (1991–1992).

Alfred, Taiaiake, *Peace, Power, Righteousness: An Indigenous Manifesto* (Don Mills, Ontario: Oxford University Press, 1999).

Alfred, Taiaiake, "Sovereignty," in Joanne Barker (ed.), *Sovereignty Matters: Locations of Contestation and Possibility in Indigenous Struggles for Self-Determination* (Lincoln, Nebraska: University of Nebraska Press, 2005).

Allen, Paula Gunn, *The Sacred Hoop* (Boston: Beacon, 1986).

Allor, Martin, "In Private Practices: Rearticulating the Subject/Audience Nexus," *Discourse Social/Social Discourse*, 2 (1989).

Anghie, Anthony, "Finding the Peripheries: Sovereignty and Colonialism in Nineteenth Century International Law," *Harvard International Law Journal*, 40 (1999).

Anghie, Anthony, "Sovereignty: Nationalism, Development and the Postcolonial State: The Legacies of the League of Nations," *Texas International Law Journal*, 41 (2006).

Annas, George and S. Elias (eds.), *Gene-Mapping* (Oxford: Oxford University Press, 1992).

Antone, Robert, "Education as a Vehicle for Values and Sovereignty," an address given at the Third International Native American Studies Conference at Lake Superior State University (October 1991).

Aoki, Keith, "Neocolonialism, Anticommons Property and Biopiracy in the (Not-So-Brave) New World Order of International Intellectual Property Protection," *Indiana Journal of Global Legal Studies*, 6 (1998).

Aoki, Keith, "The Stakes of Intellectual Property Law," in David Kairys (ed.), *The Politics of Law* (New York: Basic Books, 1982, 1998).

Apffel-Marglin, Frédérique, "Development or Decolonization in the Andes?," in Frédérique Apffel-Marglin and Julio Valladolid Rivera, *Regeneration in the Andes* (St. Urbain, Montréal, Québec: Intercultural Institute of Montréal, 1995).

Apffel-Marglin, Frédérique and Julio Valladolid Rivera, *Regeneration in the Andes* (St. Urbain, Montréal, Québec: Intercultural Institute of Montréal, 1995).

Appadurai, Arjun, *The Social Life of Things* (Cambridge: Cambridge University, 1986).

Archaeology, "Indian Camp Ranch," (March/April 1995).

Armstrong, Jeannette, "Global trade targets indigenous gene lines," *National Catholic Reporter* (January 27, 1995).

Ayer, A.J., *Language, Truth and Logic* (Oxford: Oxford University Press, 1936).

Baker, M., "La(w) – A Note to Follow So: Have We Forgotten the Federal Rules of Evidence in Music Plagiarism Cases?," *Southern California Law Review*, 65:3 (1992).

Ballantyne, Tony and Antoinette Burton, *Bodies in Contact: Rethinking Colonial Encounters in World History* (Durham, North Carolina: Duke University Press, 2005).

Barker, Joanne, "The Human Genome Diversity Project," *Cultural Studies*, 18:4 (2004).

Barker, Joanne, "For Whom Sovereignty Matters," in Joanne Barker (ed.), *Sovereignty Matters: Locations of Contestation and Possibility in Indigenous Struggles for Self-Determination* (Lincoln, Nebraska: University of Nebraska Press, 2005).

Barnes, Barry, *Scientific Knowledge and Sociological Theory* (London: Routledge & Kegan Paul, 1974).

Barnes, Barry and David Edge (eds.), *Science in Context: Readings in the Sociology of Science* (Cambridge, Massachusetts: MIT Press, 1982).
Barreiro, José, "The Search for Lessons," *Akwe:kon*, IX:2 (1982).
Barsh, Russel, "Intellectual Property and Indigenous Peoples," *American Society of International Law Proceedings*, 95 (2001).
Barsh, Russel Lawrence, "Pharmogenomics and Indigenous Peoples: Real Issues and Actors," *Cardozo Journal of International & Comparative Law*, 11 (2003).
Batalla, Guillermo Bonfil, *Utopia y Revolucíon: El Pensamiento Politico Contemporàneo de los Indios en América Latina* (Roxanne Dunbar Ortiz, trans.). (Mexico: Editorial Nueva Imagen, SA, 1981).
Battiste, Marie and Jean Barman (eds.), *First Nations Education in Canada*, (Vancouver, British Columbia: University of British Columbia Press, 1995).
Battiste, Marie and Sa'ke'j Youngblood Henderson, *Protecting Indigenous Knowledge and Heritage* (Saskatoon, Saskatchewan: Purich Publishing, 2000).
Beckwith, Jon, "Thinking of Biology: A Historical View of Social Responsibility in Genetics," *BioScience*, 43:5 (1993).
Belliotti, Raymond, "The Legacy of Marxist Jurisprudence," in David Caudill and Steven Jay Gold, *Radical Philosophy of Law: Contemporary Challenges to Mainstream Legal Theory and Practice* (Amherst, New York: Humanity Books, 1995).
Bereano, Philip, "Body and Soul: The Price of Biotech," *Seattle Times* (August 20, 1995) B5.
Bereano, Philip, Message posted to *Native-L* on October 31, 1995. Available online at: http://nativenet.uthscsa.edu/archive/nl/9511/0014.html.
Bereano, Philip, "Patent Pending: The Race to Own DNA: Guaymi Tribe Was Surprised They Were Invented: Part II," *Seattle Times* (August 27, 1995) B5.
Berg, Jeff, "Moral Rights: A Legal, Historical and Anthropological Reappraisal," *Intellectual Property Journal*, 6 (1991).
Berkes, Fikret, "Environmental Philosophy of the Chisasibi Cree People of James Bay," in Milton M.R. Freeman and Ludwig N. Carbyn (eds.), *Traditional Knowledge and Renewable Resource Management in Northern Regions* (Occasional Publication #23, Boreal Institute for Northern Studies, University of Alberta, Edmonton, Alberta, 1988).
Berlan, Jean-Pierre, "The Commodification of Life," *Monthly Review*, 41 (1989).
"Biopiracy: The Gold Rush for Human Genes" (CBC Television Broadcast, May 1, 1994). Sunday Morning.
"Biotechnology Industry Facts," available online at: http://bio.org/speeches/pubs/er/statistics.asp.
Blackstone, Sir William, 1 Commentaries on the Laws of England: Of the Rights of Things (1st edition, Oxford, 1765).

Bleier, Ruth, "Sex Differences Research," in Ruth Bleier (ed.), *Feminist Approaches to Science* (Elmsford, New York: Pergamon Press, 1986).

Bleier, Ruth, *Feminist Approaches to Science* (Elmsford, New York: Pergamon Press, 1986).

Blomley, Nicholas K., *Law, Space, and the Geographies of Power* (New York: The Guilford Press, 1994).

"Blue Mountain Declaration," reprinted in *The Seattle Times* (August 20, 1995) and available online at: http://community.seattletimes.nwsource.com/archive/?date=19950820&slug=2137238.

Bluehouse, Philmer, "The Ceremony of Making Peace," *Native Americas* (Fall 1996).

Bluemel, Erik B., "Separating Instrumental from Intrinsic Rights: Toward an Understanding of Indigenous Participation in International Rule-Making," *American Indian Law Review*, 30 (2005/2006).

Boom, Brian, "Ethics in Ethnopharmacology," in Darrell A. Posey et al. (eds.), *Ethnobiology: Implications and Applications* (Belem, Brazil: Proceedings of the First International Congress of Ethnobiology, 1990).

Bordo, Susan, *The Flight to Objectivity* (Albany, New York: State University of New York Press, 1987).

Borrows, John, "Living Between Water and Rocks: First Nations, Environmental Planning and Democracy," *University of Toronto Law Journal*, 47 (1997).

Borrows, John, "Sovereignty's Alchemy: An Analysis of *Delgamuukw v. British Columbia*," *Osgoode Hall Law Journal*, 37 (Fall 1999).

Boyle, James, *Shamans, Software & Spleens: Law and the Construction of the Information Society* (Cambridge, Massachusetts: Harvard University Press, 1996).

Bratspies, Rebecca M., "Symposium: Lands, Liberties and Legacies: Indigenous Peoples and International Law: Theoretical Approaches to International Indigenous Rights: The New Discovery Doctrine: Some Thoughts on Property Rights and Traditional Knowledge," *American Indian Law Review*, 31 (2006/2007).

Brenner, Sydney, "Old Ethics for New Issues," *Science and Public Affairs* (August 1991).

Brockway, Lucille, *Science and Colonial Expansion* (New Haven, CT: Yale University Press, 2002).

Bruchac, Joseph, "Gluskabe and the Four Wishes," in D. Dooling and P. Jordan-Smith (eds.), *I Become Part of It* (San Francisco: Harper, 1992).

Brush, Stephen B., "The Demise of 'Common Heritage' and Protection for Traditional Agricultural Knowledge," in Charles McManis (ed.), *Biodiversity & the Law: Intellectual Property, Biotechnology & Traditional Knowledge* (Sterling, Virginia: Earthscan, 2007).

Brush, Stephen B. and Doreen Stabinsky (eds.), *Valuing Local Knowledge: Indigenous People and Intellectual Property Rights* (Washington, DC: Island Press, 1996).
Burrows, Beth, "Another Patent Update: Life, Liberty, and the Pursuit of Patents," *The Boycott Quarterly*, 2:1 (1994).
Burrows, Beth, "How Do You Spell Patent? P-I-R-A-C-Y?," *The Boycott Quarterly*, 1:3 (1994).
Butler, Declan, "Genetic diversity proposal fails to impress international ethics panel," *Nature*, 377 (October 5, 1995).
Cajete, Gregory, *Native Science: Natural Laws of Interdependence* (Santa Fe, New Mexico: Clear Light Publishers, 2000).
Campbell, David and Philip Thomas (eds.), *The Province of Jurisprudence Determined* (Aldershot, UK: Ashgate Publishing, 1998 (1832)).
Canadian Broadcasting Corporation, "Sunday Morning: Biopiracy: The Gold Rush for Human Genes" (CBC Television Broadcast, May 1, 1994).
Capps, Walter Holden and Ernst F. Tonsing (eds.), *Seeing with the Native Eye: Essays on Native American Religion* (New York: Harper, 1976).
Carroll, Amy, "Not Always the Best Medicine: Biotechnology and the Global Impact of U.S. Patent Law," *American University Law Review*, 44 (1995).
Castro, Michael, *Interpreting the Indian* (Albuquerque, New Mexico: University of New Mexico Press, 1983).
Catellano, Marlene Brant, "Updating Aboriginal Traditions of Knowledge" in George J. Sefa Dei, Budd L. Hall, and Dorothy Goldin Rosenberg (eds.), *Indigenous Knowledges in Global Contexts* (Toronto, Ontario: University of Toronto Press, 2000).
Caudill, David and Steven Jay Gold, *Radical Philosophy of Law: Contemporary Challenges to Mainstream Legal Theory and Practice* (Amherst, New York: Humanity Books, 1995).
Cavalli-Sforza, L. Luca, A.C. Wilson, C.R. Cantor, R.M. Cook-Deegan, and M.C. King, "Call for a Worldwide Survey of Human Genetic Diversity: A Vanishing Opportunity for the Human Genome Project," *Genomics*, 11 (1991).
Cavalli-Sforza, L. Luca and H.T. Greely, Message posted to *Native-L* on July 8, 1993. Available online at: http://nativenet.uthscsa.edu/archive/nl/9307/0046.html.
Chambers, David Wade, "Does Distance Tyrannize Science?," in R.W. Home and S.K. Kohlstedt (eds.), *International Science and National Scientific Identity* (Dordrecht, The Netherlands: Kluwer Academic Publishers, 1991).
Chambers, David Wade, "Locality and Science: Myths of Centre and Periphery," in A. Lafuents and A. Elena y M.L. Ortega (eds.), *Mundializacíon de la cencia y cultura nacional* (Madrid: Ediciones Doce Calles, 1993).

Chambers, David Wade and Richard Gillespie, "Locality in the History of Science: Colonial Science, Technoscience and Indigenous Knowledge," *Osiris*, 15 (2000).

Chase, Allan, *The Legacy of Malthus: The Social Costs of the New Scientific Racism* (Champaign, Illinois: University of Illinois Press, 1977).

Chay, Rigoberto Queme, "The Corn Men Have Not Forgotten Their Ancient Gods," in Pablo Piancentini (ed., Inter-Press Service), *Story Earth: Native Voices on the Environment* (San Francisco: Mercury House, 1993).

Chayes, Abram and Antonia Handler Chayes, *The New Sovereignty: Compliance with International Regulatory Treaties* (Cambridge, Massachusetts: Harvard University Press, 1995).

Chen, Jim, "There's No Such Thing As Biopiracy . . . and It's a Good Thing Too," *McGeorge Law Review*, 37 (2006).

Ching, Kara H., "Indigenous Self-Determination in an Age of Genetic Patenting: Recognizing an Emerging Human Rights Norm," *Fordham Law Review*, 66 (1997).

Christie, Gordon, "Emergent Sovereignty in the Canadian Context," presented at the Pacific Division meeting of the American Philosophical Association (March 2006).

Churchill, Ward, *Fantasies of the Master Race* (Monroe, Maine: Common Courage Press, 1992).

Churchill, Ward, *Since Predator Came* (Littleton, Colorado: Aegis Publications, 1995).

Clarke, Alan W., interviewed in Chassell, Michigan (December 1, 1997).

Clarke, Alan W. and Laurelyn Whitt, *The Bitter Fruit of American Justice* (Lebanon, New Hampshire: University Press of New England, 2007).

Clay, Jason, "Editorial: Genes, Genius, and Genocide," *Cultural Survival Quarterly*, 14:4 (1990).

Code, Lorraine, *Ecological Thinking: The Politics of Epistemic Location* (New York: Oxford University Press, 2006).

Coffey, Wallace and Rebecca Tsosie, "Rethinking the Tribal Sovereignty Doctrine: Cultural Sovereignty and the Collective Future of Indian Nations," *Stanford Law and Policy Review*, 12 (2001).

Coltelli, Laura, *Winged Words: American Indian Writers Speak* (Lincoln, Nebraska: University of Nebraska Press, 1990).

Conway-Jones, Danielle, "Safeguarding Traditional Knowledge and Cultural Heritage: Supporting the Right to Self-Determination and Preventing the Commodification of Culture," *Howard Law Journal*, 48 (2005).

Cook-Deegan, Robert, *The Gene Wars* (New York: W.W. Norton & Company, 1994).

Coombe, Rosemary J., *The Cultural Life of Intellectual Properties* (Durham, North Carolina: Duke University Press, 1998).

Coombe, Rosemary J., "Works in Progress: Traditional Knowledge, Biological Diversity and Intellectual Property in a Neoliberal Era," in Richard W. Perry and Bill Maurer (eds.), *Globalization Under Construction: Governmentality, Law and Identity* (Minneapolis, Minnesota: University of Minnesota Press, 2003).

Copenhagen European Council (1993). Available at http://ue.eu.int/ueDocs/cms_Data/docs/pressdata/en/ec/72921.pdf.

Cronon, William, *Changes in the Land: Indians, Colonists, and Ecology of New England* (New York: Farrar, Straus & Giroux, 1983).

Cunningham, A.B., "Indigenous Knowledge and Biodiversity," *Cultural Survival Quarterly*, 15:1 (Summer 1991).

Danielsen, Dan, "Book Review: *Imperialism, Sovereignty and the Making of International Law* by Anthony Anghie," *American Journal of International Law*, 100 (2006).

Davis, Michael, "Bridging the Gap or Crossing a Bridge? Indigenous Knowledge and the Language of Law and Policy," paper presented to the "Bridging Scales and Epistemologies Conference," Bibliotheca Alexandrina, Alexandria, Egypt, May 17–20, 2004. Available online at: http://www.millenniumassessment.org/documents/bridging/papers/davis.michael.pdf.

"Declaration of Indigenous Peoples of the Western Hemisphere Regarding the Human Genome Diversity Project," (February 19, 1995). Available online at: www.ipcb.org.

DeFine, Michael Sullivan, "A History of Governmentally Coerced Sterilization: The Plight of the Native American Woman" (May 1, 1997). Available online at: http://www.geocities.com/CapitolHill/9118/mike2.html.

Dei, George J. Sefa, Budd L. Hall, and Dorothy Goldin Rosenberg (eds.), *Indigenous Knowledges in Global Contexts* (Toronto, Ontario: University of Toronto Press, 2000).

Deloria Jr., Vine, *Custer Died For Your Sins* (Norman, Oklahoma: University of Oklahoma Press, 1988).

Deloria Jr., Vine, "Ethnoscience and Indian Realities," *Winds of Change* (Summer 1992).

Deloria Jr., Vine, "Out of Chaos," in D. Dooling and P. Jordan-Smith (eds.), *I Become Part of It* (San Francisco: Harper, 1992).

Dill, Jordan S., "Re: Papua New Guinea Patents," (October 29, 1995). Available online at: http://nativenet.uthscsa.edu/archive/nl/9511/0282.html.

Dion-Buffalo, Yvonne and John C. Mohawk, "Thoughts from an Autochthonous Center: Postmodernism and Cultural Studies," *Akwe:kon*, IX:4 (1992).

Dodson, Michael, "Land Rights and Social Justice," in Galarrwuy Yunupingu (ed.), *Our Land is Our Life: Land Rights – Past, Present and Future* (St. Lucia, Queensland: University of Queensland Press, 1997).

Dodson, Michael, "Social Justice for Indigenous Peoples," The third David Unaipon Lecture (October 1993). Available online at: http://catalogue.nla.gov.au/Record/1453330.

Dooling, D. and Jordan-Smith, P. (eds.), *I Become Part of It* (San Francisco: Harper, 1989).

Dulbecco, Renato, "A Turning Point in Cancer Research: Sequencing the Human Genome," *Science*, 231 (1986).

Durie, Eddie, "The Law and the Land," in Jock Phillips (ed.), *Te whenua, Te Iwi: The Land and the People* (Wellington, New Zealand: Allen & Unwin, 1987).

Dutfield, Graham, *Intellectual Property, Biogenetic Resources and Traditional Knowledge* (Sterling, Virginia: Earthscan, 2004).

Dutfield, Graham, "The Public and Private Domains: Intellectual Property Rights in Traditional Knowledge," *Science Communication*, 21 (2000).

Dworkin, Gerald, "Commentary: Legal and Ethical Issues," *Science, Technology, & Human Values*, 12:1 (1987).

Echo-Hawk, Walter, "Museum Rights *vs.* Indian Rights: Guidelines for Assessing Competing Legal Interests in Native Cultural Resources," *Review of Law and Social Change*, XIV (1986).

"Ecuador, Columbia to Have Talks on FTA with US" (December 31, 2005). Available online at: http://www.bilaterals.org/article.php3?id_article=3392.

Elisabetsky, Elaine, "Folklore, Tradition, or Know-How?," *Cultural Survival Quarterly*, 15:1 (Summer 1991).

England, Charles R., "A Look at the Indian Health Service Policy of Sterilization, 1972–1976" (1997). Available online at: http://www.dickshovel.com/IHSSterPol.html.

Ermine, Willie, "Aboriginal Epistemology," in Marie Battiste and Jean Barman (eds.), *First Nations Education in Canada* (Vancouver, British Columbia: University of British Columbia Press, 1995).

Etzkowitz, Henry and Andrew Webster, "Science as Intellectual Property," in Sheila Jasanoff et al. (eds.), *Handbook of Science and Technology Studies* (Thousand Oaks, California: Sage, 1995).

Ferguson, Ann and Bat Ami Bar-On (eds.), *Daring To Be Good: Feminist Essays in Ethico-Politics* (London, UK: Routledge, Chapman and Hall, 1998).

Firestone, Jeremy, Lilley Jonathan, and Isabel Torres de Noronha, "Cultural Diversity, Human Rights, and the Emergence of Indigenous Peoples in International and Comparative Environmental Law," *American University International Law Review*, 20 (2005).

Fischer, Lawrence M., "Mining the Genome: Big Science as Big Business," *The New York Times* (January 30, 1994) Section 1.
Fletcher, Matthew, "Theoretical Restrictions on the Sharing of Indigenous Biological Knowledge," *Kansas Journal of Law & Public Policy*, 14 (2005).
Foucault, Michel, *Power/Knowledge: Selected Interviews and Other Writings, 1972–1977* (New York: Pantheon Books, 1980): 69.
Fowler, Cary, "Biotechnology, Patents, and the Third World," in Vandana Shiva and Ingunn Moser (eds.), *Biopolitics* (Atlantic Highlands, New Jersey: Zed Books, 1995).
Fowler, Michael R. and Julie M. Bunck, *Law, Power and the Sovereign State* (University Park: Penn State University Press, 1995).
Francioni, Francesco (ed.), *Biotechnologies and International Human Rights* (Portland, Oregon: Hart Publishing, 2007).
Fraser, Steven (ed.), *The Bell Curve Wars* (New York: Basic Books, 1995).
Freeman, Milton M.R. and Ludwig N. Carbyn (eds.), *Traditional Knowledge and Renewable Resource Management in Northern Regions* (Occasional Publication #23, Boreal Institute for Northern Studies, University of Alberta, Edmonton, Alberta, 1988).
Friedman, Milton, *Essays in Positive Economics* (Chicago, Illinois: University of Chicago Press, 1953).
Fruhling, Larry, "Culture Collides With Archaeology Over Ancestors Graves," *The Santa Fe New Mexican* (April 23, 1989): CH.
Fuller, Steve, *Philosophy, Rhetoric and the End of Knowledge* (Madison, Wisconsin: University of Wisconsin Press, 1993).
Fuller, Steve, *Social Epistemology* (Bloomington, Indiana: Indiana University Press, 1991).
Galtung, Johan, "After Camelot," in Irving Louis Horowitz, *The Rise and Fall of Project Camelot* (Cambridge, Massachusetts: MIT Press, 1967).
Garver, Kenneth L. and Bettylee Garver, "The Human Genome Project and Eugenic Concerns," *American Journal of Human Genetics*, 54 (1994).
Gedicks, Al, *The New Resource Wars: Native and Environmental Struggles Against Multinational Corporations* (Boston, Massachusetts: South End Press, 1993).
Gieryn, Thomas F., "Boundaries of Science," in Sheila Jasanoff et al. (eds.), *Handbook of Science and Technology Studies* (Thousand Oaks, California: Sage, 1995).
Gieryn, Thomas F., "Boundary-Work in Professional Ideologies of Science," *American Sociological Review*, 48 (December 1983).
Gillis, Anna Maria, "Getting a Picture of Human Diversity," *Bioscience*, 44:1 (1994).

Gould, Stephen Jay, *The Mismeasure of Man* (New York: WW Norton & Company, 1981).
Gramsci, Antonio, in Quintin Hoare and Geoffrey Nowell Smith (eds. and trans.), *Selections from the Prison Notebooks of Antonio Gramsci* (London: Lawrence & Wishart, 1971).
Gray, Andrew, "The Impact of Biodiversity Conservation on Indigenous Peoples," in Vandana Shiva (ed.), *Biodiversity: Social and Ecological Perspectives* (Atlantic Highlands, New Jersey: Zed Books, 1991).
Greaves, Tom (ed.), *Intellectual Property Rights for Indigenous Peoples* (Oklahoma City, Oklahoma: Society for Applied Anthropology, 1994).
Greely, Henry, HGDP (Human Genome Diversity Project), "Summary Document" Report of the International Planning Workshop (September 9–12, 1993). Available online at: http://www.stanford.edu/group/morrinst/hgdp/summary93.html.
Greely, Henry, Message posted to *Native-L* on 12 October 1993. Available online at: http://nativenet.uthscsa.edu/archive/nl/9310/0173.html.
Greely, Henry, "Message posted to *Native-L* on 25 October 1993." Available online at: http://nativenet.uthscsa.edu/archive/nl/9310/0325.html.
Greely, Henry, "Letter from Hank Henry Greely, North America HGDP Ethics Committee Chair, to Ken, HGDP Visits Guatemala" (December 16, 1993 trip report). This is no longer available on the former Rural Advancement Foundation International (RAFI) Web site. A copy is on file with the author.
Greely, Henry, "Message posted to *Native-L* on 2 February 1994." Available online at: http://nativenet.uthscsa.edu/archive/nl/9402/0020.html.
Greely, Henry, "Message posted to *Native-L* on 6 May 1994." Available online at: http://nativenet.uthscsa.edu/archive/nl/9405/0055.html.
Greely, Henry, "Message posted to *Native-L* on 20 October 1995." Available online at: http://nativenet.uthscsa.edu/archive/nl/9510/0225.html.
Greely, Henry, "Message posted to *Native-L* on 25 October 1995." Available online at: http://nativenet.uthscsa.edu/archive/nl/9510/0319.html.
Greely, Henry, "Mapping the Territory," *The Utne Reader*, 20 (1996).
Greely, Henry T., "Proposed Model Ethical Protocol for Collecting DNA Samples," *Houston Law Review*, 33 (1997).
Green, Michael (ed.), *Issues in American Indian Cultural Identity* (New York: Peter Lang, 1995).
Grinde Jr., Donald A., "Iroquois Border Crossings: Place, Politics and the Jay Treaty," in Claudia Sadowski-Smith (ed.), *Globalization on the Line: Culture, Capital and Citizenship at U.S. Borders* (New York: Palgrave, St. Martin's Press, 2002).

Gross, Paul R. and Norman Levitt, *Higher Superstition: The Academic Left and Its Quarrel With Science* (Baltimore: Johns Hopkins University Press, 1997).
Grosz, Elizabeth, *Sexual Subversions* (Sydney, Australia: Allen & Unwin, 1989).
Gutin, Joan, "End of the Rainbow," *Discover*, 15:11 (1994).
Habermas, Jurgen, *Knowledge and Human Interests* (Boston: Beacon Press, 1971).
Halbert, Debra, *Resisting Intellectual Property* (New York: Routledge, 2006).
Hamm, Bernd and Russell Smandych (eds.), *Cultural Imperialism: Essays on the Political Economy of Cultural Domination* (Peterborough, Ontario: Broadview Press, 2005).
Hannum, Hildegarde (ed.), *Peace, Land and Community* (New Haven, Connecticut: Yale University Press, 1997).
Haraway, Donna, *Primate Visions* (London: Routledge, Chapman & Hall, 1989).
Haraway, Donna, "Situated Knowledges" in Donna Haraway, *Simians, Cyborgs, and Women: The Reinvention of Nature* (New York: Routledge, 1991).
Harding, Sandra (ed.), *The "Racial" Economy of Science: Toward A Democratic Future* (Bloomington, Indiana: Indiana University Press, 1993).
Harding, Sandra, *Whose Science? Whose Knowledge?* (Ithaca, New York: Cornell University Press, 1991).
Hardt, Michael and Antonio Negri, *Empire* (Boston: Harvard University Press, 2001).
Harmon, Amy, "DNA Gatherers Hit Snag: Tribes Don't Trust Them," *The New York Times* (December 10, 2006).
Harris, LaDonna et al., "Returning to Harmony: A Comanche Effort to Reactivate the Wisdom of the People," *Native Americas* (Fall/Winter 1996).
Harry, Debra, "Acts of Self-Determination and Self-Defense: Indigenous Peoples' Responses to Biocolonialism," in Sheldon Krimsky and Peter Shorett (eds.), *Rights and Liberties in the Biotech Age: Why We Need a Genetic Bill of Rights* (Lanham, Maryland: Rowman & Littlefield, 2005).
Harry, Debra, "The Human Genome Diversity Project," *Abya Yala News*, 8 (1994).
Harry, Debra, "The Leech and the Earthworm." Available online at: www.ipcb.org.
Harry, Debra, "Tribes Meet to Discuss Genetic Colonization" (October 28, 1998). Available online at: www.ipcb.org.
Harry, Debra and Le'a Malia Kanehe, "Indigenous Land and Property Rights: Asserting Sovereignty over Cultural Property: Moving Towards Protection of Genetic Material and Indigenous Knowledge," *Seattle Journal of Social Justice*, 5 (2006).
Harry, Debra and Le'a Malia Kanehe, "Genetic Research: Collecting Blood to Preserve Culture?" *Cultural Survival Quarterly*, 29:4 (January 6, 2006).

Hayden, Cori, *When Nature Goes Public: The Making and Unmaking of Bioprospecting in Mexico* (Princeton, New Jersey: Princeton University Press, 2003).

Henderson, James (Sa'ke'j) Youngblood, *Indigenous Diplomacy and the Rights of Peoples: Achieving UN Recognition* (Saskatoon, Saskatchewan: Purich Publishing, 2008).

Henkin, Louis, "Human Rights and State 'Sovereignty,'" *Georgia Journal of International and Comparative Law*, 25 (1995).

Henkin, Louis, "That 'S' Word: Sovereignty, Globalization and Human Rights, *et cetera*," *Fordham Law Review*, 68:1 (1999).

Henkin, Louis, et al. *International Law: Cases and Materials* (St. Paul, Minnesota: West Publishing Company, 3rd edition, 1993).

Hettinger, Edwin C., "Justifying Intellectual Property," *Philosophy and Public Affairs*, 18 (1989).

Heyd, Thomas, "Indigenous Knowledge, Emancipation and Alienation," *Knowledge and Policy*, 8 (1995).

Higginbotham, C. Dean, "Native Americans Versus Archaeologists: The Legal Issues," *American Indian Law Review*, 10 (1982).

Hinman, Lawrence, *Ethics: A Pluralistic Approach to Moral Theory* (Belmont, California: Thomson Wadsworth, 3rd edition, 2003).

Hobbes, Thomas, *Leviathan*, 2nd edition (original publication: London: Printed for Andrew Crooke at the Green Dragon in St. Paul's Church-yard, 1651) (New York: Washington Square Press, 1969).

Hobson, Geary (ed.), *The Remembered Earth: An Anthology of Contemporary Native American Literature* (Albuquerque, New Mexico: University of New Mexico Press, 1979).

Hodson, Derek (ed.), *Science and Technology, Education and Ethnicity: An Aotearoa/New Zealand Perspective* – Proceedings of a Conference Held at the Royal Society of New Zealand, Wellington, May 7–8, 1996 (1998).

Home, R.W. and S.K. Kohlstedt (eds.), *International Science and National Scientific Identity* (Dordrecht, The Netherlands: Kluwer Academic Publishers, 1991).

Horowitz, Irving Louis, *The Rise and Fall of Project Camelot* (Cambridge, Massachusetts: MIT Press, 1967).

Horwitz, Morton, *The Transformation of American Law*, 1780–1860 (Cambridge, Massachusetts: Harvard University Press, 1977).

Hubbard, Ruth, "Constructs of Genetic Differences: Races and Sex," in Robert F. Weir et al. (eds.), *Genes and Human Self-Knowledge: Historical and Philosophical Reflections on Modern Genetics* (Iowa City, Iowa: University of Iowa Press, 1994).

Human Genome Diversity Project (HGDP), "FAQ" (Answers to "Frequently Asked Questions" regarding the HGDP) (1996). Available online at: http://www.leland.stanford.edu/group/moprrinst/HGDP.html.

Human Genome Diversity Project (HGDP), "Summary of Planning Workshop 3(B): Ethical and Human Rights Implications, Human Genome Diversity Project" (Bethesda, Maryland: HGDP Organizing Committee, 1993).

Hungry Wolf, Beverly, *The Ways of My Grandmothers* (New York: William Morrow & Co., 1982).

Hunt, Alan, "Foucault's Expulsion of Law: Toward a Retrieval, Law and Social Inquiry," *Law and Social Inquiry*, 1 (1992).

Hyde, Lewis, *The Gift* (New York: Random House, 1979).

Indigenous Knowledge and Development Monitor. "Editorial," *Indigenous Knowledge and Development Monitor*, 4:1 (1996).

The Indigenous Peoples Council on Biocolonialism (IPCB). Available online at: www.ipcb.org.

Ivison, Duncan, Paul Patton, and Will Sanders (eds.), *Political Theory and the Rights of Peoples* (Cambridge, UK: Cambridge University Press, 2000).

Jacobs, John et al., "Characterization of the Anticoagulant Activities from a Brazilian Arrow Poison," *Journal of Thrombosis and Haemostasis*, 63:1 (1991).

Jacobsen, Michael and Stephanie Lawson, "Between Globalization and Localization: A Case Study of Human Rights Versus State Sovereignty," *Global Governance*, 5 (1999).

Jaimes, M. Annette (ed.), *The State of Native America: Genocide, Colonization and Resistance* (Boston, Massachusetts: South End Press, 1992).

Jamieson, Dale (ed.), *A Companion to Environmental Philosophy* (Oxford, UK: Basil Blackwell, 2000).

Jamieson, Dale, "The Poverty of Postmodernism," *University of Colorado Law Review*, 62:3 (1991).

Jaroff, L., "The Gene Hunt," *Time* (March 20, 1989).

Jasanoff, Sheila, et al. (eds.), *Handbook of Science and Technology Studies* (Thousand Oaks, California: Sage, 1995).

Jiaxuan, Tang, "Statement by Foreign Minister Tang Jiaxuan at the 54th Session of the UN General Assembly," *United Nations General Assembly*, 54th Session, (November 15, 2000). Available online at: http://www.fmprc.gov.cn/eng/gjwt/gjzzhy/2594/2602/t15218.htm.

Johnson, Deborah (ed.), *Ethical Issues in Engineering* (Old Tappan, New Jersey: Prentice-Hall, 1991).

Johnson, Liz, "Cultural Revitalization," *Identity*, 4:2 (1981).

Johnson, Martha, "Documenting Dene Traditional Environmental Knowledge," *Akwekon*, IX:2 (1992).

Johnson, Ralph W., "Fragile Gains: Two Centuries of Canadian and United States Policy Toward Indians," *Washington Law Review*, 66 (1991).

Johnston, David, "Spiritual Seekers Borrow Indian Ways," *New York Times* (December 27, 1993). A:15.

Jones, James H., *Bad Blood: The Tuskegee Syphilis Experiment* (New York: Free Press, 1981).

Kahn, Patricia, "Genetic Diversity Project Tries Again," *Science*, 266 (November 4, 1994).

Kahn, Zeshan, "Colonialism Revisited: Insights into the Human Genome Diversity Project," *Journal of Law and Social Challenges*, 3 (1999).

Kairys, David (ed.), *The Politics of Law* (New York: Basic Books, 1982, 1998).

Kaplan, Jonathan, in the transcript of "Who Owns Life?: Patenting Human Genes," *Living On Earth* (World Media Foundation, 1994): Broadcast on May 13, 1994.

Karjala, Dennis, "Biotech Patents and Indigenous Peoples," *Minnesota Journal of Law and Science*, 7 (2006).

Keeshig-Tobias, Laura, "Stop stealing native stories," *Toronto Globe and Mail* (January 26, 1990). A:7.

Kennedy, David, "Sovereignty: Responding to Anghie and Aravadum," *Texas International Law Journal*, 41 (2006).

Kenney, Martin, *Biotechnology: The University–Industrial Complex* (New Haven, Connecticut: Yale University Press, 1986).

Kimbrell, Andrew, *The Human Body Shop* (San Francisco, California: Harper, 1983).

King, Michael (ed.), *Te Ao Hurihuri Aspects of Maoritanga* (Auckland, New Zealand: Reed Publishing, 1992).

Kloppenburg, Jack, *First The Seed: The Political Economy of Plant Biotechnology*, 1492–2000 (Cambridge, UK: Cambridge University Press, 1988).

Kloppenburg, Jack Jr., "No Hunting! Scientific Poaching and Global Biodiversity," *Z Magazine* (September 1990).

Kloppenburg, Jack and Daniel Kleinman, "Seed Wars: Common Heritage, Private Property, and Political Strategy," *Socialist Review*, 95 (September/ October 1987.)

Korten, David C., *When Corporations Rule the World*, 2nd edition (Bloomfield, Connecticut: Kumarian Press, 2001).

Koshland, Daniel, "Thinking of Biology: A Historical View of Social Responsibility in Genetics," *Bioscience*, 43 (1993).

Krimsky, Sheldon and Peter Shorett (eds.), *Rights and Liberties in the Biotech Age: Why We Need a Genetic Bill of Rights* (Lanham, Maryland: Rowman & Littlefield, 2005).

LaDuke, Winona, "Traditional Ecological Knowledge and Environmental Futures," *Colorado Journal of International Environmental Law and Policy*, 5 (1994).

LaDuke, Winona, "Voices from White Earth: Gaa-waabaabiganikaag," in Hildegarde Hannum (ed.), *Peace, Land and Community* (New Haven, Connecticut: Yale University Press, 1997).

Lafuents, A. and A. Elena y M.L. Ortega (eds.), *Mundializacíon de la cencia y cultura nacional* (Madrid: Ediciones Doce Calles, 1993).

Latour, Bruno and Steve Woolgar, *Laboratory Life* (Thousand Oaks, California: Sage, 1979).

Laudan, Larry, *Science and Values* (Berkeley, California: University of California Press, 1984).

Lawrence, Thomas, *The Principles of International Law* (London: Macmillan, 1895).

Lenzerini, Federico, "Biogenetic Resources and Indigenous Peoples' Rights," in Francesco Francioni (ed.), *Biotechnologies and International Human Rights* (Portland, Oregon: Hart Publishing, 2007).

Lewontin, Richard C., "The Dream of the Human Genome," *The New York Review of Books* (May 28, 1992).

Lewontin, Richard C., et al., *Not in Our Genes: Biology, Ideology, and Human Nature* (New York: Pantheon Books, 1984).

Liddle, John, quoted in David Nason, "Tickner Warns Over Aboriginal Gene Sampling," *The Australian* (January 25, 1994).

Lind, Christopher, "The Idea of Capitalism or the Capitalism of Ideas? A Moral Critique of the Copyright Act," *Intellectual Property Journal*, 7 (December 1991).

Lock, Margaret, "Editorial: Interrogating the Human Genome Diversity Project," *Social Science and Medicine*, 39 (1994).

Lock, Margaret, "Genetic Diversity and the Politics of Difference," *Chicago-Kent Law Review*, 75 (1999).

Locke, John, *Second Treatise of Government*, 3rd edition (New York: Liberal Arts Press, 1690, 1952).

Longino, Helen, *Science as Social Knowledge* (Princeton, New Jersey: Princeton University Press, 1990).

Lyons, David, "The Balance of Injustice and the War for Independence," *Monthly Review*, 45 (1994).

Lyons, Oren, "Our Mother Earth," in Dooling, D. and Jordan-Smith, P. (eds.), *I Become Part of It* (San Francisco, California: Harper, 1989).

Lyons, Oren, R.C.A.P. Public Hearings, Akwesasne (May 1993). Available online at: http://sisis.nativeweb.org/mohawk/ovide.html.

MacKay, David, "Agents of Empire: The Banksian Collectors and Evaluation of New Land," in David Philip Miller and Peter Reill (eds.), *Visions of Empire: Voyages, Botany and Representations of Nature* (Cambridge: Cambridge University Press, 1996).

MacKenzie, Debora, "European Commission Tables New Proposals on Genome Research," *New Scientist* (November 25, 1989).

MacLeod, Roy, "On Science and Colonialism," *Science and Society in Ireland: The Social Context of Science and Technology in Ireland, 1800–1950* (Belfast: Queen's University, 1997).

MacLeod, Roy, "On Visiting the 'Moving Metropolis': Reflections on the Architecture of Imperial Science," *Historical Records of Australian Science*, 5 (1982).

MacLeod, Roy, "Reading the Discourse of Colonial Science," in Patrick Petitjean (ed.), *Les Sciences Coloniales: Figures et Institutions* (Paris: ORSTOM, 1996).

MacLeod, Roy and Philip F. Rehbock (eds.), *Nature in Its Greatest Extent: Western Science in the Pacific* (Honolulu, Hawaii: University of Hawaii Press, 1988).

Manguel, Alberto, "Equal rights to stories," *Toronto Globe and Mail* (February 3, 1990). D:7.

Manihera, T., "Foreword: Learning and Tapu," in Michael King (ed.), *Te Ao Hurihuri Aspects of Maoritanga* (Auckland, New Zealand: Reed Publishing, 1992).

Marglin, Stephen A., "Toward the Decolonization of the Mind" and "Losing Touch," in Stephen A. Marglin and Frédérique Apffel Marglin (eds.), *Dominating Knowledge* (Oxford, UK: Clarendon Press, 1990).

Marglin, Stephen A. and Frédérique Apffel Marglin (eds.), *Dominating Knowledge* (Oxford, UK: Clarendon Press, 1990).

Marks, Jonathan, "Commentary: The Human Genome Diversity Project," *Anthropological News* (April 1995).

Marks, Jonathan, *Human Biodiversity: Genes, Race and History* (Hawthorne, New York: Aldine de Gruyter, 1995).

Marsden, Maori, "God, Man and the Universe: A Maori View," in Michael King (ed.), *Te Ao Hurihuri Aspects of Maoritanga* (Auckland, New Zealand: Reed Publishing, 1992).

Martin, Calvin (ed.), *The American Indian and the Problem of History* (New York: Oxford University Press, 1987).

Matthiessen, Peter, *Indian Country*, 4th edition (New York: Penguin Books, 1984).

McGowan, Janet, "Who is the Inventor?," *Cultural Survival Quarterly*, 15:1 (Summer 1991).

McGregor, Debbie, "Coming Full Circle: Indigenous Knowledge, Environment, and Our Future," *American Indian Quarterly*, 28:3 and 4 (Summer/Fall 2004).
McIntyre, Alison, "Doing Away with Double Effect," *Ethics*, 111:2 (2001).
McLaughlin, Andrew, *Regarding Nature* (Albany, New York: State University of New York Press, 1993).
McManis, Charles (ed.), *Biodiversity & the Law: Intellectual Property, Biotechnology & Traditional Knowledge* (Sterling, Virginia: Earthscan, 2007).
McPherson, Elizabeth Clay, "Ethical Implications of the Human Genome Diversity Project," *Nursing Connections*, 8:1 (1996).
Mead, Aroha, "Letter from Aroha Mead, Director, International Association of the Mataatua Declaration, to Dr. Darrell Macer, Sub-Committee on Population Genetics," UNESCO International Bioethics Committee, UNESCO-Bioethics & Human Population Research (July 29, 1995). Available online at: http://nativenet. uthscsa.edu/archive/nl/9510/0350.html.
Merryman, John, "Two Ways of Thinking About Cultural Property," *The American Journal of International Law*, 80:4 (1986).
Messenger, Phyllis (ed.), *The Ethics of Collecting Cultural Property* (Albuquerque, New Mexico: The University of New Mexico Press, 1989).
Meyer, Manu, "To Set Right–Ho'oponopono: A Native Hawaiian Way of Peacemaking," *Complete Law* (Fall 1995).
Mgbeoji, Ikechi, *Global Biopiracy, Patents, Plants and Indigenous Knowledge* (Ithaca, New York: Cornell University Press, 2006).
Miller, David Philip and Peter Reill (eds.), *Visions of Empire: Voyages, Botany and Representations of Nature* (Cambridge, UK: Cambridge University Press, 1996).
Momaday, N. Scott, "Native American Attitudes to the Environment," in Walter Holden Capps and Ernst F. Tonsing (eds), *Seeing with the Native Eye: Essays on Native American Religion* (New York: Harper, 1976).
Mooney, Pat and Edward Hammond, "Letter from Pat Mooney and Edward Hammond, of RAFI, to Concerned Readers regarding U.S. Patent on Hagahai Persons' Cell Line" (October 25, 1995). Available online at: http://nativenet. uthscsa.edu/archive/nl/9510/0310.html.
Moore, John H., "Native Americans, Scientists, and the Human Genome Diversity Project," *Cultural Survival Quarterly*, 20:2 (Summer 1996).
Moore, John H., "Putting Anthropology Back Together Again," *American Anthropologist*, 96:4 (1994).
Morris, Glenn, "International Law and Politics: Toward a Right to Self-Determination for Indigenous Peoples," in M. Annette Jaimes (ed.), *The State of Native America: Genocide, Colonization, and Resistance* (Boston, Massachusetts: South End Press, 1992).

Murray, Thomas H., "Ethical Issues in Human Genome Research," in Kristin Shrader-Frechette and Laura Westra (eds.), *Technology and Values* (Lanham, Maryland: Rowman & Littlefield, 1997).

Myers, Norman, *A Wealth of Wild Species* (Boulder, Colorado: Westview Press, 1983).

Nader, Laura (ed.), *Naked Science: Anthropological Inquiry into Boundaries, Power, and Knowledge* (New York: Routledge, 1996).

Nason, David, "Tickner Warns Over Aboriginal Gene Sampling," *The Australian* (January 25, 1994).

National Academy of Sciences, "Methods and Values in Science," in Sandra Harding (ed.), *The "Racial" Economy of Science: Toward A Democratic Future* (Bloomington, Indiana: Indiana University Press, 1993).

National Research Council, "Study on the Proposed Human Genome Diversity Project: Request for Input and Notice of Public Meetings" (June 16, 1996). Available online at: http://nativenet.uthscsa.edu/archive/nl/9606/0078.html.

National Science Foundation (NSF), "Pilot Projects for a Human Genome Diversity Project: Special Competition," file nsf96112 (1996). Available online via the NSF homepage (http://www.nsf.gov).

Nelkin, Dorothy, "A Brief History of the Political Work of Genetics," *Jurimetrics*, 42 (2002).

Niezen, Ronald, *The Origins of Indigenism: Human Rights and the Politics of Identity* (Berkeley, California: University of California Press, 2003).

Nkrumah, Kwame, *Neo-Colonialism: The Last Stage of Imperialism* (Atlantic Highlands, New Jersey: Humanities Press International, 1965).

Noble, Cheryl, "Ethics and Experts," *Hastings Center Report*, 12:3 (1982).

Norman, Waerete, "Tikanga Wahine in a Changing World," (unpublished Ph.D. dissertation, University of Auckland, 2000).

Odek, James, "Bio-Piracy: Creating Proprietary Rights in Plant Genetic Resources," *Journal of Intellectual Property Law*, 2 (1994).

Oguamanam, Chidi, "Localizing Intellectual Property in the Globalization Epoch: The Integration of Indigenous Knowledge," *Indiana Journal of Global Legal Studies*, 11:2 (2004).

Oliveira, Paulo Celso de, "Brazil: Uru-eu-wau-wau Need Help," (March 25, 1996). Available online at: http://nativenet.uthscsa.edu/archive/nl/9603/0182.html.

Oppenheim, Lassa, *International Law: A Treatise* (2nd edition, 1912).

Osterhammel, Jürgen, *Colonialism: A Theoretical Overview* (Princeton, New Jersey: Markus Wiener, 1997).

Overing, Joanna, "Introduction," in Joanna Overing (ed.), *Reason and Morality* (London: Tavistock Publications, 1985).

Overing, Joanna (ed.), *Reason and Morality* (London: Tavistock Publications, 1985).
"Paha Sapa: The Struggle for the Black Hills" (HBO television broadcast, September 1993).
Palmer, Richard E., "Toward A Postmodern Interpretive Self-Awareness," *The Journal of Religion*, 55:3 (1975).
Parkin, David (ed.), *Semantic Anthropology* (London: Academic Press, 1982).
Patterson, John, *Exploring Maori Values* (Palmerston North, New Zealand: The Dunmore Press, 1992).
Patterson, L. Ray et al., *The Nature of Copyright* (Atlanta, Georgia: University of Georgia Press, 1991).
Penner, Keith, "Indian Self-Government in Canada: Report of the Special Committee" (Ottawa, Ontario: Government of Canada, 1983).
Perry, Richard W. and Bill Maurer (eds.), *Globalization Under Construction: Governmentality, Law and Identity* (Minneapolis, Minnesota: University of Minnesota Press, 2003).
Petitjean, Patrick (ed.), *Les Sciences Coloniales: Figures et Institutions* (Paris: ORSTOM, 1996).
Pewhairangi, N., "Foreword: Learning and Tapu," in Michael King (ed.), *Te Ao Hurihuri Aspects of Maoritanga* (Auckland, New Zealand: Reed Publishing, 1992).
Philpott, Daniel, "Sovereignty: An Introduction and Brief History," *Journal of International Affairs*, 48:2 (1995).
Piancentini, Pablo (ed., Inter-Press Service), *Story Earth: Native Voices on the Environment* (San Francisco, California: Mercury House, 1993).
Poincaré, Henri, *The Value of Science* (New York: Dover Publications, 1905).
Polanyi, Karl, *Primitive, Archaic and Modern Economies: Essays of Karl Polanyi* (New York: Doubleday, 1968).
Popper, Karl, *Unended Quest* (La Salle, Illinois: Open Court, 1982).
Porter, Robert, "The Meaning of Indigenous Nation Sovereignty," *Arizona State Law Journal*, 34:75 (2002).
Posey, Darrell A. (ed.), *Cultural and Spiritual Values of Biodiversity* (London: United Nations Environmental Programme Intermediate Technology Publication, 1999).
Posey, Darrell A. and Graham Dutfield, *Beyond Intellectual Property: Toward Traditional Resource Rights for Indigenous Peoples and Local Communities* (Ottawa, Ontario: International Development Research Centre, 1996).
Posey, Darrell A. et al. (eds.), *Ethnobiology: Implications and Applications* (Belem, Brazil: Proceedings of the First International Congress of Ethnobiology, 1990).

Posey, Darrell Addison, "Biodiversity, Genetic Resources, and Indigenous Peoples in Amazonia," prepared for: *Amazonia 2000: Development, Environment, and Geopolitics*, Institute of Latin American Studies, University of London (June 24–26, 1998). Available online at: http://www.ubcic.bc.ca/files/PDF/Posey_Biodiversity.pdf.

Proctor, Robert N., *Value-Free Science? Purity and Power in Modern Knowledge* (Cambridge, Massachusetts: Harvard University Press, 1991).

Puketapu-Hetet, Erenora, *Maori Weaving with Erenora Puketapu-Hetet* (Auckland, New Zealand: Pitman, 1989).

Puketapu-Hetet, Erenora, "Te Atiawa," in D. Nicholas (ed.), *Seven Maori Artists: Interviews* (Wellington, New Zealand: V.R. Ward, 1980).

RAFI (Rural Advancement Foundation International), "Stealing Indigenous Genes," *Abya Yala News*, 7:2 (1994).

RAFI, "US Funding of Human Biodiversity Collections Carries on Despite Contrary Scientific Advice" (1997). Available online at: http://www.etcgroup.org/en/materials/publications.html?pub_id=434.

RAFI, "Scientific Review Rejects the HGDP" (October 25, 1997). Available online at: http://www.etcgroup.org/en/materials/publications.html?pub_id=436.

"RAFI and RAFI-USA Announce Plans of Name Change for Globally-focused RAFI" (February 5, 2001). Available online at: http://www.etcgroup.org/en/materials/publications.html?pub_id=282.

RAFI Communiqué, "The Human Tissue Trade," (January–February 1997). Available online at: http://www.etcgroup.org/en/archives.htm.

Reardon, Jenny, *Race to the Finish: Identity and Governance in an Age of Genomics* (Princeton, New Jersey: Princeton University Press, 2005).

Reingold, Nathan and Marc Rothenberg (eds.), *Scientific Colonialism* (Washington DC: Smithsonian Press, 1987).

Riding In, James, "Without Ethics and Morality: A Historical Overview of Imperial Archaeology and American Indians," *Arizona State Law Journal*, 24:1 (1992).

Riley, Angela R., "Recovering Collectivity: Group Rights to Collectivity in Indigenous Communities," *Cardozo Arts & Entertainment Law Journal*, 18 (2000).

Riley, Michael, "Bury My Heart at Big Mountain," *Time*, 7 July (1986). Available online at: http://www.time.com/time/magazine/article/0,9171,961656,00.html.

Rivera, Julio Valladolid, "Andean Peasant Agriculture: Nurturing a Diversity of Life in the *Chacra*," in Apffel-Marglin, Frédérique and Julio Valladolid Rivera, *Regeneration in the Andes* (St. Urbain, Montréal, Québec: Intercultural Institute of Montréal, 1995).

Rix, Bo Andreassen, "Should Ethical Concerns Regulate Science?: The European Experience With the Human Genome Project," *Bioethics*, 5:3 (1991).
Roberts, Jenna, "Global Project Underway to Sample Genetic Diversity," *Nature*, 361 (1993).
Roberts, Leslie, "A Genetic Survey of Vanishing Peoples," *Science*, 252 (1991).
Roberts, Leslie, "Genetic Diversity Project: Anthropologists Climb (Gingerly) on Board," *Science*, 258 (1992).
Roberts, Leslie, "How to Sample the World's Genetic Diversity," *Science*, 257 (1992).
Roberts, R.J., "Is Information Property?," *Intellectual Property Journal*, 3:2 (1987).
Roberts, Roma Mere, "Indigenous Knowledge and Western Science: Perspectives from the Pacific," in Derek Hodson (ed.), *Science and Technology, Education and Ethnicity: An Aotearoa/New Zealand Perspective–Proceedings of a Conference Held at the Royal Society of New Zealand, Wellington, May 7–8, 1996* (1998).
Roberts, Roma Mere and Peter R. Wills, "Understanding Maori Epistemology: A Scientific Perspective," in Helmut Wautischer (ed.), *Tribal Epistemologies: Essays in the Philosophy of Anthropology* (Surrey, UK: Ashgate Publishing, 1998).
Roberts, Roma Mere, et al., "Kaitiakitanga: Maori Perspectives on Conservation," *Pacific Conservation Biology: A Journal Devoted to Conservation and Land Management in the Pacific Region* (1995).
Roht-Arriaza, Naomi, "Of Seeds and Shamans: The Appropriation of the Scientific and Technical Knowledge of Indigenous Local Communities," *Michigan Journal of International Law*, 17 (1996).
Rorty, Richard, "Intuition," in Paul Edwards (ed.), *The Encyclopedia of Philosophy* IV (New York: MacMillan, 1967).
Rosaldo, Renato, *Culture and Truth* (Boston, Massachusetts: Beacon Press, 1993).
Rose, Wendy, "Epigraph to Truganinny," in *The Halfbreed Chronicles and Other Poems* (Los Angeles, California: West End Press, 1985).
Rose, Wendy, "The Great Pretenders," in M. Annette Jaimes (ed.), *The State of Native America: Genocide, Colonization and Resistance* (Boston, Massachusetts: South End Press, 1992).
Rouse, Joseph, *Knowledge and Power: Toward a Political Philosophy of Science* (Ithaca, New York: Cornell University Press, 1987).
Rouse, Joseph, "The Dynamics of Power and Knowledge in Science," *The Journal of Philosophy*, 88 (1991).

Rushing, Francis W. and Carole Ganz Brown (eds.), *Intellectual Property Rights in Science, Technology, and Economic Performance* (Boulder, Colorado: Westview Press, 1990).

Sadowski-Smith, Claudia (ed.), *Globalization on the Line: Culture, Capital and Citizenship at U.S. Borders* (New York: Palgrave, St. Martin's Press, 2002).

Said, Edward, *Culture and Imperialism* (New York: Random House, 1993).

Salmond, Anne, "Theoretical Landscapes: On Cross-Cultural Conceptions of Knowledge," in David Parkin (ed.), *Semantic Anthropology* (London: Academic Press, 1982).

Samuelson, Pamela, "Innovation and Competition: Conflicts over Intellectual Property Rights in New Technologies," *Science, Technology & Human Values*, 12:1 (1987).

Sarat, Austin and Thomas R. Kearns (eds.), *Human Rights: Concepts, Contests, Contingencies* (Ann Arbor, Michigan: University of Michigan Press, 2001).

Schiebinger, Londa, *Plants and Empire: Colonial Bioprospecting in the Atlantic World* (Cambridge, Massachusetts: Harvard University Press, 2004).

Schiemann, Konrad, "Europe and the Loss of Sovereignty," *International and Comparative Law Quarterly*, 56 (2007).

Schiller, Herbert, *Communication and Cultural Domination* (New York: M.E. Sharpe, 1976).

Scott, Colin, "Science for the West, Myth for the Rest?: The Case of James Bay Cree Knowledge Construction," in Laura Nader (ed.), *Naked Science: Anthropological Inquiry into Boundaries, Power, and Knowledge* (New York: Routledge, 1996).

Scott, Craig, "Indigenous Self-Determination and Decolonization of the International Imagination: A Plea," *Human Rights Quarterly*, 18 (1996).

Selin, Helaine (ed.), *Encyclopaedia of the History of Science, Technology and Medicine in Non-Western Cultures* (Dordrecht, The Netherlands: Kluwer Academic Publishers, 2008).

Semken, Steve, "Keyah: A Geological Sense of Place," in Diné College Instructor's Guide (1997). (unpublished)

Shelton, Dinah, "Globalization & the Erosion of Sovereignty," *Boston College International and Comparative Law Review*, 25 (2002).

Sherwin, Susan, *No Longer Patient: Feminist Ethics and Health Care* (Philadelphia, Pennsylvania: Temple University Press, 1992).

Shiva, Vandana (ed.), *Biodiversity: Social and Ecological Perspectives* (Atlantic Highlands, New Jersey: Zed Books, 1991).

Shiva, Vandana, *Biopiracy: The Plunder of Nature and Knowledge* (Boston, Massachusetts: South End Press, 1999).

Shiva, Vandana, *Monocultures of the Mind* (Atlantic Highlands, New Jersey: Zed Books, 1993).

Shiva, Vandana, *The Violence of the Green Revolution* (Atlantic Highlands, New Jersey, Zed Books, 1991).
Shiva, Vandana and Ingunn Moser (eds.), *Biopolitics* (Atlantic Highlands, New Jersey: Zed Books, 1995).
Silko, Leslie Marmon, *Yellow Woman and a Beauty of the Spirit: Essays on Native American Life Today* (New York: Simon & Schuster, 1996).
Silva, José de Souza, "Plant Intellectual Property Rights: The Rise of Nature as a Commodity," in N. Patrick Peritore and Ana Karina Galve-Peritore (eds.), *Biotechnology in Latin America* (Wilmington, Delaware: Scholarly Resources, 1995).
Simpson, Leanne R., "Anticolonial Strategies for the Recovery and Maintenance of Indigenous Knowledge," *American Indian Quarterly*, 28:3 and 4 (Summer/Fall 2004).
Singeo, Lindsey, "The Patentability of the Native Hawaiian Genome," *American Journal of Law and Medicine*, 33 (2007).
Singer, Joseph William, "Legal Realism," *California Law Review*, 76 (1988).
Sinha, Gayatri, "Diatribe or Art?," *The Hindu* (September 1, 2002). Available online at: http://www.hindu.com/thehindu/mag/2002/09/01/stories/2002090100340200.htm.
Skene, Loane, "Mapping the Human Genome: Some Thoughts for Those Who Say 'There Should Be a Law on It,'" *Bioethics*, 5:3 (1991).
Smart, Carol, *Feminism and the Power of Law* (New York: Routledge, 1989).
Smith, Robert L., "DNA Probe Angers the 'Endangered,'" *Syracuse Post Standard* (September 9, 1993).
Soleri, Daniela and David A. Cleveland, "Gifts from the Creator: Intellectual Property Rights and Folk Crop Varieties," in Tom Greaves (ed.), *Intellectual Property Rights for Indigenous Peoples* (Oklahoma City, Oklahoma: Society for Applied Anthropology, 1994).
South and Meso American Indian Information Center (SAIIC), "Message posted to *Native-L* on 9 November 1993." Available online at: http://nativenet.uthscsa.edu/archive/nl/9311/0069.html.
"Sovereignty," *Stanford Encyclopedia of Philosophy*. Available online at: http://plato.stanford.edu/entries/sovereignty.
Stacy, Helen, "Relational Sovereignty," *Stanford Law Review*, 55 (2003).
Standing Bear, Luther, *Land of the Spotted Eagle* (Lincoln, Nebraska: University of Nebraska Press, 1978 (1933)).
Starr, Paul, *The Social Transformation of American Medicine* (New York: Basic Books, 1982).
Stemerding, Dirk and Jaap Jelsma, "Compensatory Ethics for the Human Genome Diversity Project," *Science as Culture*, 5:24 (1996).

Stepan, Nancy, *The Idea of Race in Science: Great Britain 1800–1960* (London: MacMillan, 1982).

Stepan, Nancy, "Race and Gender: The Role of Analogy in Science," in Sandra Harding (ed.), *The Racial Economy of Science: Toward a Democratic Future* (Bloomington, Indiana: Indiana University Press, 1993): 360.

Sunder, Madhavi, "The Invention of Traditional Knowledge," *Law and Contemporary Problems*, 70 (2007).

Swazey, Judith, "Those Who Forget Their History: Lessons From the Recent Past for the Human Genome Quest," in George Annas and S. Elias (eds.), *Gene-Mapping* (Oxford, UK: Oxford University Press, 1992).

Swidorski, Carl, "Constituting the Modern State," in David Caudill and Steven Jay Gold, *Radical Philosophy of Law: Contemporary Challenges to Mainstream Legal Theory and Practice* (Amherst, New York: Humanity Books, 1995).

Tafoya, Terry, "Coyote's Eyes: Native Cognition Styles," *Journal of American Indian Education* (February 1982).

Tate, Warren, "A Report on the HRC Consensus Development Conference," *Centre for Gene Research Newsletter* (August 1995). This was available at http://biochem.otago.ac.nz:800/cgr/cgrnews.html, but the issue has been deleted from the site. However, a copy is on file with the author.

Tauli-Corpuz, Victoria, "We Are Part of Biodiversity. Respect Our Rights," *Third World Resurgence*, 36 (1993).

Taylor, Eli, *Towards Rebirth of First Nations Languages* (Assembly of First Nations, Ottawa, Ontario: Assembly of First Nations Education Secretariat, 1992).

Thomas, Nicholas, *Colonialism's Culture* (Princeton, New Jersey: Princeton University Press, 1994).

Trask, Haunani-Kay, *From a Native Daughter* (Monroe, Maine: Common Courage Press, 1993).

Tremblay, Gail, Statement for Exhibition of Contemporary Native American Art, "We Are Many, We Are One," curated by Jaune Quick-to-See Smith (1997).

Tsosie, Rebecca, "Land, Culture, and Community: Reflections on Native Sovereignty and Property in America," *Indiana Law Review*, 34 (2001).

Vicedo, Margo, "The Human Genome Project: Towards an Analysis of the Empirical, Ethical, and Conceptual Issues Involved," *Biology and Philosophy*, 7 (1992).

Vizenor, Gerald, "Socioacupuncture: Mythic Reversals and the Striptease in Four Scenes," in Calvin Martin (ed.), *The American Indian and the Problem of History* (New York: Oxford University Press, 1987).

Vogel, Howard J., "Reframing Rights From the Ground Up: The Contribution of the New U.N. Law of Self-Determination to Recovering the Principle of

Sociability on the Way To a Relational Theory of International Human Rights," *Temple International and Comparative Law Journal*, 20 (2006).
Waldouz, Michael and Hilary Stout, *The Wall Street Journal*, CCXIX:76 (April 17, 1992).
Walker, Ranginui, "The Relevance of Maori Myth and Tradition," in Michael King (ed.), *Te Ao Hurihuri Aspects of Maoritanga* (Auckland, New Zealand: Reed Publishing, 1992).
Walker, R.B.J. and Saul H. Mendlovitz, *Contending Sovereignties: Redefining Political Community* (Boulder, Colorado: Lynne Rienner Publishers, 1990).
Wallis, Roger and Krister Malm, *Big Sounds From Small Peoples* (New York: Pendragon Press, 1984).
Warren, Karen, "A Philosophical Perspective on the Ethics and Resolution of Cultural Properties Issues," in Phyllis Messenger (ed.), *The Ethics of Collecting Cultural Property* (Albuquerque, New Mexico: The University of New Mexico Press, 1989).
Warrior, Robert Allen, *Tribal Secrets* (Minneapolis, Minnesota: University of Minnesota Press, 1995).
Wartenberg, Thomas, *The Forms of Power: From Domination to Transformation* (Philadelphia, Pennsylvania: Temple University Press, 1990).
Washburn, Wilcomb, "Distinguishing History from Moral Philosophy and Public Advocacy," in Calvin Martin (ed.), *The American Indian and the Problem of History* (New York: Oxford University Press, 1987).
van de Wateringen, Susanne, "USA Pushes Ecuador to Sign IPR Agreement," *Biotechnology and Development Monitor*, 33 (December 1997). Available online at: http://www.biotech-monitor.nl/3309.htm.
Watson, Helen (with the Yolngu Community at Yirrkala) and David Wade Chambers, *Singing the Land, Signing the Land: A Portfolio of Exhibits* (Geelong, Victoria: Deakin University, 1989).
Watson, James D., "The Human Genome Project: Past, Present and Future," *Science*, 248 (1990).
Watson-Verran, Helen, "Re-Imagining Land Title and Ownership," in *Science in Society Working Papers: Working Disparate Knowledge Systems Together* Vol. 2, No. 5 (Geelong, Victoria: Deakin University School of Social Inquiry, 1994).
Wautischer, Helmut (ed.), *Tribal Epistemologies: Essays in the Philosophy of Anthropology* (Surrey, UK: Ashgate Publishing, 1998).
Weber, Max, *On Law in Economy and Society* (New York: Simon & Schuster, 1954).
Weber, Max, *The Protestant Ethic and the Spirit of Capitalism* (New York: Charles Scribner's Sons, 1930, 1958).

Weinbert, Bill, "Requiem for Big Mountain: The Road to Relocation Is Unrelenting," *Native Americas* (Fall 1997): 30.

Weir, Robert F. et al. (eds.), *Genes and Human Self-Knowledge: Historical and Philosophical Reflections on Modern Genetics* (Iowa City, Iowa: University of Iowa Press, 1994).

Westlake, John, *Chapters on the Principles of International Law* (Cambridge, UK: Cambridge University Press, 1894).

Whelan, Marina L., "What, if Any, are the Ethical Obligations of the U.S. Patent Office? A Closer Look at the Biological Sampling of Indigenous Groups," *Duke Law and Technology Review* (2006).

Whitt, Laurelyn, "Knowledge Systems of Indigenous America," in Helaine Selin (ed.), *Encyclopaedia of the History of Science, Technology and Medicine in Non-Western Cultures* (Dordrecht, The Netherlands: Kluwer Academic Publishers, 2008).

Whitt, Laurie Anne, "Biocolonialism and the Commodification of Knowledge," *Science as Culture*, 7:1 (1998).

Whitt, Laurie Anne, "Cultural Imperialism and the Marketing of Native America," *The American Indian Culture and Research Journal*, 19:3 (1995).

Whitt, Laurie Anne, "Indigenous Peoples and the Cultural Politics of Knowledge," in Michael Green (ed.), *Issues in American Indian Cultural Identity* (New York: Peter Lang, 1995).

Whitt, Laurie Anne, "Indigenous Peoples, Intellectual Property Law and the New Imperial Science," *Oklahoma City University Law Review*, 23:1 and 2 (1998).

Whitt, Laurie Anne, "Metaphor and Power in Indigenous and Western Knowledge Systems," in Darrell Posey (ed.), *Cultural and Spiritual Values of Biodiversity* (A Complementary Contribution to the Global Biodiversity Assessment for the United Nations Environmental Programme) (London: Intermediate Technology Publications, 1999).

Whitt, Laurie Anne, "Resisting Value-Bifurcation: Indigenist Critiques of the Human Genome Diversity Project," in Ann Ferguson and Bat Ami Bar-On (eds.), *Daring To Be Good: Feminist Essays in Ethico-Politics* (London, UK: Routledge, Chapman and Hall, 1998).

Whitt, Laurie Anne, "Sovereignty and Human Rights," *National Lawyers' Guild Practitioner*, 60:33 (Spring 2003).

Whitt, Laurie Anne, "Value-Bifurcation in Bioscience: The Rhetoric of Research Justification," *Perspectives on Science: Historical, Philosophical, Social*, 7:4 (1999).

Whitt, Laurie Anne and Jennifer Daryl Slack, "Communities, Environments, and Cultural Studies," *Cultural Studies*, 8:1 (January 1994): 5–31.

Whitt, Laurie Anne, Mere Roberts, Waerete Norman, and Vicki Grieves, "Belonging To Land: Indigenous Knowledge Systems and the Natural World," *Oklahoma City University Law Review*, 26:2 (2001).
Whitt, Laurie Anne, Mere Roberts, Waerete Norman, and Vicki Grieves, "Indigenous Perspectives," in Dale Jamieson (ed.), *A Companion to Environmental Philosophy* (Oxford, UK: Basil Blackwell, 2000).
"Who Owns Life? Patenting Human Genes," World Media Foundation Television Broadcast, *Living on Earth*, transcript (May 13, 1994).
Wilkes, Garrison, "Current Status of Crop Germplasm," *Critical Reviews in Plant Sciences*, 1:2 (1983).
Wilkins, David, "Exiling One's Kin: Banishment in Indian Country," *News from Indian Country* (June 1997).
Williams, Jr., Robert A., "Encounters on the Frontiers of International Human Rights Law: Redefining the Terms of Indigenous Peoples' Survival in the World," *Duke Law Journal* (1990).
Williams, Jr., Robert A., "Large Binocular Telescopes, Red Squirrel Pinatas, and Apache Mountains: Decolonizing Environmental Law in a Multicultural World," *West Virginia Law Review*, 96 (1995).
Williams, Jr., Robert A., *Linking Arms Together: American Indian Treaty Visions of Law & Peace 1600–1800* (New York: Oxford University Press, 1997).
Williams, Jr., Robert A., "Linking arms together: multicultural constitutionalism in a North American indigenous vision of law and peace," *California Law Review*, 82 (1994).
Wilson, Angela Waziyatawin, "Indigenous Knowledge Recovery is Indigenous Empowerment," *American Indian Quarterly*, 28:3 and 4 (Summer/Fall 2004).
Winner, Langdon, "The Social and Professional Responsibility of Engineers," in Deborah Johnson (ed.), *Ethical Issues in Engineering* (Old Tappan, New Jersey: Prentice-Hall, 1991).
Woodmansee, Martha, "The Genius and the Copyright," *Eighteenth-Century Studies*, 17 (1984).
Worthen, Kevin, "The Grand Experiment: Evaluating Indian Law in the 'New World,' " *Tulsa Journal of Comparative and International Law*, 5 (1998).
Wright, Shelley, "Property, Information and the Ethics of Communication," *Intellectual Property Journal*, 9 (1994).
Young, Iris Marion, "Five Faces of Oppression," in Thomas Wartenberg (ed.), *Rethinking Power: From Domination to Transformation* (Albany, New York: SUNY Press, 1992).
Young, Iris Marion, "Hybrid Democracy: Iroquois Federalism and the Postcolonial Project," in Duncan Ivison, Paul Patton, and Will Sanders (eds.),

Political Theory and the Rights of Peoples (Cambridge, UK: Cambridge University Press, 2000).
Young, Iris Marion, *Justice and the Politics of Difference* (Princeton, New Jersey: Princeton University Press, 1990).
Young, Iris Marion, "Responsibility and Global Labor Justice," *Political Philosophy*, 12 (2004).
Young, Iris Marion, "Two Concepts of Self-Determination," in Austin Sarat and Thomas R. Kearns (eds.), *Human Rights: Concepts, Contests, Contingencies* (Ann Arbor, Michigan: University of Michigan Press, 2001).
Young, Robert J.C., *Postcolonialism: An Historical Introduction* (Malden, Massachusetts: Wiley-Blackwell, 2001).
Yunupingu, Galarrwuy (ed.), *Our Land is Our Life: Land Rights – Past, Present and Future* (St. Lucia, Queensland: University of Queensland Press, 1997).
Zook, Darren C., "Decolonizing Law: Identity Politics, Human Rights, and the United Nations," *Harvard Human Rights Journal*, 19 (2006).

LEGAL CITATIONS

1869 *Act for the Gradual Enfranchisement of Indians and the Better Management of Indian Affairs Act* c. VI ß 10, Available online at: http://www.ainc-inac.gc.ca/ai/arp/ls/pubs/a69c6/a69c6-eng.pdf.
"Affidavit of Alice Benally" *P* 56, *at* 248, *Manybeads v. United States*, 730 F. Supp. 1515 (D. Ariz. 1989) (No. 88–410).
"Affidavit of Kee Shay" *P* 15, *at* 230, *Manybeads v. United States*, 730 F. Supp. 1515 (D. Ariz. 1989) (No. 88–410).
"Affidavit of Mae Tso," *Manybeads v. United States*, 730 F. Supp. 1515 (D. Ariz. 1989) (No. 88–410).
Bleistein v. Donaldson Lithographing Co. 188 U.S. 239 (1903).
Canadian Constitution (Constitution Act, 1982) pt. II, ß 35(1).
Cherokee Nation v. Georgia, 30 U.S. 1; 8 L. Ed. 25, (5 Pet.), (Decided: 18 March 1831).
Convention on Biological Diversity, 5 June 1992, art. 8(j), 1760 United Nations Treaty Series at 149. Available online at: http://www.un.org/Depts/dhl/resguide/spectreat.htm#unts.
1791 *French Constitution*, (Paris), adopted by the French National Constituent Assembly, (September 1791), Article 3.
Goldstein v. California, 412 U.S. 546, 93 S.Ct. 2303, 37 L.Ed.2d 163 (1973).
Helsinki Summit Declaration 1992. Available online at: http://www1.umn.edu/humanrts/peace/docs/helsnk92.htm.

Huber, Max (Arbitrator), Island of Palmas Case (*U.S. v Netherlands*), 2 R.I.A.A. 829, 838, (Judge Anzilotti), (1928).

Little Traverse Bay Band of Odawa Indians, Waganakising Odawak Tribal Code, Title IV, ch. 10, Act Prohibiting the Patenting of Organisms (2004). Available online at: http://www.ltbbodawa-nsn.gov/TribalCode2005/LTBBTribalCode 2005.htm.

Porter, John, "A Resolution Affecting the GATT Negotiations on Intellectual Property Rights for Genetic and Biological Resources," Congressional Record, 101st Congress, 2nd Session, Vol. 136, No. 94, (20 July 1990), E 2425.

"Report of the High Level Panel on Threats, Challenges and Change," *A More Secure World: Our Shared Responsibility*, U.N. Doc. A/59/565 (2 December 2004). Available online at: http://www.un.org/secureworld.

Sequoyah v. Tennessee Valley Authority, 620 F.2d 1159, 1160 (6th Cir. 1980).

United Nations Commission on Human Rights (UNCHR), Sub-Commission on Prevention of Discrimination and Protection of Minorities, *Study on the Protection of the Cultural and Intellectual Property of Indigenous Peoples*, P 24, U.N. Doc. E/CN.4/Sub.2/1993/28 (28 July 1993) (prepared by Erica-Irene Daes).

United Nations Conference on Environment and Development, Convention on Biological Diversity, concluded 5 June 1992, 1760 U.N.T.S. 79, reprinted in 31 I.L.M. 818 (entered into force 29 December 1993). Available online at: http://www.biodiv.org/convention/articles.asp.

United Nations Educational, Scientific and Cultural Organization (UNESCO), "Report of Subcommittee on Bioethics and Population Genetics of the UNESCO International Bioethics Committee," (15 November 1995). Available online at: http://portal.unesco.org/shs/en/files/2303/10596456491populationCIB3_en.pdf/populationCIB3_en.pdf.

United Nations General Assembly, "Declaration on Principles of International Law," (24 October 1970). Available online at: http://www.un.org/documents/ga/res/25/ares25.htm.

United States v. Wheeler, 435 U.S. 313; 98 S. Ct. 1079; 55 L. Ed. 2d 303, (Argued: 11 January 1978; As amended: 22 March 1978).

16 *United States Code*, Section 470.

U.S. Constitution, Art. 1, Sec. 8, Cl. 8.

United States v. Sandoval, 231 U.S. 28 (1913).

United States Senate, "Human Genome Diversity Project: Hearing before the Committee on Governmental Affairs." 103rd Congress, 1st Session (1993). (Washington, DC: United States Government Printing Office, 1993). Available online at: http://www.archive.org/stream/humangenomediveroounit/humangenomediveroounit_djvu.txt.

United States Senate, "Statement of Pat Lefthand," Improvement of the American Indian Religious Freedom Act: Hearings Before the Senate Select Committee on Indian Affairs, United States Senate on S. 2250, 100th Congress, 2nd Session 217 (1988).

Waitangi Tribunal, "Muriwhenua Land Report" (1997). Available online at: http://www.waitangi-tribunal.govt.nz/reports/.

Worcester v. Georgia, 31 U.S. 515; 8L. Ed. 483 (6 pct.), (Decided: 3 March 1832).

Index